ALL IN THE FAMILY

A Critical Appraisal

Published with the co-sponsorship of the
Aspen Institute for Humanistic Studies

ALL IN THE FAMILY

A Critical Appraisal

Edited by Richard P. Adler

PRAEGER SPECIAL STUDIES • PRAEGER SCIENTIFIC

LC 79 - 89505
ISBN 0 - 03 - 053996 - 8

PRAEGER PUBLISHERS, PRAEGER SPECIAL STUDIES
383 Madison Avenue, New York, N.Y., 10017, U.S.A.

Published in the United States of America in 1979
by Praeger Publishers
A Division of Holt, Rinehart and Winston, CBS Inc.

9 056 987654321

"Can Bigotry Be Laughed Away? It's Worth a Try," by Jack Gould, in *The New York Times,* January 21, 1971. Copyright 1971 by *The New York Times* Company. Reprinted by permission.

"The Message Sounds Like 'Hate Thy Neighbor,' " by Stephanie Harrington, in *The New York Times,* January 24, 1971. Copyright 1971 by *The New York Times* Company. Reprinted by permission.

"CBS Gambles on Reality with New Comedy Series," by Kay Gardella, in the New York *Daily News.* Copyright 1971, New York News, Inc. Reprinted by permission.

"TV Review" by Don Freeman in *The San Diego Union,* January 14, 1971. Reprinted by permission of *The San Diego Union.*

"Introduction to a Bigot," by Dwight Newton, in the *San Francisco Examiner,* January 12, 1971. Copyright 1971 by *The San Francisco Examiner.* Reprinted by permission.

" 'All in the Family': TV Social Departure," by Alan Bunce, in *The Christian Science Monitor,* January 18, 1971. Reprinted by permission from *The Christian Science Monitor,* copyright 1971, The Christian Science Publishing Society. All rights reserved.

"New TV Comedy Takes Hard, Realistic Poke at Bigotry" by Pamela Haynes, in the *Los Angeles Sentinel,* January 28, 1971. Copyright 1971 by the *Los Angeles Sentinel.* Reprinted by permission.

"Irresponsible Television Production Aids Racism," by Whitney M. Young, Jr., in the *Los Angeles Sentinel,* February 4, 1971. Copyright 1971 by the *Los Angeles Sentinel.* Reprinted by permission.

" 'All in the Family' Gets Better as Weeks Go By," by Norman Mark, in *The Chicago Daily News,* February 23, 1971. Copyright Chicago Daily News, 1971 by Norman Mark. Reprinted with permission from Field Enterprises, Inc.

" 'All in the Family': Review," by Cleveland Amory, in *TV Guide,* February 27, 1971. Reprinted with permission from *TV Guide* Magazine. Copyright 1971 by Triangle Publications, Inc., Radnor, Pennsylvania.

"Bigotry as a Dirty Joke," by John Leonard, in *Life,* January 18, 1971. Copyright 1971 by *Life* Magazine. Reprinted by permission of John Leonard.

"Love That Hate," by Robert Lewis Shayon, in *Saturday Review,* March 27, 1971. Copyright *Saturday Review,* 1971. All rights reserved.

"As I Listened to Archie Say 'Hebe . . .' " by Laura Z. Hobson, in *The New York Times,* September 12, 1971. Copyright 1971 by The New York Times Company. Reprinted by permission.

"As I Read How Laura Saw Archie . . ." by Norman Lear, in *The New York Times,* October 10, 1971. Copyright 1971 by The New York Times Company. Reprinted by permission.

"Can Bigotry Be Funny?" by Joseph Morgenstern, in *Newsweek,* November 29, 1971. Copyright 1971 by Newsweek, Inc. All rights reserved. Reprinted by permission.

"How Funny Can Bigotry Be?" by John Slawson, in *Educational Broadcasting Review,* April 1972. Copyright 1972 by the National Association of Broadcasters.

"Archie Bunker's Bigotry: A Study in Selective Perception and Exposure," by Neil Vidmar and Milton Rokeach, in *Journal of Communication,* Winter 1974. Copyright *Jounal of Communication,* 1974. Reprinted by permission.

"The Impact of 'All in the Family' on Children," by Timothy P. Meyer, in *Journal of Broadcasting,* Winter 1976. Copyright 1976 by *Journal of Broadcasting.*

"Bunkerism," by Crawford Woods, in *The New Republic,* December 22, 1973. Copyright 1973 by *The New Republic.* Reprinted by permission.

"The Gospel According to Edith Bunker," by Edward McNulty. Copyright 1974 by The Christian Century Foundation. Reprinted by permission from the March 27, 1974 issue of *The Christian Century.*

Acknowledgements

The editor would like to express his thanks to the following: to the Rockefeller Foundation for a grant supporting development of a television criticism curriculum, of which this book is a part; to the Aspen Institute Program on Communications and Society and its first director, Douglass Cater, for sponsoring the Television Workshop where the idea for this book originated; to Michael Novak, Maria Savage, Sue Rumsey, and Jim Arntz for their editorial help; to Gertrud Pacheco, Diane Willis, Christina Simoni, and Teresa Mallen for helping turn the manuscript into a book; and to Rich Kuhn of Cambria Press and Mary Curtis of Praeger Publishers for their support for the project. Thanks also to all those who took the time to contribute a statement to the "symposium" on the significance of *All in the Family*. And finally, special thanks to Norman Lear and his associates Barbara Brogliatti, Virginia Carter, and Lynn Naylor, for their patience in answering my many questions and their generosity in providing material for the book.

Preface

For several reasons, *All in the Family* deserves attention from all those interested in television or in contemporary American culture. First, *All in the Family* has been the most popular TV series of the past three decades. It was the top rated prime time program for five years and was watched regularly by nearly one-third of all Americans. Archie and Edith Bunker and the others on the show have become part of the American popular imagination.

Second, from its first appearance in 1971, the series has been the subject of lively controversy. One debate has focused on the question of whether the portrayal of Archie Bunker has defused or reinforced prejudice among the program's vast audience. This book presents a group of research studies which attempt to answer this question empirically.

Third, *All in the Family* broke new ground in entertainment programming. In the subjects it dealt with and the language it used, the series successfully violated many of the taboos that have previously determined what could be done on prime-time TV. Yet despite its many innovations, it did not alter the basic framework of commercial network television. What did and did not change as a result of the series is worth considering.

Finally, *All in the Family* is worth examining from an aesthetic viewpoint. A number of critics have favorably compared the series' writing and acting to that of Broadway theater. As an example of commercial programming at its best, *All in the Family* provides an opportunity to assess what the medium is capable of accomplishing —and the ways in which it is still limited.

Organization of This Book

The materials in this volume are intended to permit the reader to look at *All in the Family* from more than one perspective. The editor's Introduction provides a context for what follows by describing the origins, development, and history of the series. It also discusses why the series has been so popular, and so controversial.

The first section of the book presents the scripts of three episodes: the series' initial episode, written by Norman Lear; an episode from the series' third season which shocked viewers by defying the convention of the mandatory happy ending; and an unusual episode from the eighth season which is based on the revelation of character rather than the more typical confrontation over some particular issue.

The next two sections present a sample of the program's initial reivews, then commentary from the second season which focused on the impact of Archie Bunker's bigotry. Included in this third section is the exchange between Laura Z. Hobson and Norman Lear on this issue.

Section IV contains research studies assessing the effects of the program on the viewing audience. Three studies examine the differing responses of "high and low prejudiced" viewers to the series; a fourth study is concerned with its impact on young viewers.

The fifth section is made up of later, longer, and more analytical essays which attempt to render a critical judgement on *All in the Family* or place the program in a larger context. The next section offers a report from "behind the scenes"—a detailed account of how one episode of *All in the Family* (from the 1972-73 season) was produced.

Section VII offers examples of an unusual development stimulated by the series: articles which describe a "real Archie Bunker"—that is, a real person who resembles the TV character. These articles represent fascinating if unscientific attempts to determine how true to life the series is.

The final section is a "symposium" on the significance of *All in the Family*, made up of contributions from TV critics and TV industry leaders, as well as from people connected with the series. Statements in this section were written expressly for the book.

The book concludes with a complete listing of all episodes in the series from 1971 through the 1978-79 season, and a bibliography of further readings. A group of photographs appears on pages 171-178.

Note: There is no standard form for citing the names of television programs. Italics (*All in the Family*) is probably most often used, but also common are the use of quotation marks ("All in the Family") and no marks (All in the Family). Program titles appearing in the articles and essays reprinted in this volume follow the form found in the original.

Richard P. Adler
Palo Alto, California
May 1979

Contents

III. CRITICAL REACTION: The Second Season

IV. AUDIENCE REACTION: Research Reports

V. CRITICAL REACTION: Later Articles

Introduction

Richard P. Adler

On the evening of January 12, 1971, a new weekly comedy program called *All in the Family* was broadcast on the CBS television network. In September 1978, Archie and Edith Bunker's chairs were placed on permanent display at the Smithsonian Institution. In a ceremony marking the occasion, Smithsonian secretary S. Dillon Ripley remarked that the chairs—and the television series—had become "part of the nation's cultural legacy." How *All in the Family* contributed to that legacy is the subject of this book.

The critics of television have often observed that there is little correspondence between the world of the viewing audience and the world as portrayed on prime-time TV. But seldom has the discrepancy between the two worlds been greater than it was at the end of the 1960s.

This was, above all, the time when the country's agony over the Vietnam War was at its height. The withdrawal of U.S. combat troops had begun in the summer of 1969, but the pace was far too slow to appease the growing number of Americans opposed to the war at home. In November more than a quarter-million protesters gathered in Washington, the largest antiwar demonstration in U.S. history. The following spring, President Nixon announced the invasion of neutral Cambodia. In the demonstrations that followed, four Kent State students were killed by National Guardsmen and more than 100 colleges and universities across the country were shut down. As 1970 came to a close, Lt. William Calley's courtmartial for the My Lai massacre was about to begin; while out in California, the murder trial of Charles Manson and his followers was coming to an end.

It was not the best of times. Yet, a television viewer would have been hard-pressed during these years to find evidence from prime-time entertainment that there was anything wrong in the world that could not be set right by a cop, a cowboy, or a doctor. At the end of 1970, for example, the ratings were dominated by melo-dramas such as *Ironside, Mannix, Marcus Welby, Medical Center, Gunsmoke,* and *Bonanza.* Even more insulated from reality were the comedy programs, which ranged from the slapstick and silliness of *Here's Lucy* and *Bewitched* to the rusticated humor of *Hee Haw* and *Mayberry, RFD.*

The characters who inhabited these programs were almost wholly devoid of opinions, either pro or con, about any of the political or social issues of the day. There was some mild satire from Rowan and Martin's *Laugh-In* and occasional irreverence from Flip Wilson, but otherwise a seemingly unbridgeable chasm yawned between the bloodshed and strife reported on the six o'clock news and the escapist fare that followed.

No institution had been more careful to avoid offending public sensibilities than the television industry. According to the theory proposed at the time by one network executive, viewers wanted neither to be challenged nor to be stimulated by television. Rather, they sought only to find the "least objectionable program" among the choices available to them at any given time. This may or may not have been true of the viewing audience, but it definitely seemed to explain the behavior of the network programmers. Commercial TV had prospered mightily by being innocuous, and the risks of doing otherwise seemed too great. Material which might be controversial could not only alienate viewers, who were the industry's most important commodity, but also advertisers, who provided commercial TV with its revenues, and, ultimately, the government, under whose authority broadcasters operated.

Thus, when *All in the Family* appeared in January 1971, it represented an abrupt and unexpected departure from television's policy of providing bland escapist entertainment. The program's realistic urban setting was highly unusual for a comedy series. Even more unusual was its language and its frank treatment of sexual and ethnic-religious themes. Then there was the program's main character.

By now, Archie Bunker has become so familiar, so much of an American institution, that it is not easy to recall how startling he was when he first appeared. For here was no long-suffering, henpecked TV husband, nor a benignly wise bachelor father. Archie was impatient, stubborn, intolerant, and outspoken. Most shocking of all was his unabashed bigotry. The first episode[†] is marked by his robust and unapologetic use of racial and ethnic epithets never heard before on television.

Here was a new kind of television comedy. Whether the viewing audience would embrace or reject it, no one knew. In fact, just about everyone in the industry was wondering how a program like *All in the Family* got on the air at all—especially on CBS.

The Least Likely Network

Based on its prior history, CBS was the network least likely to broadcast a program like *All in the Family*. Ever since competition among the three national networks began in the late 1940s, CBS had been the perennial leader in audience ratings. Its position seemed impregnable. Each year, NBC would come in second; while ABC, the newest and weakest of the three, would follow a distant third.

The CBS formula for success was wonderfully simple: Hire the biggest stars and build audience loyalty around them. By the 1960s, performers like Lucille Ball, Jackie Gleason, Red Skelton, and Ed Sullivan had been drawing the largest audiences to CBS for nearly 20 years. The network's prosperity and prestige had enabled it not only to keep its own stars happy but also to raid the competing networks for any performers who might threaten the CBS supremacy. Because the formula had worked so well for so long, CBS executives showed little interest in questioning it. Then, at the end of the 1960s, the rules of the rating game changed, and CBS was suddenly in trouble.

What had happened was this: Advertisers had begun to realize that, for their purposes, not all TV viewers were equal. Marketing research had shown advertisers that within the larger viewing audience, there was a particular group who were the most active consumers, and were, therefore, the most desirable target for the

---

[†]The script of the first episode appears on page 3. In the remainder of this introduction (†) will be used to indicate material reprinted in this volume.

advertisers' messages. This group was made up of people who were younger (under 35) rather than older; urban rather than rural; and more affluent than average.

From then on, demographics—the characteristics of the viewing audience—simple audience numbers would be considered along with weighing a program's value to advertisers: Programs with a desirable demographic profile could sell commercial time at premium rates; programs with less desirable demographics sold at a discount.

Unfortunately for CBS, its audience, though impressive in size, had a demographic profile which made it increasingly less attractive to advertisers. The network's prime-time schedule featured programs like *The Beverly Hillbillies* and *Hee Haw*, which appealed particularly to rural viewers. CBS also had a disproportionate number of programs that had been successful for many years, and the audiences for these programs had grown older along with the shows. By contrast, the smaller audiences drawn by ABC (with programs like *The Mod Squad*) tended to be younger, more urban, and more affluent.

In 1969, Robert Wood, the newly hired president of the CBS television network, was given a mandate to revamp the network's offerings. Wood's first major decision was to drop both Jackie Gleason and Red Skelton from the prime time schedule for the Fall of 1970. Their shows were immensely popular, but their appeal was strongest among the older, rural viewers. In addition, their programs had become increasingly expensive to produce, and the revenues they produced were barely keeping up with their costs.

The problem with Wood's decision was that he had no new programs of remotely comparable appeal to put in their place. He knew he would have to find alternatives quickly. Thus, when he saw the pilot for a new comedy series which revolved around the battles between a middle-aged, working-class bigot and his liberal son-in-law, Wood hoped that he had found what he had been looking for.

Norman Lear, the creator of the new series, was not well-known to the public, but he had established a solid reputation as a writer and producer of television and movie comedy. Wood decided to take a gamble.

The Rise of Norman Lear

Born in New Haven in 1922, Norman Lear had spent virtually his entire working career in show business. He grew up in Connecticut, the son of a salesman who sold "garages, playrooms, small appliances, anything and everything." After attending college briefly, he dropped out to write for gossip columns in New York newspapers. He eventually emigrated to Hollywood to seek his fortune as a writer. True to tradition, he found it necessary to peddle baby pictures for a time to support himself. Then in 1951, he sold a comedy routine to Danny Thomas. He was soon working full-time as a writer for a series of live television shows, including *The Colgate Comedy Hour*, with Dean Martin and Jerry Lewis. In the mid-50s, he worked on *The Martha Raye Show* (as both writer and director), *The Tennessie Ernie Ford Show*, and *The George Gobel Show*.

In 1959, eager to try something new, Lear joined with a successful producer of TV specials named Bud Yorkin to form Tandem Productions ("we thought of ourselves as two guys on a bicycle pedalling uphill"). Their initial effort was a dramatic television series, *Band of Gold*, which featured James Franciscus and Suzanne Pleshette playing a couple in a different romantic story each week. Lear recalls that "the show was scheduled on a Friday night and went off the schedule on Monday morning."

Their next venture, a film version of Neil Simon's *Come Blow Your Horn*, proved more successful. Yorkin directed and Lear wrote the screenplay and produced the film, which starred Frank Sinatra. In the next few years, Lear continued in the movie business, writing and producing *Divorce American Style* (1967) and *The Night They Raided Minsky's* (1968). Then, once again, Lear moved in a new direction.

Shortly after completing *Minsky's*, Lear happened to see a brief item in *Variety* about *Till Death Us Do Part*, a hit British comedy series about a bigot who is constantly at odds with his family, especially his liberal son-in-law. Without having seen an episode, Lear acquired the American rights to the program, and began developing a series of his own based on it. Lear insists that although the *Variety* notice provided the original impetus for the series, his own experience was the real basis of the program:

> I would never have thought of doing *All in the Family* had I not known of *Till Death Us Do Part,* but what I eventually saw was not what inspired me. What inspired me was simply reading that somebody had done a show in which a father and son-in-law were arguing, were totally apart—not just a generation gap, but were divided on every ideological issue, and fought about race, religion, politics, economics, up and down the line. That was all

I needed to excite me, because I had lived that with my father.

Herman Lear, according to his son, was an "extremely outgoing and affectionate but enormously insensitive man." Like Archie, he was conservative and opinionated, referred to his wife as a "dingbat" and would tell her to "stifle" herself. But despite continual conflict with his father, Norman Lear's filial feelings were more complex: "I always knew I liked my father; but it was many, many years later till I realized how much I loved him." It seems clear that some of the texture of that father-son relationship played a significant part in the creation of Archie Bunker.

Once Lear obtained the rights to *Till Death Us Do Part,* he quickly prepared a "treatment"—some 80 pages of sample dialogue and notes describing the characters. Martin Starger, president of ABC-TV, liked the idea, and over the next year, the network paid some $250,000 for a sample script and the production of two pilot episodes, which were taped in January and March 1969. This is typical of the process by which program concepts are developed by the networks, except that merely a single pilot is normally commissioned. That ABC paid for two suggests that the network was both seriously interested and unusually cautious about the show.

Ultimately, ABC chose not to buy the series. The pilots had not done well in tests with sample audiences, and the network apparently decided the concept was too unorthodox and risky. Lear did not spend much time lamenting the decision, however. He turned back to the movie business, directing his first feature film, *Cold Turkey.* While he was shooting the film on location in Iowa, his agent called to report that CBS had decided to consider the pilot.

CBS Decides

What CBS president Robert Wood found appealing about *All in the Family* was precisely what had frightened ABC—its potential for provoking controversy and the unconventionality of its concept. Wood was fully aware that the show "was fraught with problems," but he also believed that it had the potential to become a runaway hit.

Wood's enthusiasm for *All in the Family* was not shared by his fellow executives at CBS, however; and their skepticism was confirmed by the network's audience tests with the two Lear pilots. The results were as negative at CBS as they had been at ABC. None of this swayed Wood's belief in the program. He stood by his decision to include it in the schedule and arranged a special screening for the ultimate arbiter at CBS—William S. Paley, the man who had built CBS into a vast media empire and was now chairman of the board of CBS, Inc.

As Wood recalls the occasion, Paley did not laugh much as he watched. After it was over, he turned to his new president and asked him whether he believed "it should be shown on *your* network." Wood said that he was convinced that the medium was ready for it and that CBS should do it. Paley merely replied, "You may be right . . ." But with this less than ringing endorsement, Wood understood that he had been given the authority to go ahead.

By the time CBS began considering *All in the Family*, it was too late to include it in the schedule for September 1970. Wood decided to introduce the series the following September, or in January 1971, as a mid-season replacement for another program that was faltering in the ratings. The network kept Lear waiting, then informed him late that Fall that his show would be broadcast in January.

The cast had to be hastily reassembled; a production team had to be brought together. The most pressing need, however, was for scripts for the 13 episodes which would comprise the first season. Don Nicholl, who was hired as story editor for the series,* vividly recalls the frantic pace of the first season:

> If we were lucky, we had three scripts ready when we went on the air . . . We were writing week by week until the last minute. The first 13 weeks were a very hectic period. It was very exciting because what we were doing was so new to American television, but also very hard. Norman was writing very hard at that time . . . We were all writing tight to the wire all the time.

The production process for *All in the Family* was largely typical of most television comedy series. But in the final production step, Lear introduced a major innovation. Instead of filming the

---

*In the second season, Nicholl was joined in the role of story editor by Michael Ross and Bernie West. Others who have played key behind the scenes roles in creating the series include: Paul Bogart, Hal Cantor, Bill Davenport, Lou Derman, Milt Josefsberg, Mort Lachman, Larry Rhine, John Rich, and Mel Tolkin.

show on a sound stage, in starts and stops and without an audience, Lear *videotaped* the actors in a continuous performance in front of a live audience. This procedure was often used for television variety shows and talk programs, but it was unusual for an acted series. (A few series, such as *I Love Lucy*, had been filmed before live audiences, but filming necessarily involved stopping the action frequently to set up each new scene.)

Perhaps because of his experience producing live TV shows in the 1950s, Lear liked the more immediate, more theatrical quality of continuous videotaped performances before an audience. He also liked the economy of the technique: The cost of each half-hour program was significantly less than similar, filmed shows at the time. The technique proved so successful it was used in most of Lear's subsequent series and was adopted by several other producers as well.*

Thus, at 5:30 on Friday evening, after a week of rehearsals, the cast of *All in the Family* would give its first performance in front of an audience and the cameras. The writers were present at the taping, and if they detected any weaknesses in the first performance (e.g., a joke that had worked well in rehearsal but not with the audience), they would make quick changes in the script which were incorporated into a second performance in front of a different audience at 8:00 p.m. The final broadcast tape was selected from the better of the two performances, although material from the other performance was sometimes edited into the final version. This process was to be repeated more than 200 times over the next nine years.

Tensions and Apprehensions

Not all those involved with the program initially were as enthusiastic about it as Lear and Wood. One of the most skeptical was the man who was playing Archie Bunker. Carroll O'Connor was a classically trained actor who had studied drama at Dublin's National University and played in Shakespeare at the Edinburgh Festival. He had established a solid record in supporting roles on the stage, in films, and on television. Although *All in the Family* provided him with his first leading role, he had little faith in the show's prospects.

---

*The taping of *All in the Family* in front of an audience was discontinued during the 1978-79 season. This was done to accommodate Carroll O'Connor, who preferred working without an audience.

O'Connor was convinced that the series would generate so much protest that CBS would be forced to cancel it before the end of the first season. The actor was so certain that the program would fail that he agreed to come to California from his home in Rome only after a provision was inserted in his contract guaranteeing return air fare to Europe for himself and his family upon cancellation of the series.

No less skeptical was William Tankersley, head of "standards and practices" at CBS—the network's chief censor. The network censors are the guardians of the corporate "image," and their major concern is to avoid alienating any substantial portion of the viewing audience. Tankersley's guiding principle was his belief in "a universal television that played to everyone and offended no one." As he began to review the *All in the Family* scripts, it became obvious that the show could not conceivably be made to conform to traditional CBS standards.

Tankersley also discovered that he would have trouble not only with the program but with the people who were producing it. Producers customarily complain that the censors impose arbitrary judgments on their creative freedom and violate the integrity of their work. But in the end, the censor almost always prevails. Lear, however, did more than complain; he declared himself unwilling to accept any changes. He had decided that if he allowed a precedent for compromise to be set at the beginning, it would be impossible to overcome later, no matter how successful the show might prove to be.

Thus, the lines were drawn, and as the date for the first episode grew nearer, the tension escalated. Robert Wood realized that a program which succeeded in being totally inoffensive would also fail to attract the more sophisticated viewers he wanted to reach. Wood therefore stepped in as arbitrator, and Lear eventually made a few concessions on the material Tankersley found most objectionable. In the first episode, for example, the sexual relationships between Mike and Gloria was deemphasized and Archie's use of the word "goddamn" was eliminated (it reappeared successfully during the second season). The racial and ethnic epithets remained, however, and the basic character of the show was unchanged.

There was one final crisis before the premiere. The day before the first broadcast, several CBS executives decided it would be more prudent to begin the series with what was to be the second episode, which was deemed slightly less shocking than the first. Once again,

Lear was adamant. He insisted that if the series contained elements that would disturb the audience, it was best to let them know it at the beginning. Lear prevailed. For better or worse, *All in the Family* would be introduced to the country with the story that was essentially unchanged from the original pilot he had developed for ABC in 1968.

On the Air: Initial Responses

On the night of January 12, CBS took several steps to prepare for the wave of protest it expected following the broadcast. Robert Wood ordered extra operators for the network switchboard to take the complaints of viewers. He also sent a message to all CBS affiliate stations suggesting that they do the same. As a final precaution, CBS introduced the program with an announcement explaining that the series was intended to throw "a humorous spotlight on our frailties, prejudices, and concerns."

As it turned out, the preparations proved unnecessary. The program was watched by a comparatively small number of viewers, most of the audiences having chosen to stay with the movies which had begun earlier in the evening on both NBC and ABC. (The 9:30 p.m. "slot" on Tuesdays was dominated by the 8 p.m. "ABC Movie of the Week," which was regularly capturing a 40-share of the audience. *All in the Family*'s predecessor on CBS, another half-hour comedy called *To Rome with Love*, had never drawn more than a meager 28-share.)

Not only did *All in the Family* attract a small audience, it also failed to generate a response of any kind from those who watched. The extra operators standing by at the network and the local stations were not needed. Wood was relieved but also disappointed and puzzled. His belief in the sophistication of the television audience had apparently been vindicated, but he had simply not expected that a comedy about an intemperate and unapologetic bigot would be accepted by the public with such indifference.

The initial reviews from the country's television critics were far from indifferent, however. *All in the Family* provoked sharply polarized opinions, perhaps most dramatically illustrated by the reviews which appeared in *Variety* and its sister publication *Daily Variety*. The review for the New York-based *Variety*[†] began by asserting that *All in the Family* was "the best TV comedy since the original *The Honeymooners*. It should be the biggest hit since *Laugh-In*, or the Nielsen sample is in need of severe revision." The reviewer observed that the "prime element [of the show] is audacity, generally a benchmark of really imaginative work," and that "the ultimate effect" of the satire was "one of pleasure and relief."

By contrast, the Hollywood-based *Daily Variety*[†] found nothing funny about "Norman Lear's raw, plotless wonder." Conceding that the show was "innovative," the reviewer found it "nothing less than an insult to any unbigoted televiewer" and concluded that it was "too bad this bundle from Britain wasn't turned back at the shoreline."

This response was relatively mild compared to the review by John Leonard in *Life* magazine.[†] Leonard's review began with a remarkable series of images implying that *All in the Family* was not so much an objectionable television program as a public meance which should be eradicated:

> *All in the Family* is a wretched program. Why review a wretched program? Well, why vacuum the living room or fix the septic tank? Every once in a while the reviewer must assume the role of a bottle of Johnson's No-Roach with the spray applicator: let's clean up this culture.

Leonard's principal objection to the program was that its basic subject matter was not suitable for comedy. He also found it impossible to accept a character who is clearly prejudiced yet likeable, and he argued that the concept is a dangerous one, a position shared by several other reviewers.

The *New York Times* hedged its bets by running three different reviews of the show.[†] The first review, by Fred Ferreti appeared under the title "TV: Are Racism and Bigotry Funny?" On balance, Ferreti decided the answer to that question was "no"—that Archie's use of epithets was shocking but not amusing. The second review, written by the *Times'* regular television critic, Jack Gould, appeared under the headline, "Can Bigotry Be Laughed Away? It's Worth a Try." As the title suggests, Gould was basically approving. The third *Times* review, by Stephanie Harrington ("The Message Sounds Like 'Hate Thy Neighbor' ") ran three days after Gould's. Like Ferretti, Harrington did not find *All in the Family* funny and doubted whether the show would have a salutory effect on its audience: "By making the expression of hostility more commonplace, do we really exorcise it? Or do we, in fact, make it more acceptable?" (A similar ambivalence toward the series was displayed by the *Los Angeles*

Sentinel, a black newspaper. A highly favorable initial review by Pamela Haynes was quickly followed by an extremely negative article by Whitney Young, Jr. attacking the series as "irresponsible."[†])

The critics universally acknowledged that *All in the Family* represented a sharp break from the medium's prevailing blandness But they were deeply divided over whether this was a change for the better. And most of the reviews included a note of tentativeness: Many of the critics had little idea how the viewing audience would respond to the Bunkers and were uncertain how well the characters would hold up over the course of a season.

Ultimately, however, the opinions of TV critics mean little in determining the fate of a series compared to the verdict rendered by the Nielsen Company. And during the spring of 1971, the news from Nielsen was not encouraging for Lear or Wood. *All in the Family* managed to attract, on average, a 29-share of the viewing audience, just one point better than the program it had replaced. Apparently, the viewers, like the critics, were having a difficult time making up their minds about the show. Although *All in the Family* won several Emmy awards, reports began appearing in the trade press that the show would not return in the fall.

The Second Season

Despite the rumors and the low ratings, *All in the Family* was never in serious danger of cancellation after its first season. Robert Wood had no intention of abandoning it hastily. Moreover, during the summer, audience ratings for the reruns of the show increased substantially. Evidently, viewers who had watched competing programs during the spring decided to see what they had missed. Wood was so encouraged by the improved ratings that he decided to move *All in the Family* from 9:30 p.m. Tuesday to Saturday at 8 p.m., which made it the lead-in show for that evening's prime-time schedule on CBS.

During the first week of the fall season in September, *All in the Family* ranked 12th in the Nielsen ratings of prime-time programs. In the second week's Nielsen report, *All in the Family* captured first place. It placed fourth during the next two weeks, then was preempted for a couple of weeks, then placed first again—and stayed there throughout the rest of the season. During the 1971-72 season, *All in the Family* was viewed on average by half of all persons watching television during its time period. For several weeks, its share of the viewing audience reached 60 percent. The show proved to be the outstanding success of the season.

Along with success, however, came controversy. After the series' initial reviews the previous winter, most of the subsequent articles about the show tended to be the sort of innocuous fare regularly produced by television columnists to fill their daily quota of space: Was Carroll O'Connor really like Archie Bunker? How was Jean Stapleton reacting to fame? By mid-fall of 1971, however, it was becoming obvious that *All in the Family* was going to be more than an interesting but short-lived experiment. Its success seemed to signal the beginning of a new trend in television comedy, and a few articles began to take a closer look at Norman Lear's brand of humor.

The most important of these was a long piece by Laura Z. Hobson, "As I Listened to Archie Say 'Hebe' . . ."[†] which appeared in the *New York Times* on September 12, 1971. The theme of Hobson's article was that rather than satirizing and hence exorcising bigotry, *All in the Family* was actually (if unintentionally) legitimizing and therefore encouraging bigoted attitudes. The article was of special importance for several reasons: First, the author had impressive credentials as a writer and an enemy of prejudice. Hobson was the author of *Gentlemen's Agreement*, an earnest expose of the evils of anti-Semitism in the United States. (The film version won the Academy Award for best picture in 1947.) Second, although Hobson was not the first critic to suggest that *All in the Family* was having negative social effects, she was the first to provide a detailed argument as to why she thought so. Third, the article provoked a response from Lear himself.

Hobson's objection to the show focused on the portrayal of the principal character. She argued that *All in the Family* transformed what should be an unambiguous evil into the figure of a "lovable bigot." Mrs. Hobson strongly objected:

> I don't think you can be a bigot and be lovable. I don't think you can be a black-baiter and lovable, nor an anti-Semite and lovable. And I don't think the millions who watch this show should be conned into thinking you can be.

Not surprisingly, Norman Lear thoroughly disagreed in his reply, entitled "As I Read How Laura Saw Archie."[†] He rejected her contention that there is no such thing as a lovable bigot. Most prejudice, he argued, comes not from villains motivated by irrational hatred, but from otherwise good people whose bigotry springs from ignorance and fear. It is Archie's complexity and inconsistency which makes him recognizably human and, therefore, representative: "If prejudice were to disappear tomorrow from the hearts of all the good people in the world, there would be no problem."

Lear also pointed out that Archie's expressions of prejudice were carefully balanced with rebuttals from other members of his family, most often his son-in-law, Mike. It is Mike's statements that consistently make sense, while Archie's convoluted logic is inevitably shown to be false and foolish. Thus, Lear insisted, the message of the show as a whole is quite different from the views expressed by Archie.

Perhaps the most interesting aspect of the Hobson-Lear debate is that Lear did not respond to Hobson's charges with the customary defense of writers and producers that his program was intended merely to be entertaining, not to influence its viewers one way or another. Rather, Lear claimed that comedy in general, and *All in the Family* in particular, exposes our flaws, thereby encouraging us to acknowledge them and, ultimately, to overcome them.

Thus, the controversy had little to do with the artistic standards of the series. The real issue here was what was happening in the hearts and minds of the viewing audience as they watched the show. But neither Lear nor Hobson could call upon any knowledge of how the program's millions of viewers were actually responding to Archie's bigotry. As a result, as Benjamin DeMott observed, the exchange produced

> much ferocity, zero illumination. Nobody knew whether the Hobsons or Lears or their successors in the dispute down to the present . . . were right. All that's become clear is that if the former were correct, incalculable social damage has been done in this country, week by week, for enormous profit, and that if the latter were correct, a profoundly important opening toward moral education for a mass audience has been obscured in a murk of piety and superstition.

DeMott concluded that the only way to resolve the controversy would be to conduct research on the audience response to the series.

What the Research Says

Both the detractors and defenders of *All in the Family* were convinced that it was having *some* impact on public attitudes. Eventually, a number of social scientists became interested in the controversy; and in the past few years, there has been more empirical research conducted on audience reaction to *All in the Family* than on any other TV entertainment program. While these studies provide some intriguing findings, they also reveal the limitations of current methods for assessing mass media effects. Taken as a whole, the studies confirm David Reisman's observation that

> no public opinion poll, no matter how large or how imaginatively stratified the sample, turns up enough cases or data to answer the questions its results raise . . . Polls are detective stories in which the reader must supply essential clues.

Interestingly, the first study of audience response was conducted by CBS itself. Based on a small telephone survey of viewers, conducted shortly after *All in the Family* went on the air, the study simply determined that most people who had seen the show liked it, found it funny, and were not offended by it. The fact that it was conducted at all is additional evidence of CBS's unusual concern about the possibility of an adverse reaction. The study did not probe why viewers liked the show nor whether it had any effect on their attitudes, but its results were apparently sufficient to satisfy the network's curiosity and concern. No further research on *All in the Family* was undertaken by CBS.

Beginning in 1974, however, a series of studies were undertaken by academic researchers. Most of them began with the premise that different members of the viewing audience might be seeing the same show in different ways. These studies were designed to test what Neil Vidmar and Milton Rokeach described as the "selective perception hypothesis": that while unprejudiced viewers appreciated *All in the Family* as a satire on bigotry, prejudiced viewers would not. Specifically, they hypothesized that more prejudiced viewers would be more likely to admire Archie, would perceive him as making the most sense and winning family arguments most often. They would also be less likely to object to Archie's use of racial epithets.

In their study utilizing a group of Midwestern high school

students and a second group of Canadian adults, Vidmar and Rokeach found support for their hypothesis.[†] Several other studies also found a relationship between viewers' prejudice or dogmatism and the extent of agreement with Archie Bunker's views. Based on these results, the authors of one study concluded that "it appears reasonable to argue that the effects of the show lie in reinforcing existing beliefs."

All of these studies, however, are surveys rather than experiments. This means that they provide no direct evidence that any viewers have become *more* prejudiced as a result of watching the program. Such a conclusion would require both before-and-after testing to detect shifts in attitudes. This type of research would, of course, be considerably more difficult and time-consuming, and no experimental studies involving *All in the Family* have been reported to date.[*]

At the same time, the existing studies contain some results which support a more positive view of *All in the Family*'s impact. For example, Vidmar and Rokeach found that a large majority of the people they interviewed expressed the belief that Mike "makes sense" more often than Archie. Even among the "high prejudice" viewers, who tended to like and agree with Archie, four times as many thought that Mike made better sense than his father-in-law. In addition, among the Canadian participants in the study, 20 percent indicated that watching the series "had made them aware that they had prejudices they didn't know about." The "high-prejudice" viewers were not significantly less likely than the "low-prejudice" viewers to report that they had gained such insight from watching the program.[**]

The impact of *All in the Family* has also been studied in The Netherlands, where the series was first broadcast in 1972 and quickly became one of that country's most popular programs. In a study similar to the U.S. and Canadian efforts, researchers G. Cleveland

---

[*]However, one study has attempted to approximate a "longitudinal" measurement of the effect of the series over time. In the study, a group of adults were asked whether they agreed or disagreed with the statement, "The more I watch *All in the Family*, the more I find myself agreeing with Archie." Overall responses were evenly divided, but those respondants most similar to Archie were more likely to answer affirmatively. (Stuart H. Surlin and Beth Bowden, "The Psychological Effect of Television Characters: The Case of Archie Bunker and Authoritarian Viewers," Paper presented to the Association for Education in Journalism, College Park, Maryland, August 1976.)

[**]This question, the only one in the study which addresses the impact of the series on viewers, was asked only of the Canadian participants in the study.

Wilhoit and Harold de Bock found a relationship between the test scores of individuals for "ethnocentrism, parental authoritarianism, and lifestyle intolerance" and the feelings they expressed about the program's characters.[†] However, "an overwhelming majority" of the participants in their study stated that they felt "Mike was usually right" in his disagreements with Archie.

Wilhoit and de Bock concluded that the series did not seem "likely to have a reinforcement effect on persons high on parental authoritarianism, ethnocentrism, and lifestyle intolerance." And while they did find some evidence of "selective perception" at work, they concluded that it did not appear strong enough "to prevent the basic satirical message from getting through, at least to the Dutch."

Despite their limitations, these studies clearly demonstrate that all viewers of *All in the Family* do not see the program in the same way. Viewers who are most like Archie tend to like him better and agree with him more often than viewers who are less like him. On the other hand, even while viewers' hearts may be with Archie, their heads are more likely to be with Mike.

Evidence from a very different kind of study offers an additional clue to the social impact of the series. This study by David Loye, measured the responses of 260 Los Angeles couples to a variety of prime-time programs.[*] Participants were asked to watch certain programs and rate each one on a scale of 1-4 in terms of the degree to which they found the program "emotionally, aesthetically, morally, and intellectually arousing and/or satisfying." Figures 1 and 2 represent average ratings by the participants for *Bewitched* and *All in the Family*. (The black bar in the middle is a general rating of how entertaining the program was judged to be.) The author commented:

> Most of the top comedy shows impact on the left side of the entertainment bar—for emotional and aesthetic arousal. *All in the Family*—and also *Good Times*, both Norman Lear productions—were unusual among the comedies in showing impact on the right side of the E bar, for *moral and intellectual arousal*.

---

*David Loye, "Mass Entertainment and Human Survival: Television's Potential for Prosocial Effects on Adults," Paper presented at American Psychological Association annual convention, Chicago, August 1975.

Question: "Did you find the program emotionally, aesthetically, morally, and intellectually arousing and/or satisfying?"

Figure 1: Profile for *Bewitched*

Figure 2: Profile for *All in the Family*

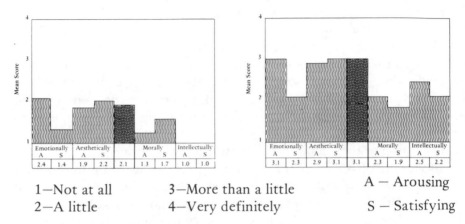

1—Not at all	3—More than a little	A — Arousing
2—A little	4—Very definitely	S — Satisfying

These findings suggest that *All in the Family* does affect its viewers in ways which are unusual for television comedies. However, the study does not tell us whether these effects are positive or negative, nor does it help answer the specific question about whether the program encourages or diminishes bigotry. Despite the number of studies *All in the Family* has stimulated, we still know relatively little about its impact. It would be hard not to agree with the authors of one study who concluded that:

> Assessing the effects of *All in the Family* and of ethnic humor as a whole upon both the viewers of the humor and the ethnic groups who are the objects of that humor is a task of critical importance. It has only just begun.

Responses of Children

A second strand of research has been concerned with children's responses to *All in the Family*. Despite the program's frank language and adult-oriented themes (e.g., menopause, abortion, impotence, lesbianism, homosexuality), *All in the Family* has been one of the most popular programs among younger as well as older viewers. Calling children "the show's forgotten audience," Timothy P. Meyer notes that *All in the Family*'s audience regularly included as many as nine million children under age 12.

Meyer was interested in discovering how much of the program's plot is understood by children; which characters children admire most and least and why; and what information the show is conveying to children about standards of adult and family behavior.[†] To find answers to these questions, Meyer interviewed a group of first, second, and third graders immediately after they had been shown an episode of *All in the Family*. Among the findings reported by Meyer:

- Archie was named by most children as the character liked *best* (by 44 percent of the children) and the character liked *least* (25 percent). "Curiously the same major reason is given why he is liked most or least (i.e., 'Archie yells at Edith when she acts stupid')."

- Moral and ethical behavior has little impact on most children's character preferences. "Doing what is right" seemed to be much less relevant than being funny, having a nice physical appearance, being nice.

- Older children demonstrated a much better understanding of the show's plot than younger children, but even the oldest children (third graders) often failed to understand some important aspects of the plot.

- One of the most interesting—and unexpected—findings was that differences in "ability grouping" among children at the same grade level (based on reading ability) showed no relation to understanding the program's content. Thus, "it may be that differences in ability to read print messages do not apply to the ability to 'read' audio-visual messages."

The Appeal of the Series

While the social impact of *All in the Family* remains an open question, there is no doubt about the fact of the program's appeal: *All in the Family* has been one of the most popular programs in the history of television. For much of the decade, the series was the number one prime-time program, watched regularly by nearly one-third of all Americans. Even in its ninth year, after both Rob Reiner and Sally Struthers had left the series, it still finished the season among the top ten prime-time programs. Along the way, *All in the Family* set some impressive records: Four episodes won places on Nielsen's list of the top 25 programs with the largest all-time audiences, an unprecedented feat for a regular continuing series. *All in the Family* even managed to get itself into the *Guinness Book of World Records*. In the 1975 edition, it was listed as holding the record—since eclipsed—for charging the highest advertising rate of any TV program ($128,000 for 60 seconds of commercial time.)

How to explain the program's immense appeal? Although the shock value of Archie's bigotry probably stimulated some of the initial interest in the series, it cannot account for its sustained popularity. In fact, bigotry was never really the primary focus of either the program or the character of Archie. From the beginning, the series has dealt with a broad range of other issues—law and order, patriotism and protest, religion and morality, politics and economics —not as abstractions, but in terms of their meaning for the lives of a recognizably American family. In addition, the series also showed the characters attempting to cope with more personal problems and pressures—impotence, homosexuality, menopause, aging, drug addiction, unemployment, mental retardation. These "sensitive" issues are now almost commonplace in prime-time, but they had seldom it ever been acknowledged by television before *All in the Family*. Lear has said that he believes the series succeeded because it "presented real people dealing with real issues."

Both halves of the equation are equally important: It is the reality of the people in the series that made the issues real. Clearly, a large part of the popularity of *All in the Family* was due to the appeal of the characters created by Lear and portrayed by Carroll O'Connor, Rob Reiner, Jean Stapleton, and Sally Struthers.

The key figure in the series, of course, was Archie Bunker. In the hands of a less gifted actor, he could have quickly become grating and tiresome. But the energy Carroll O'Connor brought to the role redeemed Archie, even in his most stubborn and wrongheaded moments. When he is on the screen, it is he who dominates; giving orders, delivering opinions, trading wisecracks, trying—and often failing—to stay in control of what is happening to him. He may be bested in an argument, caught in a strategm, but he is never wholly defeated.

At the same time, O'Connor permits us to see enough of the vulnerability beneath the bravado so that we recognize that Archie's tirades and put-downs are, as Lear claimed, motivated not by hatred but by a need to maintain his identity in a relentlessly changing world. Archie is a conservative in the strictest sense of the word. He not only supports the *status quo*, he longs to return to a time when things were simpler. He is unable to accept change because he is incapable of changing himself. As Carroll O'Connor observed in a 1973 *Playboy* interview, "It would take a miracle for Archie to change his attitudes. Christ would have to come down personally and speak to him."

Archie is also a provincial. He instinctively reacts against whatever is different from himself. Archie is *for* himself, his family, and for those who are like him; everyone and everything else he views as a potential threat. The following speech encapsulates Archie's attitude toward his country and his fellow citizens:

ARCHIE   Here in America—the land of the free where Lady Liberty holds her torch sayin' send me your poor, your deadbeats, your filthy . . . so they come from all over the world pourin' in like ants . . . like your Spanish, your P.R.s from the Carribuan, your Japs, your Chinamen, your Krauts and your Hebes and your English fags . . . all of them free to live together in peace and harmony in their own little separate sections where they feel safe, and break your head if you go in there. That there is what makes America great!

Rob Reiner's Mike is Archie's perfect foil—a genuine bleeding-heart liberal who enthusiastically embraces whatever cause is fashionable at the moment. As a result, it is Mike who most frequently confronts Archie and who is given the role of stating the ideologically "correct" position:

MIKE   What do you mean—America: Love it or leave it?

ARCHIE   That's right, it's a free country so amscray.

MIKE   But what would our leaving solve? With or without protesters we'd still have the same problems.

ARCHIE   What problems?

MIKE   The war. The race problem. The economic problem. The pollution problem.

ARCHIE   Well, if you're gonna nitpick.

Mike is Archie's opposite in other ways as well. He is a college student (later a college professor), while Archie is a high school drop-out. He is open in dealing with sexual matters, while Archie is deeply inhibited. Yet they are also alike. Both derive great pleasure from their confrontations. (Lear once remarked that the Bunkers, like his own family, "live at the top of their lungs"). And Mike is as capable of intransigence and self-contradiction as his father-in-law; he frequently demonstrates that he is not entirely undeserving of Archie's favorite description, "meathead."

Then there is Edith. As Mike is Archie's ideological counterpart, so Jean Stapleton's Edith is his emotional opposite. Although she shares many of her husband's old-fashioned values (both are deeply embarrassed by any discussions concerning sex, for example), her openness and tolerance contrast with his rigidity and hostility toward the world at large. As a number of observers have noted, her acceptance is close to saintly. It encompasses not only the targets of Archie's wrath, but Archie himself, with all of his imperfections. In one episode, Edith explains to a friend how she has kept her marriage going:

EDITH   Oh, I ain't got no secret. Archie and me still have our fights. Of course, we don't let them go on too long. Somebody always says, "I'm sorry." And Archie always says, "It's okay, Edith."

Edith is surprisingly complex. She is capable of tuning out what she does not like, of hearing what she wants to hear—often to Archie's dismay: "I'm talkin' English, Edith, but you're listenin' in dingbat." But she is also firmly in touch with reality, the one character who is able to break the impasse between opposing sides. She can be counted on to make peace, to lighten the mood. Without Edith, in fact, the Bunker family quarrels would become intolerably strident.

Finally, Sally Struthers as Gloria provides the link between the two generations. She balances her commitment to her husband and his values with an undisguised affection for her anachronistic parents.

From the beginning, Struthers' character has been allowed to express the greatest range of emotions—from fury to hilarity and from sorrow to elation. She is also the character who has changed the most over the course of the series. Her development has, in particular, reflected the impact of the women's movement during the 1970s. While the other characters seem to have *aged*, the character of Gloria has *grown*.

As important as the performers' individual strengths has been their ability to play together. They have honed their interaction so well that it is easy for viewers to forget that they are watching actors rather than an actual family. One of the distinguishing characteristics of their ensemble performance has been their eloquence in nonverbal communication. In an episode from the third season, for example, Archie returns home one evening to find a couple of obnoxiously gregarious swingers in his living room. Edith has invited them over, having completely misunderstood their classified ad seeking "companionship." This essentially contrived situation is handled deftly as the Bunker's progression from confusion to embarassment to indignation is communicated entirely in a series of facial expressions exchanged between Archie and Edith.

Also important in explaining the sustained popularity of the series is that it retained the capacity to surprise the audience. From one season to the next, *All in the Family* continued to experiment with new themes, to test the limits of the situation comedy format. For example, in the episode from the third season entitled "Archie is Branded,"[†] Archie is offered "protection" by a militant Jewish self-defense group after he finds a swastika painted on his door. The episode was especially shocking because it violated the most fundamental convention of both comic *and* dramatic TV series: the happy ending.

The fourth season brought episodes in which: Edith confronts the prospect of cancer when she discovers a lump in her breast; Gloria must deal with a retarded boy who develops a crush on her; Mike gets upset when Gloria decides she has the right to take the sexual initiative; and Edith "adopts" a resident of an old age home, forcing Archie to deal with his fear of growing old. The seventh (1976-77) season opened with a one-hour episode in which Archie jeopardizes his marriage as the result of a near-affair with another woman. The eighth season included another hour-long episode in which Edith is the victim of a graphically portrayed rape attempt.

A number of critics have charged that such subjects are simply too serious and complex to be treated adequately within the confines and conventions of TV comedy. Thus, Kenneth Pierce objects to what he terms *All in the Family*'s "use of burlesque caricature to call forth a serious emotional response."

It should be noted that a number of critics have charged that such subjects are simply too serious and complex to be treated adequately within the narrow confines of TV comedy. Thus, Roger Rosenblatt argues that situation comedy formulas unavoidably trap characters in lives that are "impervious to change." Despite what happens to them in each weekly installment, these characters don't learn anything, and therefore they don't develop. As a result, viewers can have "no feelings for the people involved" in these programs. Other critics have criticized *All in the Family* for indiscriminately mixing wisecracks with serious emotions. In a long essay in *The New Yorker*, Michael Arlen takes note of the tendency in Lear's comedies for the mood to "shift, almost in mid-dialogue, from (seriousness) into an old-timey gag or a cheap laugh."

In fact, there are times when the contrast between subject matter and situation comedy style is jarring. For example, the long sequence in which Edith, at home alone, struggles with the would-be rapist is extremely effective: The scene is intensely dramatic, even though it contains moments of real humor. Comedy and menace are kept in balance. However, in the scene that follows, Archie and Mike, two bufoons with baseball bats, are seen timidly creeping into the room (after first getting stuck in the door—a frequently recurring sight gag the series' writers seem unable to resist). The mood of the previous scene is shattered by this sudden plunge into low comedy. The shift has been too abrupt: after the realism of the rape attempt, we are not ready to believe that the husband and son-in-law of the victim would be so preoccupied with trading insults.

Yet even in awkward moments such as this, *All in the Family* remains more provocative and rewarding than the slick predictability of most other TV drama. And it is not true that viewers did not care about the characters in the series. The reason the rape scene worked is precisely because, after seven years, the audience believed in and cared about Edith. While the characters in some of Lear's weaker series (such as the short-lived *Hot L Baltimore*) were little more than one-dimensional vehicles for jokes, the characters in *All in the Family* were able to evoke responses that went well beyond the usual limits of situation comedy.

Finally, beyond the quality of its writing and acting, beyond the interest generated by its willingness to break new ground and take on difficult issues, there is one more reason, perhaps most important of all, for the enormous appeal of the series: *All in the Family* succeeded in symbolizing and dramatizing the conflicts which had arisen throughout the country during the 1960s. The divisions within this one family—conservative vs. liberal, patriot vs. skeptic, old vs. young—mirrored in comic form the polarizations which threatened to divide the society as a whole. The Bunker household was, in short, a microcosm of America.

Prior to *All in the Family*, social problems were portrayed as something that happened "out there," in the public arena. By contrast, home was a refuge and the family was sacrosanct, the realm of the purely domestic. Lear ignored these conventions and portrayed the family as a political arena—as *the* political arena.

The conception was audacious and powerfully dramatic. But it was also true to life: the crises of the 1960s were acted out in living rooms across the country. Perhaps not since the Civil War had America experienced a conflict that had cut through families in such an intimate way. Better than any book or film or play of the time, *All in the Family*, for all its flaws, helped us to see what was happening to ourselves and our society.

The message was not entirely comforting: Although Archie reacts to change by rejecting it and Mike responds by embracing it, neither one has much ability to control it. They do not initiate, they react—to a strike, a troublesome neighbor, a Presidential proclamation, an act of violence, a computer mix-up, a medical emergency. But because this *is* a television program, and because Lear himself is an optimist, the show's ultimate message was positive. The series repeatedly demonstrated that no matter how great the strain, how heated the argument, the family's bonds of love are stronger. The idea is old-fashioned but appealing. In the final analysis, the series represented an affirmation of the power of the family to endure.

Family's Offspring

When Norman Lear decided to leave film-making to go back into television, many of his colleagues and friends—including his wife—tried to persuade him that he was making a mistake. After all, it was TV people who wanted to get into films, not the other way around. But Lear knew what he was doing. Following the explosive success of *All in the Family*, he became the most sought-after producer in the industry. The networks love a winner, and Lear was winning in a big way.

New programs began emerging at a remarkable rate from Tandem productions (still in partnership with Bud Yorkin) and his own company, T.A.T. Productions: *Sanford and Son* and *Maude* in 1972, *Good Times* in 1974, *One Day at a Time* and *The Jeffersons* in 1975. Although Lear could not claim credit for inventing the idea of a spin-off, he exploited it with great skill. Thus, *All in the Family* begat *Maude* and *The Jeffersons*, while *Maude* begat *Good Times*. These series also flourished, and by the end of the 1975 season, the three most popular prime-time programs were Lear's (*All in the Family*, #1; *Sanford and Son*, #2; *Maude*, #3).

Lear's programs, along with series such as *The Mary Tyler Moore Show, Rhoda, Bob Newhart* (from MTM Enterprises), and *M*A*S*H* pioneered a new, more sophisticated brand of comedy. They were programs that mature viewers could watch—and discuss—without apology, and they helped earn a new respect for the potential of commercial television. But it was Lear's shows which continued to attract the most attention and to provoke the most controversy

There was much debate, for example, about whether his "black" comedies were a good thing, because they gave blacks greater visibility in prime-time, or a bad thing, because characters like Fred Sanford and J.J. of *Good Times* were demeaning to blacks. Among the many controversial episodes of *Maude* was one in which Bea Arthur underwent an abortion and another in which she had to seek help for depression. Lear prided himself on continuing to test the limits of what he could present on television—even in smallest matters. Thus, in an angry moment Maude calls her husband a "son of a bitch." And a 1976 episode of *All in the Family* brought prime-time TV's first example of "frontal nudity" when Archie changes the diaper of his infant grandson.

Throughout the 1970s, Lear's struggles with the networks seemed to grow more heated. The popular success of his programs had not lessened the vigilance of the networks' censors. Lear remained willing to do battle with them, but he felt the networks were becoming increasingly arbitrary and restrictive. In fact, pressure was building on the industry to do something about what came to be known as "sex and violence."

The result was a policy called Family Viewing Time (FVT).

In 1975, in response to intense pressure from the chairman of the Federal Communications Commission, Richard Wiley, broadcasters adopted a requirement that programs broadcast before 9 p.m. be suitable for viewers of all ages. What the policy meant at CBS was that *All in the Family*, which had been carried for years at 8 p.m., would either have to be "toned down" or moved to a later time period. Lear refused to alter the program's character, and the network rescheduled it to 9 p.m.

Lear was furious and, along with other producers, directors, and writers, brought suit challenging the legality of the family viewing policy. Characterizing FVT as "ridiculous" and "a gutless give-in" to the government by the networks, Lear claimed that the new policy represented an unconstitutional violation of his right of free speech.

In November, 1977, Federal Court Judge Warren Ferguson ruled that the Family Viewing policy was illegal, and that FCC Chairman Wiley had exceeded his authority by using the threat of government intervention to coerce broadcasters into adopting FVT. The networks quickly announced that they would individually continue to schedule programs suitable for family viewing before 9:00 p.m. However, the following season *All in the Family* was moved back to 8:00 p.m. by CBS.*

Nine Seasons

Lear had won a major victory, but he was beginning to grow tired of the constant battles he had to fight to get his shows on the air. In addition, his more recent series had not been proving as successful as his earlier efforts. Viewers had shown little interest in *Hot L Baltimore, The Dumplings,* or *The Nancy Walker Show*, and they had all been quickly cancelled. *All's Fair* lasted a single season, then was not renewed.

Lear also discovered that the networks were more interested in having him continue to imitate his past successes than offer them something really new. For several years, Lear had worked on the concept for a satirical soap opera. Like a conventional soap opera, it would have five episodes a week which told the continuing story of an interrelated group of characters, but it would also contain comic elements. Lear tried to sell the idea to the networks, but was

---

*For a detailed account of the struggle over Family Viewing Time, including Lear's role in it, see *See No Evil* by Geoffrey Cowan (New York: Simon and Schuster, 1979).

turned down by all three. Unwilling to abandon the project, Lear decided he would sell the show directly to individual stations.

Mary Hartman, Mary Hartman turned out to be the most interesting program of the 1975-76 season.* But even though it was a critical and popular success, it lost more than $1½ million due to the high cost of selling and distributing the program via syndication. In its second season, *MH, MH* did manage to show a profit, but it was discontinued shortly after its star, Louise Lasser, left the series. Lear tried several more times to create a successful syndicated program (*All That Glitters, Fernwood 2-Nite, America 2-Nite*), but was unable to sign up enough stations to make them profitable. It was becoming increasingly clear that there were no simple alternatives to the networks.

Meanwhile, Lear's original series were beginning to fade. As the 70s progressed, times changed, and both the networks and the public seemed to lose interest in controversial programs. With the end of the war in Vietnam, students turned their attention from protest to grades and job training, and the campuses quieted down. The Carter Presidency seemed to signal a shift in the mood of a country grown weary of conflict and confrontation.

By 1977, Lear's brand of comedy was giving way to another kind of comedy. *All in the Family* had been replaced at the top of the ratings by ABC's *Happy Days*, a distinctly uncontroversial comedy about teenage hijinks in the 1950s. Second and third in the ratings were *Laverne and Shirley* and *Three's Company*. And even though *All in the Family* remained among the top ten shows, it too seemed to reflect the apparent change in the mood of the country. The arrival of a grandson for the Bunkers took some of the passion out of the generational conflict which had previously given the show much of its energy. Mike seemed to lose some of his idealism and passion as he made the transition from student to teacher. Even Archie seemed to grow more mellow.

The series remained capable of surprise, however. The episode entitled "Two's a Crowd,"[†] broadcast in February 1978, begins by setting up a relatively contrived situation: Mike and Archie get stuck in the storeroom of Archie's tavern. The two antagonists trade the

---

Mary Hartman, Mary Hartman, like *All in the Family*, inspired as much comment on its sociological significance as its artistic merits. See, for example: "The Mary Hartman Craze" by Harry F. Waters and Martin Kasindorf, *Newsweek* (cover story), May 3, 1976; and "MH[2] Recycles Our Garbage" by Ted Morgan, *New York Times Sunday Magazine*, October 3, 1976.

usual insults for a while, but then the tone shifts as Archie, under the influence of a few drinks, begins reminiscing about his childhood and his father. The wisecracks fade away as Archie reveals himself in a way neither Mike nor the audience has seen before. Thanks in large part to Carroll O'Connor's performance, the episode turned out to be one of the most moving and memorable in the series.

Also in February 1978, Norman Lear announced that he had decided to "take a leave" from day-to-day involvement in television production. For eight years, he had been intimately involved in almost every episode of every series produced by his companies, and now he wanted an opportunity to change focus and begin developing some new projects.

Shortly thereafter, Rob Reiner and Sally Struthers let it be known that the 1977-78 season would be their last in *All in the Family*. Lear felt that with their departure, the program had reached a natural stopping place. With *All in the Family* finishing the season still among the top ten programs, it seemed a good time to call it quits.

However, there was to be one more season. Alan Horn, the new head of Lear's company, and Robert Daly, the new president of CBS Entertainment, overruled Lear and persuaded Carroll O'Connor and Jean Stapleton to sign on for a ninth season. To round out the cast, Danielle Brisebois was added in the role of Stephanie, a precocious nine-year-old who moves in with the Bunkers as a kind of foster daughter. Even with a diminished cast, *All in the Family*'s audience appeal remained potent, and the series finished the 1978-79 season among the top ten prime-time programs.

With the departure of Jean Stapleton at the conclusion of the ninth season, the program seems finally to have reached the end of the line. Archie Bunker will apparently continue in a new program set primarily in his bar, but it will no longer be *All in the Family* as American viewers have come to know it.

Still, the series will probably never disappear entirely from TV screens; for in the Fall of 1979, the more than 200 episodes of *All in the Family* will begin syndicated reruns on individual stations across the country.

After nine years, it is now possible to look at *All in the Family* in some perspective. Yet, as the statements in the final section of this book demonstrate, much about the series remains controversial.

One major unanswered question concerns the series' social effects. We still cannot make a definitive judgement about the impact of *All in the Family* on its vast and heterogeneous audience. The evidence to date indicates that not all viewers have responded to the program and its characters the same way. In particular, highly bigoted viewers and young viewers are likely to miss the not-very-subtle satire of Archie's prejudices. Yet on the whole, the existing research suggests that Archie has been "understood" by the great majority of viewers.

A second, even more controversial question concerns the program's aesthetic achievement. Several critics (Michael Arlen, Roger Rosenblatt, Dorothy Rabinowitz) have found the series to be seriously, even fatally flawed. Their objections relate directly to the requirements of commercial television for a predictable, standardized product—26 weekly half-hour segments per year, to be delivered for as many years as the ratings and the creators hold up. Yet within these stringent limitations, *All in the Family* represents a considerable achievement, especially in terms of performance and complexity of character.

Perhaps the reason that *All in the Family* has resisted easy evaluation is that it embodies a series of striking contradictions—contradictions that mirror the personality of its creator. Thus, Norman Lear is a man who cares passionately about ideas, yet is comfortable practicing the broadest kind of vaudeville humor; he is an outspoken liberal who shows deep respect for traditional, even reactionary values; and, most interesting of all, he is a fierce individualist who has thrived in the atmosphere of collaboration and compromise required for commercial TV production.

A final question about *All in the Family* concerns its ultimate impact on television itself. A few years ago, it seemed clear that the series had, in Robert Wood's phrase, "changed the face of television." The series seemed to have destroyed the old taboos and opened up new vistas for treating controversial subjects in prime time. In light of the largely witless programming currently dominating the network schedules, the claim now seems dubious. In fact, one might well ask if anything really changed as a result of *All in the Family*. Censorship continues. The network decision-making process remains intact. Program choices are still dictated by ratings and revenues. Quality remains a luxury and imitation, not innovation, remains the guiding principle for selecting new programs.

It is possible that *All in the Family* represented part of a transient cycle rather than the vanguard of a permanent change. If so, we may some day look back on the early 1970s as a Golden Age of TV Comedy, the era of *All in the Family, Maude, The Mary Tyler Moore Show, Rhoda, M*A*S*H, Barney Miller,* and *Mary Hartman, Mary Hartman.* These series proved that commercial television could be both entertaining and have something to say. And none provided more entertainment or had more to say than *All in the Family.*

ALL IN THE FAMILY:
A TEN YEAR CHRONOLOGY

January 1969	First pilot taped in New York under the title *Those Were the Days*
March 1969	Second pilot taped in Los Angeles with same script, but with roles of Mike and Gloria re-cast with Rob Reiner and Sally Struthers
Summer 1970	CBS decides to buy *All in the Family* (*AITF*) after ABC turns it down
January 12, 1971	Series premieres on CBS
May 1971	*AITF* wins Emmy as outstanding comedy series
September 1971	*AITF* begins second season at 8:00 p.m. on Saturady nights; quickly becomes the #1 prime time series
Sept-Oct 1971	Hobson-Lear exchange in the *New York Times*
November 1971	*AITF* on cover of *Newsweek*
May 1972	*AITF* wins 7 Emmies, including best series, best lead actor (O'Connor), best lead actress (Stapleton), best supporting actress (Struthers), best director (John Rich)
Summer 1974	O'Connor threatens to leave series; first two episodes of fifth season taped without him
December 1974	100th episode special, narrated by Henry Fonda
September 1975	Family Viewing Time begins; *AITF* moved to 9:00 p.m. on Tuesday nights
December 1975	*AITF* begins daytime reruns on CBS; Archie's grandson arrives

November 1976   Judge Warren Ferguson rules FVT illegal

February 1978   Lear takes leave from day-to-day involvement in television production

September 1978   Archie and Edith Bunker's chairs installed at Smithsonian Institution; ninth season begins without Rob Reincr and Sally Struthers

February 1979   200th episode celebration of *AITF* taped as 90-minute special with Norman Lear

September 1979   *AITF* begins syndicated reruns; *Archie Bunker's Place* begins on CBS

TELEVISION SERIES PRODUCED BY NORMAN LEAR

1.   Tandem Productions

All in the Family	CBS	January 1971—April 1979
Sanford and Son	NBC	January 1972—March 1977
Maude	CBS	September 1972—April 1978
Good Times	CBS	February 1974—April 1979
Sanford Arms	NBC	September 1977—October 1977
Diff'rent Strokes	NBC	November 1978—

2.   T.A.T. Productions

The Jeffersons	CBS	January 1975—
Hot L Baltimore	ABC	January 1975—June 1975
One Day at a Time	CBS	December 1975—
The Dumplings	NBC	January 1976—March 1976
All's Fair	CBS	September 1976—March 1977
The Nancy Walker Show	ABC	September 1976—March 1977
Year at the Top	CBS	August 1977—September 1977
In the Beginning	CBS	September 1978—October 1978
Apple Pie	ABC	September 1978 (2 episodes)
Hello, Larry	NBC	January 1979—

Syndicated programs

Mary Hartman, Mary Hartman	January 1976–July 1977
All That Glitters	April 1977–July 1977
Fernwood 2-Nite	July 1977–September 1977
Forever Fernwood	October 1977–March 1978
America 2-Nite	April 1978–July 1978

I. On the Screen:
Three Scripts

Meet the Bunkers

written by Norman Lear
First season, broadcast January 12, 1971

Produced by
Norman Lear

Directed by
John Rich

CAST

ARCHIE BUNKER	Carroll O'Connor
EDITH BUNKER	Jean Stapleton
MICHAEL STIVIC	Rob Reiner
GLORIA STIVIC	Sally Struthers
LIONEL	Michael Evans

OPENING CREDITS

FADE UP:

Archie & Edith at Piano

Music: "Those Were the Days"

ARCHIE Boy, the way Glenn Miller played[*]
　　　　　Songs that made the Hit Parade!
　　　　　Guys like us, we had it made—
　　　　　Those were the days!

DISSOLVE TO FILM AND CREDITS

MUSIC CONTINUES:

EDITH And you knew where you were then,

ARCHIE Girls were girls and men were men,

BOTH Mister we could use a man
　　　　　Like Herbert Hoover again!

ARCHIE Didn't need no welfare state,

EDITH Everybody pulled his weight,

BOTH Gee our old La Salle ran great!
　　　　　Those were the days!

FADE TO BLACK

ACT ONE

FADE UP:

> (*Gloria in dining room setting table. Mike enters front door*)

MIKE   Gloria—I hurried back.

GLORIA   Good, you can take out the garbage.

MIKE   Garbage is not exactly what I had in mind. Come here.

GLORIA   Not now, Michael.

MIKE   Why not?

GLORIA   I want everything ready for when the folks get back from church. *(Comes D.S. to table)* It's different, isn't it, an anniversary brunch.

MIKE   Yeah, well I think your mother will love it. But your father —he doesn't care about anniversaries. I mean, you hadda pick out the present for him to give to your mother. And I had to get the card. And he doesn't know anything about any of this. What do you think he's gonna do when he finds out?

GLORIA   He'll have a fit. But then, he wouldn't get her anything and it'll make Mom's day.

MIKE   What are you running from me? Come here. *(He kisses her)* Gloria, we've been living with your folks since we're married. We don't get the house alone that much!

GLORIA   Oh we're not alone. Lionel's upstairs.

MIKE   Lionel? Why?

GLORIA   He's fixing the portable TV for Dad.

MIKE   *(Reacts)*

5

GLORIA   And then later he's gonna take the present and get some fresh-cut flowers and deliver them together, just to make it more romantic.

LIONEL   *(Entering)* Set's good as new Gloria. Hey, how's it going, Mike?

MIKE   Hey Lionel, how are you?

GLORIA   I'll get the present.
    (Gloria exits)

LIONEL   Hey, so what's new on the campus with all you angry white social democrats?

MIKE   Oh, we're shaking them up.

LIONEL   *(Laughs)* Okay. *(Looking around)* Hey, where's your father-in-law?

MIKE   Oh, he's at church.

LIONEL   Good.

MIKE   Why? Is he still giving you a hard time?

LIONEL   Oh, I'm used to him by now. You know his latest kick?

MIKE   What?

LIONEL   Asking me what I'm gonna be when I get to college. He likes to hear me say: "Ahm gwana be a 'lectical ingineer."

MIKE   And you say that for him?

LIONEL   Give the people what they want, man. How else do I get to become an electrical engineer?

GLORIA   *(Entering with small package)* Here's the present and the card. Mom likes just about any kind of flowers, so—will a dollar be enough?

LIONEL   Crazy. Where I get my flowers this represents a buck profit! *(To Mike)* See ya', man.
　　　　(He exits)

MIKE   See ya, Lionel.

GLORIA   *(Turns into his arms)* Alright now, Michael. Promise me something. For today. For their twenty-second anniversary. No fighting with Daddy? Okay?

MIKE   Okay.

GLORIA   Thank you.
　　　　(They kiss. He nods "yes" and she nods "no")

GLORIA   No Michael, not now. I don't have any time.

MIKE   Gloria, they won't be out of church 'till eleven thirty; it's a ten minute walk; we got time to spare.

GLORIA   Not now, Michael. I've got too much on my mind.
　　　　(She exits into kitchen. He follows)

MIKE   One little thing more it's not gonna hurt . . .

GLORIA   But we have to be downstairs to yell 'surprise'.

MIKE   They'll be downstairs. Let *them* yell 'surprise'.

GLORIA   For their own anniversary!

MIKE   Come here!
　　　　(He starts kissing her, muttering "Yeah, for their own anniversary"—and she responds)
　　　　(Cut to: front door area)
　　　　(Two other voices are heard coming toward the apartment from the outside)

ARCHIE'S VOICE   *(O.S.)* If you don't like what I do then what the hell did you bring me there for? Anyway?

EDITH'S VOICE   *(O.S.)* I ain't gonna quarrel with ya', Archie. *(As they enter)* It's maybe the fourth time in twenty-two years you been to church with me, so I'm grateful for the half'a sermon we sat through.

ARCHIE   Half a sermon was plenty. He said all I wanted to hear. And I've been to church with you more than four times in twenty-two years, too.

EDITH   Well maybe it's six times, seven, if you want to include the time we were married in church. *(She takes off her hat)* Look, I don't wanna make no World War Three out of this . . . *(Archie sees the table set and the party streamers)*

ARCHIE   Whaddya call all this?

EDITH   The table's set with the good glasses and all—oh, it's for our anniversary! Look Archie, Gloria and Mike, they made us a brunch!

ARCHIE   A "what"?

EDITH   A brunch.

ARCHIE   "BRUNCH." *(He picks up magazine)* It figures. She's reading *Cosmopolitan* again!
   (At this moment, Mike enters, carrying Gloria. They are locked in a kiss as they head for the stairs. Archie and Edith regard them wordlessly. Gloria and Mike suddenly sense Archie's presence)

GLORIA   Hi!

MIKE   You're early.

ARCHIE   So are you.

MIKE   *(He puts Gloria down)* We were just gonna go sit down over there.

ARCHIE   Eleven ten of a Sunday mornin'.

(Gathering themselves together, Gloria and Mike begin to sing:)

GLORIA AND MIKE   Happy anniversary to you
                      Happy anniversary to you
                      Happy anniversary dear mom and dad
                      Happy anniversary to you.

EDITH   Oh my, Archie, ain't this nice?

ARCHIE   Five minutes more and we would've got it remote from the bedroom!

GLORIA   Gee, Mom, would you tell him it's normal!
(Exits)

EDITH   *(She goes to Archie)* Oh, Archie, why do you wanna pick on them, when you've just had such a nice surprise?

ARCHIE   *They* was the ones that had the surprise! Used to be, the daylight hours was reserved for the respectable things of life.

MIKE   Come on, Archie, certain things're no different now than they ever were.

ARCHIE   Whaddya talkin'! Get your feet off the furniture! In my day we was able to keep things in their proper suspective. *(To Mike)* Take keepin' company, for instance. When your mother-in-law and me was goin' around together—it was two whole years—we never—I never—I mean there was nothin'—I mean absolutely *nothin'*—not 'till the wedding night.

EDITH   Yeah, and even then . . .
(Gloria brings a tray of orange juice around. She speaks gaily to change their mood)

GLORIA   Now—here we are—we have the juice in here—then we go in there for brunch.

EDITH   My, my, how fancy.

ARCHIE   Alright leave it there, huh. *Cosmopolitan*!

GLORIA   Oh, stop it, Daddy. I think it's very "today."

EDITH   That's right. The "in" crowd never has a whole meal in one room anymore. *(Archie looks at her)* That's what they say.

ARCHIE   You're a pip, you know that. A real pip!

GLORIA   You're married twenty-two years today, Daddy, so talk real nice to Mom, okay?

ARCHIE   *(To Gloria)* Listen little girl—you just go on and mind your own beeswax, huh? *(Gloria bends to set tray down)* And pull down that skirt. Everytime you sit down in one of them things, the mystery is over. What the hell is it nowadays! Will ya tell me! Girls wit' skirts up to here, guys wit' *hair* down to there! Gee. I stopped in a Gent's Room the other day. So help me there was a guy in there with a ponytail. My heart turned right over in me—I thought I was in the wrong toilet!

MIKE   Why do you fight it? The world's changing.

EDITH   That's right. That's what the Reverend Felcher was sayin'. You two should have heard him. Of course, Mr. Religion here wasn't seeing eye-to-eye with the sermon.

ARCHIE   What sermon! That was Socialist propaganda, pure and simple. And don't give me that look. You didn't think it was so hot, neither.

EDITH   I said it was different, that's all. But I didn't curse the Reverend from right there in the front pew.

ARCHIE   He never heard me. Besides, I ain't sittin' still for no preacher tellin' me that I'm to blame for all this here break-down in law and order that's goin' on.

MIKE   Why not? We're all to blame for not paying enough attention to the cause of it.

ARCHIE   The cause of it? I'll tell ya the cause of it. The cause of it is these sob sisters like the Reverend Felcher. And the bleedin' hearts and weepin' Nellies like youse two!

MIKE   Like us?

ARCHIE   Yea.

EDITH   I think we better eat now.

MIKE   No, wait a second. It's you.

ARCHIE   Me?

MIKE   Yeah, that's right. You—the property owners, with your twenty-four inch TV's and your four-slice toasters and your ice-maker refrigerators. That's all you care about, Archie, is what you got and how you can keep it.

ARCHIE   You'd care about it, too, sonny boy, if you *had* anything. If you wasn't livin' offa me—without a pot to peel a potato in!
(*Archie crosses to dining room and Mike follows*)

MIKE   Wait a second. You're the one who said I could stay here while I'm in school—

ARCHIE   Yeah, but I thought you was gonna be for a year while you learn a trade or something. I didn't think you was gonna wind up in college learnin' how to be a subversive!

MIKE   What are you talkin' about?—I just want to know a little bit about society so I can help people.

ARCHIE   People—your mother-in-law an' me is people—help us—will ya go to work!

MIKE   I know what's bothering you—you're upset because I was nailing you on that law and order thing.

ARCHIE   You nailin' me!

11

MIKE   Yeah, that's right. Now I'm gonna tell you something.

GLORIA   Michael!

MIKE   Wait a second. I'm sorry, Gloria, I know I promised—but I feel I have to say this. You know why we got a breakdown in law and order in this country, Archie, because we got poverty, real poverty, and we got that because guys like you are afraid to give the black man and the Mexican-American and all the other minorities their just and rightful hard-earned share of the American dream.

GLORIA   Who said he wasn't smart? That's beautiful, Michael. Beautiful.

ARCHIE   *(Aping her)* Oh, that's gorgeous. *(Gets up and crosses into living room)* Now let me tell you something. If your Spics and Spades want their rightful share of the American Dream, let 'em go out and hustle for it just like I done.

MIKE   *(Following him)* Yeah, but Archie you're forgetting one thing. You didn't have to hustle with black skin.

ARCHIE   No, and I didn't have to hustle with one arm and one leg neither. So what?

MIKE   So you're admitting that the black man is handicapped.

ARCHIE   Oh no. No more'n me. He's just as good as me.

MIKE   Now I suppose you're gonna tell me that the black man has had the same opportunity in this country as you.

ARCHIE   More. He's had more. I didn't have no million people out there marchin' and protestin' to get me my job!

EDITH   No, his uncle got it for him.

ARCHIE   *(After a withering look to Edith)* All I'm saying is. don't blame me—you and that Reverend Bleedin' Heart Felcher up there in his ivory shower.

12

(Edith crosses in from dining room)

EDITH   Now, that's enough—talking about a man of the cloth that way. God could punish you for that.

MIKE   God! What God?

GLORIA   Yeah. What God?

ARCHIE   What was that? *(To Edith)* Did you hear him? Did you hear her? *(To Mike)* What was that remark, sonny?

EDITH   *(Heading back to dining room—Mike follows)* I think we better eat now.

ARCHIE   *Not yet. (To Mike)* I wanna know what you meant by "What God?"

MIKE   It's nothing Archie. It's nothing. You need God, so forget it. *(Archie moves to table)*

EDITH   That's no way to talk on the Sabbath, Mike.

ARCHIE   Stifle, Edith.

EDITH   And no way to talk to your father-in-law either.

ARCHIE   Edith, I told you to—

EDITH   I mean, you know Sunday's a day of rest and peace. And you eat a nice brunch.

ARCHIE   Edith, will you stifle.

EDITH   Archie, we're all hungry.

ARCHIE   Will you stifle!! *(Archie moves to his chair. Mike and Gloria reach for toast)* Don't touch nothing. Nobody eats nothing around here until we get this thing straight. *(Waits a beat; speaks to Mike)* Now, sonny boy, you made a certain referential remark there a minute or so ago along the following

13

lines. "What God?" you said. And I heard *your wife*, my flesh and blood, repeated it. So let's hear it, okay? What did you mean by, "What God?"

MIKE   We just don't see any evidence of God, that's all.

GLORIA   That's right, Daddy.

ARCHIE   "That's right, Daddy" . . . *(Explodes standing and pacing D.S.)* Well, I knew I had a couple of pinkos in this house; but I didn't know we had atheists. Did you know that's what we had—a pair of atheists under the roof, Edith!

EDITH   Maybe if we could just eat a little something.

ARCHIE   Will you stifle, you silly dingbat!

EDITH   I don't want no more arguments.

ARCHIE   *(Sitting)* We are not arguing, we are discussing.

EDITH   I don't care what you call it, it's still arguing.

ARCHIE   We're having what we always have around here—a discussion.

EDITH   I don't see the difference.

ARCHIE   That's cause you're a dingbat! Now—will you stay the hell outta this! *(Edith puts hat on)* And get that ridiculous hat off your head!

EDITH   So long as you don't argue.

ARCHIE   Edith! Stay the hell outta this! *(Reaches for coffee handle and grabs spout instead)* OW! Owwwww! Oh my God!
    (He paces up and back, waving his arm, cupping it between his knees, whining all the while the family crosses to him)

MIKE   What's the matter?

ARCHIE   Get away from me, you meathead. It's all your fault. You nearly burnt the hand off of me.

GLORIA   What did he do?

ARCHIE   He helps himself to coffee then he turns the handle around the other way.

GLORIA   *(Mike and Gloria leave)* Daddy, he didn't do it on purpose.

EDITH   *(Going to him)* Let me see . . . It really hurts, huh?

ARCHIE   *(Answers with a grunt of pain)* Yeah.

EDITH   Right about in there?

ARCHIE   *(Another grunt)* Yeah.

EDITH   You know what I think we oughta do?

ARCHIE   What do you think?

EDITH   I think we oughta eat.
(She heads for the table. Camera holds on Archie's reaction)
(Applause)

FADE TO BLACK

ACT TWO

FADE UP:

(The table. The family is eating. Table talk. One change in mood, they are wearing the paper party hats)

ARCHIE   Gimme over the ketchup there, will ya?

GLORIA   Ketchup on eggs? Daddy, really!

ARCHIE   "Daddy Really's" been eatin' ketchup on eggs since before you was born, little girl, so don't let it concern ya, huh?
(He belches)

EDITH   Archie, that's terrible.

GLORIA   *(Getting up)* Well, who's for more eggs?

EDITH   Sure I can't help you, dear?

GLORIA   Not today, Mom. Today you sit. If I need any help, Michael can do it.

ARCHIE   It won't do him no harm neither. The last time I seen him lift a hand around here, he was testing his deodorant.

GLORIA   Mom!

EDITH   Archie—leave him alone!

MIKE   Ya! What do you want from me, anyway! I don't have *time* to do anything. I'm in class six hours, I'm studying six hours. It's not easy going to college; it's hard work!

ARCHIE   For you, it's like building the pyramids. I'll tell you, studyin' sociology, and all that welfare stuff—I don't call that no hard work!

GLORIA   Oh, leave him alone, Daddy. I think it's beautiful that Michael wants to help the underprivileged.

ARCHIE   He wants to help the underprivileged, let him start with himself. He's got no brains. He's got no ambition, and if that ain't underprivileged, I don't know what is.

GLORIA   *(Stands)* That's it! Mother, we're moving out of here.

I'm not gonna stay here another minute to see my husband insulted like that.

EDITH *(An arm around Gloria's waist)* Archie, say you're sorry! If she leaves here, she'll be dead inside a year.

ARCHIE You don't have to worry. They ain't goin' nowheres.

EDITH You don't know what it is, Archie. She can't be cleaning an apartment and cookin' and marketing—Dr. Feinstein says she's anemic.

ARCHIE Don't gimme that. For ten bucks some of these doctors'll tell ya anything you wanta hear.

EDITH He's the best there is when it comes to blood. My own cousin from the hospital said so.

ARCHIE Your cousin from the hospital empties bedpans, don't make him out no specialist. And, I know what Dr. Feinberg said.

EDITH Fein*stein*—

ARCHIE Feinstein, Feinberg, it all comes to the same thing, and I know that tribe.

EDITH I'm telling you, Archie, them kids don't leave this house until Mike can provide for her proper.

MIKE Oh boy! Four years before I even begin to make a living! It seems like forever!

ARCHIE Lemme tell you, sonny boy, the same thought crosses my mind at least once a day.

GLORIA Mom!

ARCHIE Gloria, you married the laziest white man I *ever* seen.

MIKE Alright, alright, it's bad enough you gotta make fun of me, you don't have to make it worse by attacking a whole race.

ARCHIE   Who's attacking a whole race?

MIKE   You are. You said I was the laziest white man you ever met.

ARCHIE   What's the matter with that?

MIKE   *White* man you ever met?

ARCHIE   Yeah, you!

MIKE   Implying that the blacks are even lazier.

ARCHIE   Now wait a minute, you meathead. You said that, not me. I never said your black beauties is lazy. It's just their systems is geared slower than the rest of us.

MIKE   Aw, come on, Archie.

ARCHIE   If you don't believe me, look it up!

GLORIA   There's just no fighting his prejudice. There's no hope for him. No hope at all.

ARCHIE   I'm not prejudiced! Any man deserves my respect, he gonna get it. Irregardless of his color!

MIKE   Then why do you call them names like "black beauties" for?

ARCHIE   Now, that's where I got you, Mr. Liberal. Because there's a black guy who works with me down the building's got a bumper sticker on his car that says "Black is Beautiful," so what'sa matter with black beauties?

EDITH   It's nicer than when he called 'em coons.

SOUND: DOORBELL RINGS

ARCHIE   If black beauties is kosher with them, it's kosher with me.
>   *(Mike goes to the door and opens it to reveal Lionel, with a spray of wild flowers)*

MIKE   Hey, Lionel. How you doin'? Come on in. You know, in a way we were just talking about you.

GLORIA   Michael!

ARCHIE   Talkin' about prejudice, I'm glad you're here Lionel.
>   *(Gets up and goes to living room)*

LIONEL   Yes, sir. Mr. Bunker, sir. *(Hands flowers to Edith)* These are for you, Mrs. Bunker. A present from an admirer.

EDITH   *(Overwhelmed)* For me? Oh my goodness, I ain't had a present for ten years.

GLORIA   I wonder who it's from.

ARCHIE   *(Coming back to table)* There's something I want to ask you, Lionel.

GLORIA   Wait a minute, Daddy. Let her open her gift first.

ARCHIE   She waited ten years; another minute ain't gonna kill her! *(Puts gift on table, takes Lionel to living room)* Come here, Lionel. Let me ask your opinion of somethin' there, Lionel. When you started doin' odd jobs in the neighborhood, wasn't I one of the first guys to throw a little work your way— by the way, didya fix the TV up in the bedroom?

LIONEL   Sure did, Mr. Bunker.
>   *(Lionel nods. Archie slips him some change)*

ARCHIE   Swell. Good boy . . . Here, put this in your pocket.

EDITH   Cheaper than a repairman, believe me.

ARCHIE   Is anybody talkin' to you . . . Now, Lionel, you could say by throwin' you these little jobs, in a way I was helpin' you get some money so you can get through college so's you can become . . .

LIONEL   A 'lectical ingineer.

ARCHIE   *(Loves it)* Yeah. Ya hear that?

MIKE   *(Impatient)* Archie, ask your question already!

ARCHIE   Will you keep your drawers on? Hey, by the way, that's a pretty nice looking suit you got on there. I mean it's classy, it's quiet. Where'd you get it?

LIONEL   Up in Harlem.

ARCHIE   *(Looks)* Nah.

LIONEL   Now I got two more, but one's in yellow with stripes, the other one's in purple with checks. You know, for when I'm with *my* people.

ARCHIE   Well, anyway Lionel, I'd say you know me pretty good, wouldn't you?

LIONEL   Oh, yes, sir. I got a bead on you, all right. I know you real good.

ARCHIE   Good, good.

MIKE   *(Crossing to living room)* Alright, alright, let's get to the point. Lionel, what he wants to know, is if you think he's prejudiced.

LIONEL   *(Feigning innocence)* Prejudiced?

ARCHIE   Yeah.

LIONEL   Prejudiced against who?

MIKE   Against Black People.

LIONEL Against Black People! Mr. Bunker! That's the most ridiculous thing I ever heard!
    (Archie turns proudly to the others)

ARCHIE There, you see that, wise guy. *(Turns to Mike)* You thought you knew him. You thought you knew me. Oh these liberals—they're supposed to be so sensitive, ya know. I'll tell you where this guy's sensitive, Lionel—right in his tochas.
    (Archie goes to dining room table)

LIONEL *(Surprise)* Where?

MIKE It's a Yiddish word. It means—
    (Points)

LIONEL Oh, I know where it's at. I was just wonderin', Mr. Bunker—what's with the Jewish word?

ARCHIE I hear them. We got a couple of Hebes working down the building.

LIONEL Does he use words like that very often?

MIKE Now and then.

ARCHIE I told ya, I work with a couple of Jews.

LIONEL Beggin' your pardon, Mr. Bunker, but you wouldn't happen to be one of them, would you?

ARCHIE *(No humor about this)* What??

LIONEL I mean people don't use Jewish words just like that, do they, Mike?

MIKE *(Crossing to table, sits)* No, not in my experience.

ARCHIE Maybe people don't but *I* do! And I ain't no Yid!

MIKE Come to think of it . . . when your father was visiting last year . . . wasn't his name Davie, or somethin'?

21

ARCHIE   David, my father's name is David.

MIKE   Yeah, David. And your mother's name . . . uh . . . Sarah, wasn't it?

ARCHIE   *(To Lionel)* Sarah, my mother's name is Sarah—So what?

LIONEL   David and Sarah, two Jewish names.

ARCHIE   David and Sarah. Two names right out of the Bible— which is got nothin' to do with the Jews.

LIONEL   You don't wanna get up tight about it, Mr. Bunker. There's nothing to be ashamed of being Jewish.

ARCHIE   But I ain't Jewish!

MIKE   Look at that—see the way he uses his hands when he argues. A very Semitic gesture.

ARCHIE   What do you know about it, you dumb Polack.

MIKE   All right, I'm a Polack.

ARCHIE   You sure are! You're a Polack Joke!

MIKE   Okay, I don't mind, so I'm Polish. I don't mind. I'm proud of it!

LIONEL   There you are, Mr. Bunker. Now you oughta be proud that you're Jewish.

ARCHIE   *(Whining)* But I ain't Jewish.

EDITH   I didn't know you was Jewish.

ARCHIE   What the hell are you talking about? You, of all people, should *know* that I ain't Jewish.

EDITH   You *are* talking with your hands.

LIONEL   See, the Jews tend to be emotional.

ARCHIE   *(Blowing)* Now listen to me Lionel. I'm going to give it to you just once more and that's all. I am not Jewish.

LIONEL   Yes, Sir, Mr. Bunker. But even if you are, it doesn't change things between you and me. I mean I'm not gonna throw away nine years of friendship over a little thing like that. So long, everybody.
    (He exits)

ALL   Bye, Lionel!
    (Archie watches him go and turns to others. They resume eating quickly)

ARCHIE   Well, I hate a smart aleck kid, and I don't care what color he is!
    (Applause)

FADE TO BLACK

TAG

FADE IN:

    (Family at table)

ARCHIE   *(Rising)* Well, I think I'll go up and lay down and watch a little TV.

GLORIA   Wait a minute, Dad. Mom hasn't opened her gift yet. Open it now, Mom.

MIKE   Yeah, Mom, go ahead.
    (Feigning it)

EDITH   *(Opening gift)* I can't hardly believe it. Look, my hands are shaking. Oh! My! Lace hankies! Look, Gloria, two beautiful lace hankies!

ARCHIE   Is that all?
  (He starts to walk away)

MIKE   Hey, wait a second, don't you want to know who it's from?

GLORIA   Yeah, sit down, Daddy. There's a card there—open it!
  (Archie sits)

EDITH   *(As she puts on glasses to read it)* Oh these are the most beautiful lace hankies. That's real nice. And flowers. I just never seen such—*(Reads the card now)* Oh—my glory!

ARCHIE   Come on Edith . . . Who are they from?

EDITH   They're from you, Archie. *(Archie coughs)* Archie, I can't believe it. I ain't seen an anniversary gift from you since the first— *(Archie coughs)* Pound his back, Mike—

ARCHIE   Keep away from me, meathead.
  (He crosses to his chair)

EDITH   *(Who hasn't stopped talking)* You know what I'm going to do? I'm going to try using one. See how I look with it. Some people don't look natural with fancy things.
  (She crosses to her chair as she talks and dabs her nose daintily. The kids applaud her)

GLORIA   You look wonderful, Mom.

MIKE   Perfectly natural.

ARCHIE   Just don't blow in it; it'll go right through.

EDITH   *(Warmly)* Oh, Archie. I just don't know what to say. Except—thank you, sweetheart. Oh, I do thank you, Archie dear.
  (Gets up and kisses him)

ARCHIE   *(Not altogether untouched)* All right, Edith. You're getting me all wet.
  (Mike and Gloria into living room)

GLORIA   *(Handing her the card)* Read the card, Mom.
   (Archie throws them both a look)

EDITH   Oh, Archie, I'll bet it's a Hallmark. *(Looks at the back of it)* Well, pretty near. Oh—and inside there's a verse inside. *(She clears her throat)*
   Together.
   Through all the years I've been with you
   We've had our ups and downs, 'tis true.
   But life with us has just begun
   We've yet to have all of our fun
   As long as we're together.
   (A long beat as Edith looks warmly toward Archie and he looks uncomfortable over at the kids. They laugh)

ARCHIE   What are you looking at?
   (He shoots them a look, then he starts to rise—and Edith catches him off-balance by starting to read a second verse)

EDITH   And when my dear we're old and gray
   And life for us is sunny weather
   We'll look back on our lives and say
   It's been a gay, gay lark together.
   (Another long moment. Edith dabs at her eyes with a hanky. Archie clears his throat. Then pulls himself together)

ARCHIE   Alright, alright—come on, party's over. Let's clean this mess up. Them eggs over there are starting to foment.

EDITH   Archie, I don't know what to say. That was so beautiful. *(Afraid she might cry, Edith hurries from the room)*

ARCHIE   *(Noticing Mike and Gloria kissing)* Do you always have to be doing that? It's as if she was a hamburger.

GLORIA   Mom!
   (Exits)

MIKE   The card kinda got to you, eh?

ARCHIE   What do you mean it got to me? It got to you mother-in-law. Women . . .

MIKE   No, no, no. It got to you, too. I never knew you were so soft and sentimental.

ARCHIE   Yeah—well, you don't know much anyhow. I want to tell you something about yourself. You are a person of very little quality. You got no appreciation for some of your finer things.

MIKE   Archie, we're talkin' about a greeting card.

ARCHIE   They got some damn good writers writin' for them cards.

MIKE   Come on.

ARCHIE   Some of your best song lyrics come right from them cards.

MIKE   Alright, alright. What're you so excited about, anyway! One stinkin' little poem on a greeting card. It's not like you wrote the thing!

ARCHIE   No, I didn't write it. But who had the good taste to pick it out? *(Mike jiggles his thumbs indicating himself. Archie reacts)* Go on will you, meathead.
        (Hold on Archie)
        (Applause)

FADE TO BLACK

Archie Is Branded

written by Vincent Bogert
Third season, broadcast February 24, 1973

Executive Producer
Norman Lear

Produced by
John Rich

Directed by
John Rich and
Bob La Hendro

CAST

ARCHIE BUNKER	Carroll O'Connor
EDITH BUNKER	Jean Stapleton
MIKE STIVIC	Rob Reiner
GLORIA STIVIC	Sally Struthers
PAUL BENJAMIN	Gregory Sierra
MUNSON	Billy Halop
JERRY	Michael Gregory
BOY SCOUT	John Putch
MAILMAN	Patrick Campbell

ACT ONE

FADE UP:

INT. LIVING ROOM — DAY

> *(Archie comes downstairs)*

ARCHIE   *(Calls)* Edith, you got the coffee made out there?

EDITH   *(O.S.)* Yeah, Archie.

ARCHIE   Did you bring in the Sunday paper?

EDITH   *(O.S.)* No, not yet!

ARCHIE   *(Mumbles as he goes to door)* She knows it's out there she leaves it there. Well, what're you gonna do. You can't teach an old dingbat new tricks.
> *(He unlocks door. Goes outside to get the paper. He leaves the door wide open. On the door is painted a large swastika. Archie comes back. Closes the door behind him. He crosses to his chair—then halts. He crosses back, opens the door, and stares in utter disbelief at the swastika)*

ARCHIE   *(Yells)* Edith!
> *(Edith enters from kitchen with breakfast)*

EDITH   I'm sorry I'm late, Archie, here's your breakfast.

ARCHIE   Never mind the breakfast! Come over here and take a look at the front door.

EDITH   Oh, my!! Who did that?

ARCHIE   I wouldn't know Edith. The artists didn't sign it! *(Archie slams door and crosses to phone)* I'm callin' the cops.

EDITH   Oh yeah, call the cops, that's a good idea.
> *(Mike comes downstairs)*

MIKE   Call the cops? What's going on?

ARCHIE   Look at the door!

MIKE   *(Looks — shrugs)* Yeah.

ARCHIE   You meathead! Open the door and look on the outside!

MIKE   You didn't tell me to open the door. All you said was "Look at the door." You didn't say, "Open the door and look at it from the outside." All you said was, "Look at the door."

ARCHIE   Open the damn door and look at the outside of it.

MIKE   All right. You didn't say open the door.

ARCHIE   Open it!
        (Opens door)

MIKE   A swastika!!
        (Gloria comes downstairs)

Mike   Hey Gloria did you see this?

GLORIA   Yeah, what? Oh, Michael. Who could've done that?

ARCHIE   *(On phone — dialing)* It's probably the same crummy kids who busted the street lamp last week.

MIKE   I wonder if they did it to any of the other houses? I'm gonna look.
        (He exits to look at other houses)

ARCHIE   Who cares. I know they done it to my house and they ain't getting away without calling the cops. *(On phone)* Hello? . . . hello, hih! How do you like this. I call the cops and I get a recorded announcement here. *(Mimics)* 'The lines are all busy. Do not hang up the phone. Your call will be answered when the lines are clear?' *(He holds out phone)* The lines would be cleared if they wasn't playin' records.
        (Mike enters)

GLORIA   Michael, did they paint any of the other doors on the block?

MIKE   No — just this house.

GLORIA   Why do kids do things like that?

MIKE   I don't think it was kids! There are a lot of fanatics running around loose these days.

ARCHIE   *(To Mike)* Who cares. Whoever done it, I'm gonna get 'em for it. That's all. Now here, you stay on the blower till the cops answer. *(Gloria and Archie join Edith at table)* What about you little girl. You hear anythin' last night? The cops'll want to know that when they get here.

GLORIA   No, daddy, all I heard was your alarm clock when it went off this morning.

ARCHIE   And that's another thing, why did the alarm clock go off on a Sunday morning, huh? I was outta bed and halfway to the toilet before I remembered I didn't have to get up!

EDITH   I'm sorry, Archie, but I wanted to get up and put a cake in the oven for Louise Jefferson. It's her anniversary tomorrow.

ARCHIE   Tomorrow. Why you ringin' the alarm today.

EDITH   Well, I figured if the cake didn't turn out good today I'd have another chance at it tomorrow.

ARCHIE   Oh, why do I ask her anythin'?

MIKE   Hey, Arch! I've got the police . . .

ARCHIE   Gimme the phone.

MIKE   *(Into phone)* Hold on a second.

ARCHIE   Gimme that phone there. *(Grabs phone)* Hello? The Police? Yeah, this is Archie Bunker, 704 Hauser Street. Well

I gotta complaint. Last night sometime, during the night someone come around here and painted a swastika on my front
door. Swastika, swastika. No, one of 'em German things from
W.W. 2! Yeah well, can you come over? All right, good. That's
all I want. Thanks very much. *(Hangs up)* Alright, we'll get
to the bottom of this. The cops are coming over and they're
gonna have a little investigation here.

EDITH   Oh well, I'd better get something to wipe that off the door.

ARCHIE   No. What'll you wipe it off the door for, I want it on the
door. I want the cops to see that. That's evidence. Catch on?

GLORIA   But daddy, in the meantime everyone else can see it.

ARCHIE   Good thinkin' little girl! All right we'll fix it so nobody
else sees it till the cops get here. I'm gonna cover that thing
up right.

EDITH   With what, Archie?

ARCHIE   Oh, wait till you see Edith. I'll cover that thing up with
Old Glory here. *(Archie goes to closet and takes American flag
off the shelf)* This put the kibosh on them Nazis once before
and it's gonna do it again. Get the thumb tacks.

EDITH   Oh, why don't you stick it up with tape?

ARCHIE   Thumb tacks, Edith.

EDITH   Oh, tape would be better.

ARCHIE   Why would tape be better?

EDITH   'Cause I know where the tape is.

ARCHIE   Would somebody get the thumb tacks!!

GLORIA   All right, daddy, would you calm down. Geez, I know
where the tacks are. *(She shoves her hand in the drawer. Comes
up with tape)* Oh . . . it's the tape!

31

ARCHIE   Bring me the tape. The tape! The tape! Come on, put it up there.
   (Gloria brings tape and helps Archie hang up the flag)

EDITH   I wonder why they call it a swastika?

ARCHIE   Why they call it a swastika? Look at the damn thing.

EDITH   Yeah!?

ARCHIE   What the hell else would you call it?

EDITH   *(Sees something lying on the porch)* Archie, did you drop something? *(She exits to porch, picks up paper)* There's a piece of paper here.
   (Comes inside)

ARCHIE   Huh!

EDITH   It's a note.

ARCHIE   Huh?

EDITH   *(Reads)* "This swastika is just the beginning. We'll be back."

ARCHIE   Gimme that. I'll read that. *(Takes note — reads)* "This swastika is just the beginning. We'll be back." What is this?

MIKE   Well, do you still think that's a bunch of kids?

GLORIA   Michael. I'm scared! What if they try something else? It's like burning a cross outside a black person's home—sometimes they follow it up with a bomb!

ARCHIE   Ah cut that out! In the first place, this ain't a black person's house.

MIKE   Arch, why would they just pick our house? Huh?

ARCHIE   Well listen. Maybe because of you — 'cause you live here!

MIKE   That's crazy!

ARCHIE   It ain't so crazy. You're always mixed up in those things, carryin' signs around. Maybe somebody's here to pin a sign on you!

MIKE   What are you talking about?

EDITH   Oh, no, Archie, I don't think that could be right . . .

MIKE   Thanks, ma . . .

EDITH   I don't think anybody cares what Mike does.

MIKE   Thanks, ma!

EDITH   Oh, I'm sorry Mike. I didn't mean it that way.

ARCHIE   This guy, and everybody knows it, is always puttin' this country down. As far as he's concerned, nothin' is right unless it's left!

MIKE   Hey, I happen to believe in this country more than you do!

ARCHIE   What was that??

MIKE   That's right! Because I believe it's strong enough to accept some changes.

ARCHIE   Well, it ain't gonna accept communism buddy!

MIKE   Who's talking about communism? I'm talking about civil rights.

ARCHIE   That's communism!

MIKE   You know something your thinking is really neanderthal.

ARCHIE   If you're gonna talk to me, talk American or clam up!

SOUND: DOORBELL

ARCHIE   Clamp up anyhow. Get away from there, get away from
there. I'll answer the door. Go on little girl, you just sit down
and have your breakfast. I'm talking to the cops. *(Archie opens
door — it is Munson)* Oh, Munson, come on in.

EDITH/MIKE/GLORIA   Hello, Mr. Munson . . .

MUNSON   Hello — Mrs. Bunker! Hey what's with the flag on your
door? This ain't the 4th of July.

ARCHIE   I know it ain't the 4th of July — I don't have to wait
till the 4th of July to hang Ol' Glory out there — show my
country I love it.

EDITH   And it looks better than a swastika.

ARCHIE   *(Over-riding)* Your cake is burning in the kitchen. Get
out of here. No, no, no, don't pay no attention to Edith. You
gonna let me drive the cab tonight?

MUNSON   That's what I came over for. I was gonna give you the
keys.

SOUND: DOORBELL

ARCHIE   Hold it, hold it.
    (He opens door to a Boy Scout)

SCOUT   Hey mister, you know you got your flag hung up wrong?

ARCHIE   Oh, listen, boyscout, you're talking to a veteran of W.
W. Two — this is the way we used to hang the flag under fire.

SCOUT   You were doin' it wrong. The stars are supposed to go in
the other corner. Want me to hang it the right way for you?

ARCIIIE   Oh yeah, yeah, all right, you can do that — but

listen, no tip or it ain't a good deed!
*(As the Scout removes the flag — the swastika becomes
visible. Munson sees it)*

SCOUT   Hey, mister, you know you got a swastika on your door?

ARCHIE   *(Snatches flag from Scout)* Ahh, gimme the flag, kid.
Get lost, huh.
(The Scout runs away)

MUNSON   What's a swastika doing on your door?

ARCHIE   Ahhh, how do I know. It ain't got nothin' to do with me.

MUNSON   I don't like the looks of this! Somebody's got ya'
marked out for somethin'.

ARCHIE   Nobody's got me marked out for nothing there Munson.
It's just that somebody's sore at the meathead here!

GLORIA   Michael's done nothing.

MIKE   C'mon, quit it, will ya?

MUNSON   Well, Arch, I don't think you better take the cab out
tonight.

ARCHIE   Why not?

MUNSON   Well, if somebody's after your son-in-law, you ain't
safe, neither!

ARCHIE   I certainly am safe.

MUNSON   Look, you know what follows those things up on the
door? The next thing you know when you ain't lookin' they'll
plant a bomb in the cab. You'll get in, start it and ka-boom!

ARCHIE   What do ya mean. Kaboom??

MUNSON   I wouldn't want that to happen, Arch.

ARCHIE   Ahh, don't worry about me . . .

MUNSON   I can't afford to lose that cab.
(Archie reacts)

EDITH   *(Enters from kitchen)* It's all right, Archie, the cake ain't burning. It'll be done in a little while.

ARCHIE   Ain't that good news!

SOUND: DOORBELL

ARCHIE   Do something useful, answer the bell. *(Edith goes to door)* Munson, you come in here and get my family all excited here!
(While they argue, we cut to Edith opening door to mailman with a Special Delivery package)

MAILMAN   Special Delivey for Bunker.

EDITH   Oh,thank you.
(The mailman has been eyeing the swastika)

MAILMAN   Say, lady, d'you know you've got a swastika on your door?

EDITH   Yeah. Thank you.
(Mailman takes off fast. Edith closes door. Munson goes to door)

ARCHIE   Wait a minute, I want to drive . . .

MUNSON   No way! No way! I'll be seein' ya.
(He exits)

EDITH   Goodbye Mr. Munson.

MUNSON   Goodbye Mrs. Bunker
(Edith holds out the package)

EDITH   Archie, look what came for you.

ARCHIE   What?

EDITH   A package. Special Delivery!

ARCHIE   Can you believe that Munson . . .

MIKE   Hey — hey, wait a second! That package is ticking. Listen.

GLORIA   It is ticking! The package is ticking!
         (She screams)

ARCHIE   Let me listen to the thing!
         *(One more scream from Gloria. There is a beat of silence
         from everyone. In it — quite clearly — we hear the ticking)*

ARCHIE   It's ticking!!

GLORIA   It's a bomb!! Throw it away!
         (Edith reaches for it)

MIKE   No, no! Don't touch it! Don't touch it! Put it in water!

ARCHIE   Put it in the toilet.

EDITH   No, not the toilet.

ARCHIE   The sink.

MIKE   Put it in the sink.

ARCHIE   Put it in the sink.

MIKE   You put it in the sink.

ARCHIE   You do it!

MIKE   You do it.

ARCHIE   You . . .

MIKE   You . . .

GLORIA   Michael!!
   (*Edith hands package to Mike. He runs into the kitchen with the package, the others running after him*)

ARCHIE   Everybody out! Get out the back door!
   (*They all exit through back door*)

FADE OUT:

END OF ACT ONE

ACT TWO

FADE UP:

INT. KITCHEN — DAY

   (*Archie and Mike are standing by kitchen sink. Gloria and Edith are still outside*)

ARCHIE   (*Calls out*) I think we're all right. I don't hear it tickin' no more. You go give them the all clear.

MIKE   All right. Gloria, Ma, come on in — it's all right.

EDITH   (*In door*) Are you sure?

ARCHIE   Yeah.

EDITH   Come on, Gloria.
   (*They enter*)

GLORIA   (*Talking away nervously*) The house almost exploded and nobody even ran to save my wedding pictures . . .

MIKE   Hey, wait a second!

ARCHIE   Huh?

38

MIKE   It's still ticking.
   (*Gloria screams*)

ARCHIE   Shut up, will ya!! Listen to this thing. Wait a minute. This thing ain't tickin' at all here.
   (*Archie looks at Edith — walks over to her and brings Edith's kitchen timer out of her apron pocket*)

ARCHIE   You run us out of our own home with your rotten lousy kitchen timer!
   (*A beat*)

SOUND: TICKING FOLLOWED BY A TING

   (*Edith takes cake out of oven*)

EDITH   My cake's done.

ARCHIE   Yeah, Edith just beautiful. You know, we got a Special Delivery package over there in the sink, I don't know what's in it but it better be rubber goods 'cause it's under water.

EDITH   Oh, I think . . . (*Goes to sink*) It's soaked through.

ARCHIE   I wouldn't be surprised.
   (*Edith is fishing out the soggy package which has broken up in the water*)

EDITH   Here's a note. It's from cousin Amelia! "Russ has given up smoking so he's sending Archie these cigars."

ARCHIE   Hold it. Cigars, get away from that sink! Holy . . .
   (*Archie is fishing frantically in the remains*)

EDITH   ". . . Russell says to be sure you keep them in a humidor because they spoil if you let them get dry!!"
   (*Archie comes up with crumbling soggy mess of cigars in his fingers*)

ARCHIE   These ain't gonna be dry for a hellava long time. (*Throws "cigar mess" in the sink*) Edith, all I can say is, I ain't a happy man.

SOUND: DOORBELL

MIKE   *(Starts for door)* I'll bet that's the police.

ARCHIE   I'll get that. Stay away from that bell there, eh.
   *(Archie goes into living room, followed by Edith, Mike
   and Gloria)*

INT. LIVING ROOM

ARCHIE   *(Enters)* If that's the cops, I don't even want them talking
   to you.

MIKE   Why not?

ARCHIE   'Cause you're the one that started this whole thing.
   I'll talk to the cops. *(He opens the door to Paul Benjamin)*
   Yeah?

BENJAMIN   *(Points to swastika)* They sure did a job on you,
   didn't they? We've got our work cut out with this bunch!

ARCHIE   You don't look like no cop to me!

BENJAMIN   The reason for that — I ain't a cop!

ARCHIE   Oh what do ya want then.

BENJAMIN   *(Indicating swastika)* I got a solution to your problem.
   Can I come in?

ARCHIE   *(Grudgingly)* You're already in — I wanna warn you
   though, I wouldn't leave my car parked out there long if I was
   you. The cops put a $25 summons on it.

BENJAMIN   That's okay.
   (Benjamin enters)

ARCHIE   And if this is some salesman's gag to get into the house,
   we don't need magazines!

BENJAMIN   But you need Protection.

EDITH   Is that anything like "Cosmopolitan"?

ARCHIE   Stifle yourself!

BENJAMIN   That's terrific. Funny lady! Is that your wife?

ARCHIE   Yes, that's my wife. That's my son-in-law and my daughter over there. Who are you?

BENJAMIN   The name is Benjamin.

ARCHIE   Benjamin what?

BENJAMIN   Paul Benjamin. It's one of those names that work both ways — you know? Like James Stewart, Dean Martin.

EDITH   Pope John!

ARCHIE   Will you stifle yourself. Sit down in that chair.
   (She sits)

BENJAMIN   She's a funny lady.

ARCHIE   I never laugh at her.

MIKE   Mr. Benjamin. You say you came to help about the swastika?

BENAJMIN   Right, like I said — we're gonna make sure you get protection. Here let me get those drapes.
   (Pulls drapes closed)

ARCHIE   What're you doin'?

BENJAMIN   Protecting you.

ARCHIE   Protecting me? What for? After all, I don't even know you.

BENJAMIN 'Cause that's the way it's always been with our people. We gotta look after each other. Right, bubby.

ARCHIE Bubby??

BENJAMIN You know somethin'?? I never would've guessed it in a million years. You sure don't look Jewish!

ARCHIE Well, there's a very good reason for that — I ain't Jewish!

BENJAMIN Ahh! You're a convert.

ARCHIE No.

BENJAMIN I don't get this. What're you afraid of?

ARCHIE I ain't afraid of nothin'!

BENJAMIN Hey, listen. Don't worry about the guys that painted that thing on your door. You're not alone. I'm here now. You're with one of your own. You know what I mean.

ARCHIE I ain't one of your own. I'm one of my own!

BENJAMIN Listen, if that's the way you wanna play it, Mr. Bloom, it's fine with me. But ah . . .

ARCHIE Hold it! Hold it! Why are you calling me Bloom?

BENJAMIN You mean — you changed your name too?

ARCHIE No.

MIKE Mr. Benjamin, I think you've got the wrong house—there's no Bloom here. This is Archie Bunker!

ARCHIE Archie Bunker.

MIKE And I can testify that he is not now, nor has he ever been a member of the Jewish faith!

ARCHIE   At no time!

BENJAMIN   Then why did the goons that painted your door mistake your place for David Bloom's place?

MIKE   You mean the David Bloom that's on the School Board?

GLORIA   Oh, he lives up the end of the block. At number seven-forty. Our house is number seven-oh-four.

ARCHIE   Oh, that Bloom. That's that big mouth liberal who was always tryin' to run for the City Council. Oh, I get it now! This here swastika belongs to Bloom. Oh geez, I feel a lot better about that.

MIKE   Makes you feel better Arch. A man is being threatened.

ARCHIE   *(To Benjamin)* When he talks, never listen. Come here, Paulie. I'm gonna show you where Bloom lives. Right up at this house at the end of the corner. You better go up there . . . what the hell are you doing?

BENJAMIN   Hold it! You know that swastika was meant for Bloom, and I know it was meant for Bloom, but they think it was meant for you.

GLORIA   "They"? Who's "they"?

BENJAMIN   The creeps that painted your door. They still think this is David Bloom's place, so we've gotta be ready for 'em right here!

GLORIA   And who's "we"? You keep saying that.

ARCHIE   Yeah, who's "we"?

BENJAMIN   The H.D.A.

MIKE   Oh, boy! That's the Hebrew Defense Association.

ARCHIE   Huh?

MIKE   Arch, that's a strong-arm outfit! A vigilante group!

ARCHIE   Hold it! Vigilante sounds good to me. Wait a minute. That could be something good there. Wait a minute, what do you guys do?

BENJAMIN   What they do. If they use force — we use force.

ARCHIE   Good.

MIKE   But violence won't help!

BENJAMIN   It wouldn't hurt!

GLORIA   Michael's right — just because some people do some terrible things to other people, doesn't give you the right to do the same things. That's just revenge!

ARCHIE   What's the matter with revenge. It's the perfect way to get even.

BENJAMIN   You're catching on bubby!

MIKE   Why don't you catch on. Any thinking person has gone past the idea of revenge, a long time ago!

BENJAMIN   Any thinking person knows that Homo Sapiens is a killer.

EDITH   Homo Sapiens. Is he an Arab?

ARCHIE   No Edith. Homo Sapiens, that's a killer fag.

MIKE   Arch, Homo Sapiens is man. *(To Benjamin)* And man invented the law to protect himself.

BENJAMIN   Law, law, what law? What are you talking about? A law that let's a bunch of thugs get away with painting swastikas on doors, uh? Or killing innocent hostages? That let's them kill off one religion in the name of another religion? Look, that's your law!

ARCHIE   Yeah, that's right. Listen, if some guy, meathead, runs around doing damage to some other guy, the only decent thing to do is knock 'em off. And if you can't do that by yourself, the best thing to do is bring back the old death penalty!

MIKE   I don't believe what you're saying, Arch. That just makes murderers of us all! I don't want to murder anyone and I don't want the state doing it in my name.

ARCHIE   Ahh, go eat a marshmellow.

BENJAMIN   What are you? Some kind of saint? Look, all I'm sayin' is I know the guys that did that, and if it comes to killin' heh, *(He pinches Archie's cheek)* better them than my bubby here.

ARCHIE   That's some straight thinkin' there, Paulie.

MIKE   Straight thinking??? Arch, if this guy's lips wasn't moving, I'd have sworn those words were coming out of your mouth!

ARCHIE   That's right! 'Cause this guy is making sense.

BENJAMIN   Thanks.

ARCHIE   Don't mention it there, bubby!

GLORIA   Mr. Benjamin hasn't there been enough fighting? I mean isn't it time people sat down and talked their problems over with one another?

BENJAMIN   Oh no, no, we've had it with that up to here; we've had it! No more talk!! You can't talk to bullets! *(He slaps his brow with his hand)* Cheez! what's the use. When will people understand?

EDITH   Careful, you'll hurt yourself.

ARCHIE   Yeah. That's an awful shot in the head you gave yourself.

BENJAMIN   Better this kind of shot in the head *(Points finger to head like gun)* than this kind.

ARCHIE   You ain't kidding.

BENJAMIN   You're right, I'm not kidding bubby and that's what me and my boys are here to prevent.

ARCHIE   Hey, you got them boys with you?

BENJAMIN   *(Looks out window)* Oh yeah. They'll be here in a few minutes.

GLORIA   *(Aside)* Daddy! Daddy! I'm scared of this man—will you please ask him to leave!

ARCHIE   What are you talking about? Ask him to leave? *(Gloria sits on couch)* Some bum comes and paints a swastika on my door. Paulie's only here just to get even with them, that's all —tit for tat!

BENJAMIN   We call it 'an eye for an eye'!

MIKE   Whatever happened to 'turn the other cheek'?

ARCHIE   You can't do that no more.

BENJAMIN   He's right.

MIKE   He is not right.

BENJAMIN   You stick to your Testament and I'll stick to mine.

MIKE   Fine! Fine! Doesn't your Testament say something about "loving they neighbor"?

BENJAMIN   All right! All right! Look, say you're walkin' down the street with your wife here and some creep comes up and jumps her! What are you gonna do? Love him? Or break his head open?

MIKE   I'd probably break his head open.

BENJAMIN   Right.

MIKE   But that's not a fair example. Because that's a reflex response. What you're talking about is a cold blooded plan. Don't you see that's how violence spreads.

BENJAMIN   What are you gonna do? Just smile and let 'em keep hi-jacking and assassinating and sending their letter bombs? That's okay, eh?

ARCHIE   No. Them things are very, very wrong. Answer me — ain't them terrible things?

MIKE   Of course they are terrible, Arch. The same way it's terrible for us to be sending bombs by air mail.

ARCHIE   We never done that!

MIKE   We sure have, Arch. Addressed to women and children in Vietnam!

ARCHIE   We don't bomb no women and children on purpose.

GLORIA   Oh, I'm sure they're happy to know that daddy.

ARCHIE   You stay out of this over there. That's one of them what you call ordinary tragedies of war, that's all. Geez, you can't fight a war, without that. What ya call your "say la gwarey."

BENJAMIN   *(To Archie)* You're right again bubby— *(He jerks a thumb at the door)* And this is war!!

SOUND: DOORBELL

BENJAMIN   I'll get it. *(Benjamin moves swiftly, looks out the window, opens the door to another H.D.A. man)* It's okay, it's one of my men. Heh Jerry — what's up?

JERRY   This is the wrong house!

BENJAMIN   I know that—but they don't.

JERRY   They do now. We just got word they're on their way to Bloom's place.

BENJAMIN   All right, we'll be ready for 'em. Look, why don't you go on ahead. I'll drive on up and meet ya.

JERRY   Right.
(Jerry exits)

BENJAMIN   Well I guess you folks are off the hook! . . . So long, everybody!

ARCHIE   So long there bubby . . .

BENJAMIN   *(He shakes Mike's hand warmly)* You too, friend. I don't agree with what you say but I like your chutzpah. You know something, one of these days you're gonna find out that this . . . *(He clenches Mike's fist)* is the only answer. Right there.

MIKE   I still think you're wrong, because this *(He holds up the other fist clenched)* only gets you this.

BENJAMIN   Okay friend. You keep talking and I'll do what I have to do! Shalom.
(He waves — and exits)

EDITH   'Shalom'? What does that mean?

MIKE   Believe it or not ma — it means 'peace'!

GLORIA   Jewish people also use it to say 'hello' or 'goodbye'.

EDITH   But how do you know which one they mean?

ARCHIE   Why don't you use your common sense, Edith. If a

Jew is comin' at ya it's 'hello'. If he's goin' away from you it's 'goodbye'.

EDITH   But when does it mean peace?

ARCHIE   In between 'hello' and 'goodbye'!

SOUND: A LOUD EXPLOSION

>   *(The family reacts — stunned by the explosion in the street. Archie looks out the door. Edith and Gloria get up — Mike stops them. Archie turns back into the room with an expression of shock and horror)*

ARCHIE   Oh geez, that's Paul. They blew him up in his car.
(As they stare at each other)

FADE OUT:

END OF ACT TWO

Two's a Crowd

written by Phil Sharp
Eighth season, broadcast February 5, 1978

Executive Producer
Mort Lachman

Produced by
Milt Josefsberg

Directed by
Paul Bogart

CAST

ARCHIE BUNKER	Carroll O'Connor
MIKE STIVIC	Rob Reiner

ACT ONE

FADE IN:

INT. ARCHIE'S PLACE

ARCHIE (At register) Okay, meathead, I'm goin' to start countin' the money, so lock the front door there huh?

MIKE Okay.
      (Starts for door)

SFX: PHONE RINGS

MIKE (Answers) Archie's Place . . . Oh, hi, hi, Gloria . . . I was just down here helping Archie out tonight. We were just about to close up. Oh, that's nice. Hold on. (To Archie) Arch, it's Gloria. She said she and Ma had a great train ride, Joey slept all the way to Aunt Helen's.

ARCHIE I hate that fat Helen.

MIKE (Into phone) Yeah, yeah. I miss you, too, honey. Yeah, well I won't see you the whole weekend. Uh . . . honey, please . . . I don't wanna do it now. No, I can't do it now, honey. We're not alone. Honey, please don't make me do it. (A beat) All right, I'll do it. I'm kissing your ears. (Kisses into phone) I'm kissing your lips . . . (Kisses into phone) I'm kissing your neck . . . (Kisses into phone)

ARCHIE End it with the neck there.

MIKE I'm kissing your shoulders . . . (Kisses into phone)

ARCHIE If you're goin' to go any further, drop down to the feet.

MIKE Honey, I think I better stop at the shoulders.

ARCHIE Keep in the zone of decency here.

MIKE I'll see you Monday, honey. We'll pick up where we left

off. You remind me, okay? Goodbye.
(Hangs up)

ARCHIE   *(Finished counting the receipts)* What're you tryin'
to do — drive me nuts. I've got enough trouble with this here.

MIKE   What's the matter?

ARCHIE   The cash register come up short. I'm under fourteen
cents.

MIKE   What's so bad about that? Fourteen cents?

ARCHIE   Listen to the college man. Don't you know nothin'
about business? Every cash register's supposed to check out on
the nose. You know, what do you suppose General Motors
would do with that big cash register they keep back in Detroit,
suppose they come out fourteen cents short on that?

MIKE   They'd just stick another Chevy motor in a Buick.

ARCHIE   *(Reacts)* Wise guy . . .

MIKE   I read it in the paper. I read it in the paper.

ARCHIE   Forget it, I don't want to talk to you about that. You're
the kind of guy that goes to a John Wayne movie and roots
for the Indians there. You do that! C'mon, here, grab one of
them cases. Help me carry it into the back room.
(Picks up carton)

MIKE   Arch, you know . . . *(Picks up carton, they cross, Mike
following Archie)* Joey said something so funny the other day.

ARCHIE   Yeah, what'd he say?

MIKE   Well, we were taking a bath together, and —

ARCHIE   *(Stops, Mike bumps into him)* Hold it! Hold it! Hold it!
Hold it! You and Joey takin' a bath together?

MIKE   Yeah.

ARCHIE   I hope you was wearin' a bathin' suit?

MIKE   Who takes a bath wearin' a bathin' suit?

ARCHIE   Put the box down.

MIKE   What?

ARCHIE   The box down. Sit down here. *(They sit)* Let me tell you somethin'. A grown man ain't supposed to take a bath in the nude with a little boy.

MIKE   Why not?

ARCHIE   Oh, geez!! 'Cause when the little kid gives you the once over there, it makes him feel so hopeless.

MIKE   I don't think so.

ARCHIE   Well, maybe not in your case.

MIKE   In Japan, whole families take baths together.

ARCHIE   Who the hell cares? Japs eat fish eyes too.

MIKE   What's the matter with you? What's the matter with you? Didn't you and Ma ever take a bath togheter?

ARCHIE   Hey! Hey! Hey! Put the box down. *(They do)* Sit down. *(They sit)* Don't never ask me no questions like that there. In the first place, it's dirty, dirty, and in the second place, can you picture Edith and me floppin' around in the one tub?? *(Mike thinks)* Don't look at us! Don't look for it! It's awful! Forget about it! You . . . *(They rise, cross to door)* 'Til the end of time, I'll be tryin' to straighten you out. *(As he takes key out, puts in in door, opens it)* When they finally plant me in the end, they'll be lowerin' my box into the ground and my voice will come out of it, 'Don't be dirty . . . Don't be dirty . . .' And you won't even be listenin' then. You won't even be at the gravesite. You'll be over in Hong Kong with your family takin' a bath.

INT. STOREROOM — NIGHT

> *(They enter. Archie turns light on. The room is piled high with boxes, etc. Mike kicks door shut. Archie reacts)*

MIKE   *(Looking around)* Where do you want this?

ARCHIE   You don't know what you done there, huh?

MIKE   No. What's the matter?

ARCHIE   Put the box down. *(Mike does. Archie sits on pile of boxes)* Would you mind openin' that door a crack for me there?

MIKE   Sure. *(Reaches for door knob. Reacts)* There's no door knob.

ARCHIE   Fancy that.

MIKE   Uh, how're you supposed to open the door.

ARCHIE   With a key.

MIKE   Where's the key?

ARCHIE   Well, if you could open the door a crack, you could see the key stickin' otta the lock on the other side of that door.

MIKE   You mean we're locked in here?

ARCHIE   I think you have grasped the situation.

MIKE   All right. All right. We'll just a . . . *(Backs away)* We just break the door down, that's all.

ARCHIE   Huh . . . Huh . . . Huh . . . You hurl your shoulder into that door, you're gonna have two armpits on the same side.

(Mike tries, yells in pain)

MIKE   Oh, Gee I'm sorry I did that!

ARCHIE   If I wasn't so mad at you, I'd laugh like hell.

MIKE   *(Crosses)* Well, I am not the one who left the key on the other side of the door.

ARCHIE   I am not the one who slammed and locked the door, with the key on the other side.

MIKE   I am not the one who didn't say, 'Don't close the door, the key is on the other side.'

ARCHIE   I am not the one who sponged offa me for five years and didn't earn nothin' but the name of 'Meathead.'

MIKE   I am not the one who sits and watches Korean midgets wrestling on Channel 5 and thinks it's educational TV.

ARCHIE   I am not the one who sits in front of a television set for a whole hour starin' at the same orchestra.

MIKE   I like symphonies.

ARCHIE   If you like symphonies, you're gonna love this — *(Raspberry, crosses)* Dumbbell.

MIKE   All right, all right, let's just relax . . . calm down . . . *(Sits)* . . . we'll analyze our predicament.

ARCHIE   Ah, forget the predicament. Analyze your head.
      (Crosses and sits)

MIKE   Hey, we just have to figure out what to do.

ARCHIE   Well, there ain't nothin' to do. We're stuck here til Harry comes in and opens up tomorrow.

MIKE   *(Jumps up, crosses to stack of boxes. Steps on boxes)* I wish there was a window in here.

ARCHIE   You get your wish. There is.

MIKE   Where?

ARCHIE   It's up on the far wall there.

MIKE   Then that's it. That's it.

ARCHIE   You can't get out.

MIKE   We can get out of here.

ARCHIE   You can't get out of there.

MIKE   Why not?

ARCHIE   In the first place, there ain't no catch on that window by which you can open that window.

MIKE   So we'll force it open.

ARCHIE   In the second place, that window is painted shut until the second coming.

MIKE   Then we'll break the glass.

ARCHIE   In the third place . . .
        (*Mike breaks window*)

CUT TO:

EXT. ARCHIE'S PLACE — ALLEY OUTSIDE WINDOW)

   (*Mike is looking out through bars*)

MIKE   There's bars on the window.

CUT TO:

INT. ARCHIE'S PLACE — STOREROOM

ARCHIE   Now you got three.

MIKE   I don't believe it! We're trapped in here. We're trapped in here!

ARCHIE   Oh, stop your yellin' there. You're only trapped in here with me, but look who the hell I'm trapped in here with.

MIKE   *(Goes to window, calls)* Hey! Anybody out there! We're locked in Archie's Place in the storeroom. The door's wide open. So come on in.

ARCHIE   And be sure to take all of Archie's money, which you'll find on top of the cash register.

MIKE   *(Calls)* And be sure and take all of Archie's mon . . . *(Looks at Archie)* What???

ARCHIE   How stupid can you get? Yellin' out there into an alley-way. Don't you know the kind of people that pass through alleyways this time of the night, none other than the criminal element.

MIKE   Arch, shouldn't we at least take a chance that a decent human being will pass by?

ARCHIE   In New York?
      (Blast of wind and snow comes in. They react)

FADE OUT

END OF ACT ONE

ACT TWO

FADE IN:

INT. STOREROOM – NIGHT

> *(Mike is doing exercise)*

ARCHIE   You know what I was thinkin' there? That if we was lost in the snows up there in the Swiss Alps, they'd have to send out one of them Roman Catholic dogs to save us.

MIKE   *(Stops exercising)* Roman Catholic dogs?

ARCHIE   Saint Bernards. You never heard of them dogs? They run around the mountains there with little barrels of booze hid around their necks.

MIKE   We have booze right here.

ARCHIE   Oh yeah, well yeah, but I hafta pay for this booze. The Saint Bernard's booze is on the Pope.
> *(Mike sits, takes a swig, coughs)*

MIKE   That's good.

ARCHIE   *(Rummaging around)* Hey, hey, lookit this here. That's an old Kelcy's awning. All the guys, they thought I shoulda kept this up, but I didn't. You know, I never missed it.

MIKE   *(Looking at it)* Looks like the birds never missed it, either.

ARCHIE   Well, you know, there's a lot of good luck in bird doo-doos. You never heard that?

MIKE   No, I can't say that I have.

ARCHIE   You ain't got none of that old time knowledge you know. *(Puts canvas over his shoulder)* Well, put this around me here. I got somethin' here to keep me warm.

MIKE   Thanks a lot.

ARCHIE   Oh, gee. All right, pain in the neck, get in.

MIKE   Why is it so hard for you to be nice to me?

ARCHIE   *(Looks at him)* What the hell are you talkin' about. I always been nice to you.

MIKE   Get outta here. You've been rotten to me ever since the time Gloria brought me home to meet you. Do you remember the first thing you said to me?

ARCHIE   Hello?

MIKE   No, after that, the second thing you said was 'Are you Jewish?'

ARCHIE   Listen, if I woulda been a Jewish father, that woulda been the first thing I'da said to you.

MIKE   I wish you coulda seen the look on your face when I told you I was Polish.
            (Laughs)

ARCHIE   Well, you know from where I set now, maybe it would've been better if you had been a Jew.

MIKE   Why?

ARCHIE   Because a Jew woulda been smart enough so we wouldn't get locked in a storeroom.

MIKE   That is so awful! Do you realize how awful it is when you say things like that?

ARCHIE   What was awful? I just said somethin' nice about the Jews.

MIKE   It's not coming out of anything positive. It's coming out

59

of your prejudice. Don't you see that? Why is it so important to you for everybody to be the same? Isn't it better? Doesn't it make life more interesting, because we're different, that we're all different shapes, different sizes, different colors?

ARCHIE   Oh, go on. I know all about the differences. The Lord made all them differences. But I'll tell you somethin', the Lord wanted the sames to stay over here with the sames, and the differents to be with the differents. Hey, did you ever read the story of Noah's Ark in the Bible there.

MIKE   Yes.

ARCHIE   Well, you know then, the animals come up the gang-plank into that ark, they come up in twos and the differents with the differents. So the tiger he come up with a tigeress, a lion come up with a lionette, a Zebra he come up with a zebrella, the elephant he come up there with . . . well . . .

MIKE   With what?

ARCHIE   Well, geez, I forget the term, but you know the point I'm tryin' to make is, the elephant didn't come walkin' up there with a Pollack.

MIKE   I've told you a thousand times, I don't like it when you call me Pollack! Why do you have to call me Pollack? I'm a human being . . . a human being! Why can't you think of me as a human being?

ARCHIE   Because you're an animal. *(Mike reacts)* You was like a wolf comin' in there after my little girl.

MIKE   Oh, not this again!!

ARCHIE   Yes! This again, then and now, forever and always. It's only natural there that the fathers-in-laws is gonna hate the sons-ins-laws. When I took away Edith, Edith's old man said that was the reason that he hated me. He said he had a whole lot of other reasons, but that was the reason.

MIKE   I think there were other reasons too, Arch.

ARCHIE   Oh, that's you. You're never on my side on nothin' there. You didn't even know and you never met Edith's father, and you're even takin' his side over me! You're takin' the side of a man with no chin and a go-funny eye who used to tell longer stories than Edith, and they was worse 'cause he told 'em to you with bad breath! I ain't surprised 'cause in all family arguments, you ain't ever on my side.

MIKE   What do you mean, I've been on your side. I've been on your side.

ARCHIE   Never. Never.

MIKE   What're you talking about? What about when you wanted to buy the bar, and you forged Ma's signature.

ARCHIE   I traced! I traced! There's a hell of a difference between traced and forgery.

MIKE   All right, traced. I'm saying traced. And I understood it the time you had that little thing with the waitress.

ARCHIE   Oh, for God sake! Ain't the world ever gonna forget about my little thing??! No, I suppose not. Well, *(Gives raspberry)* to the world. The hell with the world! The world out there, kid, ain't up to no good. You don't trust nobody out there except for your own kind, and you remember that, Meathead.

MIKE   *(A beat)* There's another thing. Meathead. Why must you always call me Meathead?

ARCHIE   What the hell? Why does that bother you so much? I bet I wasn't the first one to call you Meathead.

MIKE   You were the only one to call me Meathead. They never called me Meathead in school. In school they always called me Michael.

ARCHIE   That's all they called you?

MIKE   Well, Mike, or Mikey.

ARCHIE   What a sweet little school you went to. No wonder you grew up thinkin' the world was beautiful.

MIKE   Why? What did they call you in school?
      (Ad lib resistance)

ARCHIE   Oh . . . different things.

MIKE   What? Tell me. What'd they call you in school. Tell me what they called you.

ARCHIE   *(Takes a drink)* Well, I remember one winter during the depression, we didn't have no money 'cause the old man lost a job, and we was all busted . . . and I couldn't go to school with only one shoe, but my mother, she found a boot . . . so I had a shoe on one foot there and a boot on the other. A shoe and a boot. Shoe, boot. The kids called me Shoebootie. They used to holler, Shoebootie!

MIKE   Huh?
      (Laughs)

ARCHIE   They used to holler, 'Tuttie-frutty, here comes Shoebootie.' And they kept callin' me that, 'til they find out my name was Archibald, and they thought that was funnier. And then I wished they'd go back to Shoebootie.

MIKE   Kids all made fun of you, huh?

ARCHIE   Yeah, they all made fun, well . . . all except one little black kid by the name of Winston.

MIKE   A black kid liked you?

ARCHIE   Oh, no. The black kid beat the hell outta me.

MIKE   Why?

#0819   II-I-22.

                    ARCHIE
~~Oh, well,~~ What a ~~nice~~ *swell* little ~~kid~~ *school* you

went to ~~was. You was always livin' in an~~

~~ivory shower~~. No wonder you ~~think~~ *grew up thinkin'*

the world ~~is~~ *was* beautiful.

                    MIKE

Why? What did they call you ~~?~~ *in school?*

(AD LIB RESISTANCE)

                    ARCHIE

Uh ... Different things ~~from time to time~~.
                                    ← ——— *MIKE*
(TAKES A DRINK)   *What? Tell me*
        I remember   *What'd they call you*
Well, one winter during the   *in school? Tell me*
        we didn't have no money   *what they called*
depression, ~~I was six years old~~ -- *you.*
Cause the old man ~~was out of~~ *lost* a job, and we
        all busted... and
was ~~broke~~... I wore out ~~one~~ *a* shoe, *one shoe.*
So   *only*
~~And~~ I couldn't go to school with one
        but   *one*
shoe, ~~so~~ my mother found a boot. *so I had*
        a   *on one foot there*
~~sent me to school in one~~ shoe and *on one foot there*
a   *on the other. A shoe and a boot. Shoe, boot.*
~~one~~ boot. The kids called me

Shoebootie.

They used to holler
                    MIKE
            Shoebootie? *huh?*

        (LAUGHS)

**Sample page from the script for "Two's a Crowd" showing handwritten changes
made during the production process.**

ARCHIE *(Mumbles)* I don't know. Nothin'

MIKE He musta had a reason.

ARCHIE Well, he said that I said he was a nigger.

MIKE Did you?

ARCHIE Sure.

MIKE Well then, that's the reason.

ARCHIE What the hell reason was that? That's what all them people was called in them days. I mean everybody we knew called 'em people niggers. That's all my old man ever called 'em there. What the hell was I supposed to call them? I didn't know the difference, I didn't call 'em a wop. Couldn't call 'em wops because wops was what we called the dagos.

MIKE Did you ever think that possibly your father just might be wrong?

ARCHIE Wrong, my old man? Don't be stupid. My old man, let me tell you about him. He was never wrong about nothin'.

MIKE Yes, he was, Arch.

ARCHIE Huh?

MIKE My old man used to call people the same things as your old man. But I always knew he was wrong. So was your old man.

ARCHIE No he wasn't.

MIKE Yes he was. Your father was wrong. Your father was wrong!

ARCHIE Don't tell me my father was wrong. Let me tell you somethin'. Your father, the breadwinner, the man who goes out and busts his butt to keep a roof over your head and clothes on your back, you call your father wrong? Your father,

64

the man who comes home bringin' candy. Your father's the first guy to throw a ball to you and take you for walks in the park, holdin' you by the hand. My father held me by the hand. Oh — hey . . . my father had a hand on him. *(Holds up his hand)* I'll tell you. He busted that hand and he busted it on me to teach me to do good. My father, he shoved me in a closet for seven hours to teach me to do good 'cause he loved me, he loved me. Don't be lookin' at me! Let me tell you somethin', you're supposed to love your father! 'cause your father loves you. *(A beat)* Now, how can any man who loves you tell you anything that's wrong! What's the use in talking to you.

> *(A beat, he rises, crosses and lies down on a tablecloth that is on the floor. He falls asleep. After a few beats, Mike rises, crosses to Archie, carefully covers him with awning, lies down himself, gets under cover)*

MIKE   Goodnight, Shoebootie.

> *(After a beat Mike turns, spoon fashion to Archie. Puts his arm around Archie, pats his stomach. Archie mutters about Alice Faye as he turns, facing Mike. They get into embrace which now leaves them cheek to cheek)*

FADE OUT

END OF ACT TWO

II. Critical Reaction:
The First Season

Telepic Review:
All in the Family

Variety   January 13, 1971

This is the best tv comedy since the original "The Honey-mooners." It's the best casting since Sgt. Bilko's squad. It should be the biggest hit since "Laugh-In," or the Nielsen sample is in need of severe revision.

"All in the Family" is based on the BBC series, "Till Death Us Do Part," but recreators Norman Lear and Bud Yorkin have made it as all-American as apple pie, hot dogs, bigotry, ethnic suspicion, political ignorance, social blindness and grandma Moses. This sounds like much too much for the nether tube, but the Lear-Yorkin comedy is a broad, sharp double-edged sword sliced right and left, and the ultimate effect is one of deep pleasure and relief. Prime element is audacity, generally a benchmark of really imaginative work.

The show has a strong focal character in Carroll O'Connor as the blustering, bigoted father. It must be seen to be believed, but O'Connor plays Archie Bunker with such relish, skill and style that he is quite literally a "lovable bigot." Playing with and off Archie expertly is Jean Stapleton, an excellent comedic foil and bridge over the household gap to the young marrieds, Rob Reiner and Sally Struthers as Mike and Gloria Stivic. With honest-to-lower-Jersey working class accents all around, the kids are equally successful in underpinning this broad farce with a reality in human terms, as is Michael Evans, featured as a young black counterpoint to the old man's racial cliches (Lionel would be more uncomfortable at Julia's house than at the Bunkers, which is a clue to the ingenious kidding that goes on here). And they all look like real people.

Relative to the rest of prime-time tv, the show gets shocking bite as the old man slings around such terms as Hebe, Polack, Spook, Coon, but the shots are backed up by strong scripting otherwise; as in the confrontation between the father and Lionel in the premiere. This climaxes with Lionel telling the old man that their long friendship will sustain—even if he might be Jewish.

It is no small benefit (if cheaper) that "All in the Family" is taped straight through before a live studio audience at Television City in Hollywood as was the original "Honeymooners" at the old Dumont network in New York. The real laughter and applause—although it may be touched here and there with the yock console—is an adjunct to the basic reality of the performers and the setting, while at the same time lending a theatricality that is almost totally lacking in the filmed sitcoms. And as for theatrics, this show shows promise of farce comedy which is a cut above much that's playing Broadway these days. *Bill.*

Telepic Review:
All in the Family

Daily Variety (Hollywood)   January 13, 1971

CBS-TV prexy Robert D. Wood, in commenting on midseason entry "All in the Family," noted net is putting into practice innovative rather than imitative policy. Idea is valid, but first edition of "Family," if this is example of where series is headed, though innovative, is nothing less than an insult to any unbigoted televiewer. If target is the young American liberal, he is being asked to sit still for a one-joke show—and a sick joke at that. Premise is outrageous enough to attract the curious to discover what is causing outcry.

Format concerns Carroll O'Connor as racist father in middle-class household. Gruff and malapropic, O'Connor blasts timid wife Jean Stapleton, daughter Sally Struthers (re her mini skirt: "Every time you sit down the mystery's over!"), and son-in-law Rob Reiner. Character played by O'Connor has absolutely no redeeming features

He dislikes all minorities, wallows in his ignorance like a hog in mud. Defending names of his non-Jewish parents, he says, "David and Sarah: two names right out of the Bible, which has nothing to do with the Jews." Character and show manage to slur Jews, Italians, Poles, blacks (Michael Evans appeared as bright, young black kowtowing to O'Connor's character's prejudice), liberals, conservatives. "Family" sitcom comes up with something for every prejudice.

Producer-writer Norman Lear's raw, plotless wonder, designed to shock, was directed in initial outing by John Rich, who kept actors stepping sprightly despite overall premise of show. Lear can write sharp comedy and build characters in polished fashion; too bad this bundle from Britain wasn't turned back at the shoreline.

O'Connor in pivotal role, despite lines designed to alienate everyone, is strong in his part. Miss Stapleton comes across as the put-upon wife who occasionally zings home an honest comic line at O'Connor. Miss Struthers has little to do but look stricken, which she does. Reiner is okay as supposed liberal who can't keep his mouth shut.

Presumably, idea of show is that airing prejudices in their true light can diminish them. Other side of coin, however, is that anything gamy is better buried.   *Tone.*

TV: Are Racism and Bigotry Funny?

Fred Ferretti *New York Times*   January 12, 1971

Tonight the Columbia Broadcasting System Television Network will find out if Americans think bigotry and racism, as the prime elements of a situation comedy, are funny.

Is it funny, for example, to have the pot-bellied, church-going, cigar-smoking son of Middle America, Archie Bunker, the hero of "All in the Family," fill the screen with such epithets as "spic" and "spade" and "hebe" and "yid" and "polack"? Is it funny for him to refer to his son-in-law as "the laziest white man I ever seen?" Or to look at a televised football game and yell, "Look at that spook run . . . It's in his blood"?

The answer, I say, is no. None of these is funny. They shock because one is not used to hearing them shouted from the television tube during prime-time family programs. They don't make one laugh so much as they force self-conscious, semi-amused gasps.

They are not funny because they are there for their shock value, despite C.B.S.'s protestations that what are being presented are "familiar stereotypes" with "a humorous spotlight on their prejudices . . . making them a source of laughter," so "we can show how absurd they are." What is lacking is taste.

"All in the Family" could have been funny; in fact it was funny when it was "'Til Death Do Us Part," a four-year hit on British Broadcasting Corporation television. It was offered to networks here and rejected.

And it was funny when it was "Those Were the Days," a pilot half-hour made for the American Broadcasting Company in 1969 by Norman Lear and Bud Yorkin. A.B.C. rejected it out of hand, and it was bought by C.B.S.'s Michael Dann as his last program decision before leaving C.B.S.

That first pilot, which I saw last week, was funny. Vulgar, suggestive, coarse, but funny.

Carroll O'Connor as Archie and Jean Stapleton as his wife, Edith, were, despite the vulgarity, amusing and, oddly enough, sympathetic. Mr. O'Connor so warmed to his role of blue-collar bully that he came off as well as Jackie Gleason ever did as Ralph Kramden. Miss Stapleton as his whining, wise-cracking wife was the perfect foil, saying with utmost sweetness, after Archie referred to blacks as "black beauties," that the reference was "nicer than when he called them coons."

But what happened to that pilot on its way to a network showing was a complete rewriting by Mr. Lear under network pressure; deletion of several remarks, and insertion of a remark wherein Archie calls his son-in-law "a Polish joke."

The shock lines were left in, but a rather amusing scene where son-in-law and daughter are surprised in deshabile by the Bunkers was written out. Sex is out, it would appear, but bigotry stays.

Mr. Lear disagrees with this interpretation. He sees both pilots, the one rejected by A.B.C. and bought by C.B.S. and the remake, which is tonight's first episode, as essentially similar. The first time around when Archie angrily denies that he's Jewish, despite his parents' names, David and Sarah ("the names are out of the Bible. That's got nothin' to do with Jews") he was funny. In the new pilot the line is delivered flatly. It becomes offensive.

The episode is filled with "mick" and "pinkos" and "bleedin' hearts," but they jar. They are not natural, and Mr. O'Connor doesn't seem to say them with as much gusto as he did the first time.

In the next couple of weeks we'll see episodes in which Archie writes a letter to President Nixon; he has an auto accident with a "yenta" but asks to be represented by a Jewish lawyer; in which a friend of his son-in-law turns out to be a "birdie . . . queer as a three-dollar bill."

It will be an interesting 13 weeks, for C.B.S. as well as for the viewing public.

Can Bigotry Be Laughed Away?
It's Worth a Try

Jack Gould *New York Times*   January 21, 1971

For any weekly television comedy situation series to generate an iota of controversy is akin to having network heads William S. Paley, Leonard H. Goldenson and Julian Goodman do a festive Maypole dance in Central Park Mall. Not that such pirouetting executives would be wanting in consummate grace; it just ain't going to happen.

But it has happened. On Tuesday nights the Columbia Broadcasting System has unfolded a program entitled "All in the Family" and rarely has a series set so many reviewers and viewers dashing to their memo pads to record their feelings. The variety of their comments suggests that the show may either polarize the country beyond measure or successfully treat the issue of bigotry in terms of laughter.

The central figure of "All in the Family" is Archie Bunker, played by Carroll O'Connor, who instinctively if not militantly harbors just about every known prejudice. For Jews, Blacks, Catholics, the welfare state, socialism. Archie has a string of epithets and slurring remarks which understandably provoke the affected parties.

The season, it may be recalled, opened with a sea of hogwash about "relevancy," but in many ways "All in the Family" invokes a different kind of relevancy and not one meriting instant dismissal. The world is filled with Archies—not architects of genocide, but people who have been raised in an environment of bigoted cliches which have a persistent virulence and reality.

Prejudicial epithets always make a civilized soul squirm in discomfort and wish they would go away. But, unfortunately, such is not the case. No matter how much TV or other media attempt to suppress them, they do exist. Except for "All in the Family," it is difficult to recall another TV attempt to bring the disease out into the open with the aim, one hopes, of applying the test of corrective recognition and humor.

There have been suggestions, by now growing a bit tiresome, that sophisticates east of the Hudson will detect the attempts at subtlety in "All in the Family" but that elsewhere Archie might just become an increasingly popular figure and represent a utilization of the home screen for evil ends. But as the role of Archie evolves, this convenient rationalization may fall into a measure of dispute. If Archie turns out to be a know-it-all and a truly venal bigot, off with him. But it might be worth waiting to see whether Archie doesn't end up looking like a vacuous boob in assuming that any man can live alone and not feel the influence of other faiths and races.

Although some reviewers have jumped up and down in ethnic rage—and it is easy to see why—"All in the Family" has been accorded sympathetic approval by some sensitive community groups involving blacks, whites and the clergy. The show also received a rave appraisal in a West Coast black journal. There might just be something to the argument that new tactics are needed to combat ingrained bigotry: CBS may not have found precisely the right tactic, but the experiment should not be written off precipitously.

In the first installment there was a jarring reference to Jews. But the life of Archie cannot be taken out of context. Mike, the son-in-law, acted by Rob Reiner, casually inquired if the names of Archie's parents were not David and Sarah.

"David and Sarah," Archie replied. "Two names right out of the Bible—which has got nothin' to do with Jews."

Or, more recently, Archie suddenly grew envious of a black boy and his father, a janitor, who, through settlement of an automobile accident claim, acquired enough capital to open a dry cleaning store. Archie, whose car's rear end has recently been bumped, decides to follow suit and calls in a distinguished Jewish law firm. Knowing the neighborhood where Archie lives, the firm at first sends the "house Gentile," subsequently replacing him with a distinguished senior partner.

Just as the senior partner is attempting to elicit the details of Archie's feigned accident injury, the attorney for the insurance company shows up with a list of impeccable witnesses who make it plain that the automotive mishap took place only in Archie's imagination. The senior Jewish attorney retires, citing one of the law's cardinal principles: "Never take a case where the defense has seven Catholic nuns as witnesses."

It is easy to misunderstand "All in the Family," to concentrate on Archie's disparagement of practically everyone around him. The larger lesson is that he is continually a loser, always a bit more frustrated than before.

The Norman Lear production, which John Rich directs remarkably well in front of a live audience, is blessed by the presence of the gifted Jean Stapleton. Miss Stapleton, with amusing resignation, goes about her chores seeminngly undismayed by the battles between her unreconstructed husband and a son-in-law and daughter (Sally Struthers) who disagree with everything he says.

In one such confrontation, Archie and the son-in-law, having decided to unburden themselves to President Nixon, argue whether he should be addressed as "Dear Mr. President," "Sir," or "Commander-in-Chief." Then Miss Stapleton dryly interjects, "Or Tricky Dicky." That line, mind you, on a situation comedy series.

Mr. Lear has his hands more than full in sustaining the comedy series. But there is much to be said in behalf of his attempt, derived from the British series entitled "Till Death Do Us Part." Whether he succeeds or fails, he has abjured the preposterously larger-than-life situation comedies that never even mention everyday themes. Some of Archie's words may chill the spine, but to root out bigotry has defied man's best efforts for generations and the weapon of laughter just might succeed. The possibility entitles "All in the Family" to a chance.

The Message Sounds Like "Hate Thy Neighbor"

Stephanie Harrington
New York Times   January 24, 1971

CBS's new half-hour gift to Tuesday nights, "All in the Family," is kind of like wishing for a little more frankness in political dialogue and getting your wish in the form of Spiro Agnew. A working-class family situation series with a message, "All in the Family" is vulgar and silly. And after the disgust-at-first-shock wears off, the vaudeville clinkers passed off as humor are totally predictable, both in themselves and as means of conveying the show's moral. All prejudice—racial, class, sophisticated against unsophisticated and vice versa—is bad.

In describing the means used to get this message across, it is impossible to employ any adjective that could possibly get into the same thesaurus with words like nuance or subtlety of dimension. And Carroll O'Connor as the "hero" for anti-heros, Archie Bunker, plays to the camera as if he were on a vaudeville stage instead of a set that is supposed to be someone's living room. For the home viewer, that little conceit is destroyed anyway by the laughter of the studio audience, which also makes painfully offensive lines that, if not milked for laughs they don't deserve, might at least have some shock value in terms of making people face their prejudices.

Archie is a paunchy, middle-sized, slightly more than middle-aged, white, working-class type. His victimized wife Edith, acted by Jean Stapleton, whom he repeatedly, and with great imaginative thrust, refers to as a "dingbat," is alternately insulted by him or patronized or ignored. Her only revenge is to get off some of the best lines of the show (which isn't conceding much). Living with them is their 18-year-old daughter, who looks like a 6-year-old Shirley Temple in a blonde wig and black leather mini. Her mental life consists of affirming whatever her husband says and she should have women's lib out after CBS in full cry. Her husband, a reaonsably socially concerned student with moderately long hair, is the principal antagonist to Archie (he is evidentally of Polish-American background, since Archie refers to him as a "Polack").

Archie, we can assume, is not Polish. Nor is he a "Spic," a

"Spade" or a "Yid," the epithets he uses with some satisfaction to refer to those groups. (He might, however, be Irish since he never uses the word "Mick.") The joke—and the message—of the first episode were sprung on us when the neighborhood handyman, a young black engineering student, in the course of being patronized by Archie, who insists he is not a racist, turns the tables. In put-on-Whitey Uncle Tomese, the young man asks Archie if he is Jewish, noting that he uses the word *tuchas* and talks with his hands. Everyone takes up the joke while Archie helplessly sputters his denial. Which just goes to show Archie (and us) that bigotry can boomerang.

We are also supposed to get the message that if we have categorized Archie as a bigot just because he calls people names, then we are victims of our own bigotry. Archie, after all, is moved by the corny sentiment of a verse on a not-quite-Hallmark anniversary card. And that is supposed to prove that behind the gruff exterior is a warm, sympathetic, perhaps even potentially brotherly human being just aching to be recognized. But the characterization gives us no reason to believe this. Archie does not come across as a sympathetic character who victimizes others because he himself is a victim. For 30 minutes Archie is *nothing but* bigoted about others and unrelievedly rotten to his family. And because the show is so one-dimensional, because its characters are caricatures, it cannot even claim the shock value of being courageously, uncompromisingly, true to life. In an attempt to discredit stereotyping, it resorts to stereotypes. In its sledge-hammer determination to tell it like it is, it over-tells, and, instead of being the breakthrough in courage it was meant to be, it over-kills itself.

But beyond the question of success is the question of intent. "All in the Family" is a logical extension of the kind of tell-it-like-it-is "confrontation" television in which hostile blacks, on discussion programs or documentaries, shout their long-simmering resentment at whites with a minimum of euphemisms, and whites come back with their gripes. (Indeed, had "All in the Family" succeeded, it would have been gutsier, much more shocking and much more effective than those confrontation-dialogues, which themselves quickly become predictable and stagey.) The question raised by both these attempts, or pseudo-attempts, at dramatic, consciousness-raising honesty is: Just what social purpose is being served? By making the expression of hostility more commonplace, do we really exorcise it? Or do we, in fact, make it more acceptable?

CBS Gambles on Reality
with New Comedy Series

Kay Gardella *New York Daily News* January 13, 1971

CBS rolled the dice last night with a new situation comedy, All in the Family, which will either be the biggest hit of the season or the biggest bomb, depending upon your views. Archie Bunker, the focal character in the half-hour series, is described as a "middle-class husband-father who sees the world and everyone in it only in terms of his own prejudices."

This is putting it mildly when words like "black beauties," "yids," "Spades," "pinkos" and "subversives" start being tossed around. And while Archie is superbly played by Carroll O'Connor and his dim-witted wife is brilliantly conceived by Jean Stapleton, so much of the so-called comedy hinges on Archie's prejudicial outbursts one has to assume he soon will run out of things to hate—and then where will the series be?

The actors, which also include Sally Struthers as Archie's daughter and Rob Reiner, Carl Reiner's son, as Archie's liberal son-in-law, provide a good basis for a realistic, funny situation comedy. But the emphasis had better be shifted quickly to their relationship and the fact that the young couple are living off the Bunkers, not on Archie's built-in hates, which we could barely tolerate.

Crude characters have their place in drama—situation comedy and whatever—there's no doubt about it. We're reminded when we say this of Stanley Kowalski in "Streetcar Named Desire," a role brilliantly created by Marlon Brando. O'Connor certainly has his teeth in Archie Bunker. The trouble is too much has been written into him too quickly and not enough permitted to slowly emerge from the characterization. It's too bad, because O'Connor is so good.

But prejudices, per se, are not funny. While we saw value in certain aspects of the series, we were very uncomfotable when the writers would allow these lines to take the place of real humor. For instance, it's neither offensive nor funny to hear Archie say that if Negroes have bumper stickers that say, "Black is Beautirul," there's no reason why they can't be called "black beauties." Where's a laugh in that?

Still, in the second episode of the series, when Archie samples what appears to be boiling soup on the stove only to find out his wife is dyeing trousers, the incident has good middle-class humor in it. And there are other moments—some very amusing, some not so amusing, some downright vulgar. It runs hot and cold like that, always challenging a viewer to make a basic decision. To wit: If the Archie Bunkers bore the life out of you off the home screen, can you commit yourself to a weekly half-hour to hear them insult the blacks, Jews, Poles, etc., even if it's all in the family?

Bigotry runs rampant as Archie indiscriminately takes off on anything and everything, including his son-in-law, whom he calls "a Polish joke." And when a nun comes to the door for charity, he tells his wife to limit the contribution to 50 cents. Says he: "Most of what you give them they buy golden candlesticks with it."

All in the Family is based on a hit British series, Till Death Do Us Part, which had a successful four-year run on TV. Imitating the British can be a deadly game, since their humor frequently borders on the very cruel—as witness the series, Steptoe and Son. At any rate, producers Bud Yorkin and Norman Lear put the package together on the assumption that if the British liked it, we'll love it.

For the same reason we won our independence, may we suggest that the tastes of American viewers need not be the same. America is indeed a melting pot, a fact we're proud of. If there's any direction we should be going in, it's to set the example for the rest of the world.

TV Review

Don Freeman *San Diego Union*   January 14, 1971

"All in the Family," the new CBS Tuesday night comedy series, is outrageous, shocking, probably offensive, undoubtedly insulting and it is also extremely funny. Certainly it stands alone in American television, an adult social satire reflected in farce comedy with a bite that cuts nearly, with surgical precision, to the bone.

Mostly it is audacious and adventurous, a not altogether tentative step into brisk waters. Adapted from the four-year hit British series, "Till Death Do Us Part," this CBS version produced by Norman Lear and Bud Yorkin has lost none of its crackle in the move to our shores and none of its contemporary flavor.

In at least one regard, mainly in its blunt airing of the racial epithet, "All in the Family" is an antiseptic offshoot of the movie, "Joe"—but by no means is it all that antiseptic.

Before the series hit the air, Robert Wood, president of CBS, announced: "We hope it will prove to be both entertaining and provocative, and that it will serve to ventilate some of the prejudices and misconceptions in American society today. Hopefully, a program like 'All in the Family' can contribute toward getting viewers to relax a bit and encourage them to laugh at themselves as well as at other people."

There will be those who won't laugh, who will find both the theme and the language distasteful. But none will deny the show's basic honesty or the accuracy of its probing—with skill and relish —into the stubborn realities of American life.

Certainly the family is unlike any other ever to grace television where domestic blandness has always been the rule. There's Archie Bunker, the head of the household, portrayed brilliantly by Carroll O'Connor as a sympathetic, almost lovable bigot whose outspoken prejudices are boundless and frequently uttered.

There's his wife, Edith, forlornly optimistic and played with endearing but doubtful helpfulness by Jean Stapleton. Their daughter (Sally Struthers) wears a miniskirt and a mind to match and their son-in-law (Rob Reiner) is long-haired and mustachioed, an activist firmly attached to his own set of preconceptions.

Given this explosive fuse, the arguments flourish and they are hilarious. Every incident is a confrontation, a spotlight on the gaps that separate them.

Archie wants to watch the football highlights on the TV. The youngsters prefer a special on pollution with Jack Lemmon. And the fuse ignites.

"When I wanna learn about pollution," Archie fumes, "it won't be from no millionaire actor who got nothin' to do but sit on his duff and dream up causes. If he wants to unpollute something, let him unpollute the movies. All them nudies."

They argue about John Wayne. "Let me warn you," Archie snaps, "that when you're talking about the Duke you're not just talking about an actor. You're talking about the kind of spirit that made this country great."

"Are you kidding?" says the son-in-law, incredulously.

From the kitchen, Edith calls in with: "He'd lay down his life for the Duke."

"You bet I would," says Archie.

Edith nods. "For me, no. For the Duke, yes."

Archie is all for the Duke but he's opposed to miniskirts. He peers with distress at his daughter. "Every time you sit down in one of them things," he says, "the mystery's over."

The casting, all down the line, is right on the mark and the writing is inspired. Comments in phone calls to CBS have ranged from "degrading" and "worst possible taste" to "refreshing" and "marvelous." It's that kind of a show.

Introduction to a Bigot

Dwight Newton
San Francisco Examiner   January 12, 1971

"All in the Family," premiering tonight, 9:30, Channel 5, is the first U.S. situation comedy to call a spade a spook, and to order a wife not to contribute more than half a buck to a Roman Catholic nun because "most of what you give them, they buy golden candlesticks with."

These remarks are voiced by the main character, Archie Bunker, a loving family man and blustering bigot whom Carroll O'Connor portrays as the most self-centered know-it-all to hit television since Jackie Gleason created Ralph Kramden for "The Honeymooners."

"The Honeymooners" show, now in repeats, is where it was: Fantasyland. A bombastic ado about lower middle class trivia, circa 1950.

"All in the Family" is where it is: Todayland. A bombastic ado about lower-middle class frailties, prejudices and concerns, circa 1971.

"All in the Family" also is outrageously, shockingly funny.

CBS-TV did not run it through a TV strainer conforming to the antiseptically superficial tradition of "Father Knows Best" and "Family Affair." This "all-in-the-family" affair wades belly-deep in nearly every challenge confronting nearly every family today—sex,

81

religion, law and order, students, hair, racism, communism—you named it, bumptious Archie Bunker has an opinion.

Next question: Is the U.S. televiewing public ready for Archie Bunker? The British public was ready when he arrived as outspoken Alf Garnett in "Till Death Us Do Part," a series that ran four years. David Frost told me that "the British press presumed that bigots could never raise their heads again after this television mockery, but instead of a mockery, Alf Garnett became a national hero."

"All in the Family" is a U.S. rewrite of the British series. Segment No. 1, scheduled for tonight, pulls no visible nor audible punches. The dialogue will variously be construed as nasty, hilarious, vicious, biting, mean, wonderful, defamatory and delightful.

"All in the Family" will be talk of the country tomorrow morning. It will hit home screens with the impact of the first "Laugh-In" and the first and only "Turn-On" which was cancelled the morning after its premiere.

"All in the Family": TV Social Departure

Alan Bunce
Christian Science Monitor   January 18, 1971

Look at Archie for a minute and try to guess what entertainment medium you'd be likely to find him in. He chomps a cigar, wears white socks, malaprops broadly. He's an arrant bigot, calls people "spics" and "spooks." To him, welfare is a fraud, black men are natural athletes, and the radical ideas of his young daughter and husband—who live with him in a lower-middle-class townhouse—are shocking. That the kids are tentative atheists is bad enough, but slurring John Wayne is the last straw.

"He'd lay down his life for the Duke," explains his wife Edith. "Not for me, but for the Duke."

No, Archie isn't filmdom's "son of 'Joe' " or a "relevant" Broadway character. Actually he is the antihero of a new situation comedy on CBS-TV that marks the first major social departure for this commercial genre.

Called "All in the Family" and based on a BBC series, the startlingly different half-hour show caused the network some misgivings before its premiere last week, even though the pilot film had apparently been softened a bit, and each episode has a preamble about laughing at our own frailties.

The main jolt is finding such material cropping up when you're used to seeing, say Andy Griffith. While it is frank in other areas— the newlyweds' affection, for instance—the real break is the sudden entrance of this social dimension, which isn't attempted in other current premieres, such as ABC-TV's "The Smith Family," a Henry Fonda vehicle airing Wednesday.

Is it being exploited? Undoubtedly, Archie's gross prejudice is milked for laughs, and the show offers merely routine production values. Some viewers resent Archie's very presence on the tube, even as a step toward the kind of satire praised to the skies in other media —and even though most other series are berated for their blandness and unreality (that is, for the absence of people like Archie).

Yet this series is often funny, and in a sense more humane than most of its prime-time peers. Racial canards aren't a bit comic, of course, but people are, and it doesn't take long to discover that Archie comes closer to being a person than most TV figures. Once viewers see someone they recognize (do you recognize anyone on "Green Acres"?), they can also begin to laugh at him.

Carroll O'Connor plays Archie with authority and enough Jackie-Gleason-like braggadocio to make him the butt of gags. It works well against the foil of Jean Stapleton's Edith. She torpedoes his grandest moments with wisecracks tossed off in a voice that sounds like a bad oboe. While made too goofish, the young couple is nicely done by Rob Reiner and Sally Struthers, and Michael Evans portrays their black friend Lionel with a gleeful amusement at Archie's Neanderthal outlook.

Last week's premiere saw a long, humorous buildup to a senti-mental anniversary for Edith. Tomorrow night Archie writes a letter to President Nixon, and pity anyone in the family who thinks it's funny that he dresses formally to pen the great epistle, or that he begins it with "Dear Mr. President, your honor, sir:"

New TV Comedy Takes Hard, Realistic Poke at Bigotry

Pamela Haynes
Los Angeles Sentinel   January 28, 1971

You will not believe the new CBS-TV program "All in the Family" which premiered Tuesday night at 9:30.

You will not believe it because for years we have been snowed under with nonsensical pap which masqueraded as "situation comedy" on television.

These so-called comedy shows about "average American families" bore about as much resemblance to real life as Richard Nixon does to Mahatma Ghandi.

But now we have Archie Bunker, hilariously played by Carroll O'Connor. Archie is a damned sight closer to where real "American" lower middle families are at.

Archie is a racist, a religious bigot, a card-carrying member of Spiro Agnew's Silent Majority.

If you saw the movie "Joe," then you know Archie Bunker. If you remember Joe's tirade against "nigger, commies, hippies" and practically everyone else you will recognize Archie as his soul brother.

"When I was looking for a job, nobody got out and picketed and marched for me," he growled repeating the cant of the white working class.

"Yeah," put in his wife (the long-suffering Jean Stapleton), "your uncle got it for you."

Archie is the kind of gentle soul who has nothing against "yids" as a matter of fact, he even works with a couple of "Hebes" (his words, not mine).

Archie outrages the sensibilities of just about every minority group on earth. But his ranting serves an important purpose and I hope that these upset liberals or uptight viewers won't lose sight of that fact.

The paramount thing about "All in the Family" is that for the first time, instead of trying to pass off an expensively groomed and immaculately coiffed Doris Day as "the typical American housewife" and a distinguished, suave and ever so tolerant Robert as everyone's father, they have presented a fat, ignorant, angry middle aged pig who swears at his wife, belches at the table and gets choked up over sugary tributes on greeting cards. In other words, Archie Bunker is real.

Far from protesting, members of the minorities slandered by Archie should rejoice at this non-cosmetized portrait of the "master race."

It remains to be seen whether, once the shock of seeing and hearing the uglier side of "typical American" attitudes is over, Archie Bunker will be welcomed into our homes as a funny and instructive cat or turned off as a big-mouthed bore.

What is hoped is that the show will be given a chance to go on doing its outrageous thing and not be strangled by the outrage of some narrow, uptight people.

Archie Bunker lives in millions of American homes, and it's about time that we saw him in all of his white-sock-wearing glory.

Credit for the authentic ring and general true-to-life bearing of the show must go to Norman Lear, of the Bud Yorkin-Tandem outfit turning out "All in the Family."

It's Lear's genius which shines through and one can understand why he supervises all scripts closely and nurses each show all the way through to the TV screen.

Irresponsible Television Production Aids Racism

Whitney M. Young, Jr.
Los Angeles Sentinel   February 4, 1971

Recently, bigotry reared its ugly head in a place we least expected it, and disappeared from a platform from which it usually holds forth.

Nationwide television is one place where, at least in recent years, we don't expect to hear racial slurs and insults. But two weeks ago a network unveiled a new situation comedy series, "All in the Family." It has to be a new low in taste. Just about every ethnic group is insulted on this show. Blacks, Puerto Ricans, Jews, Poles, and others all come in for their share.

The central character is a bigoted blue-collar worker who drops racial insults like some people drop comments on the weather.

I suppose the show's producers intended to satirize that kind of mentality. They play him off against his cretinous daughter and liberal son-in-law, who mouth the usual liberal platitudes and in general try to make the hero look bad.

But this doesn't compensate for the gratuitous insults that fill the public airwaves.

Even when our hero gets his come-uppance, racial stereotypes predominate. The black youth who makes the bigot look foolish, for example, is given some money and sent on an errand to buy flowers.

"Where I get my flowers," he says, "this represents clear profit."

After all these years, we're back to the stereotyped black who is irresponsible and who steals.

I suppose the people who wrote and produced the show think they're being "in" by following the trend toward ethnic frankness and honesty.

But all they've succeeded in doing is outraging minority groups and, indeed, all decent individuals, by filling the public airwaves with hate-filled epithets.

They probably think that by showing the hero to be a narrow-minded bigot, they're providing a message.

But the only message that comes through is that such a program ought to be taken off the air and relegated to wherever they're storing the old Amos 'n' Andy programs.

And it's about time clever liberal writers started easing up on their portrayal of working-class whites as bigots. Some are; some aren't.

Purveying that stereotype is just as objectionable as the racial slurs we heard. Studies show that the Wallaceites are drawn from the middle-class as much as from workers, and many of the upper-class men who control the racist institutions in our society are more deserving of exposure than workers, some of whom are used by racists to keep them from natural alliances with black workers.

It is irresponsible to air a show like this at a time when our nation is polarized and torn by racism.

Some future day might find a situation where such slurs are meaningless but right now, it is a luxury we can't afford.

While the show tries to satirize bigotry, it only succeeds in spreading the poison and making it—by repetition—more respectable.

If we don't expect bigotry from network entertainment broadcasts, we sadly have come to expect it from southern politicians.

So all people were deeply gratified when the new governor of Georgia, Jimmy Carter, stated in his inaugural address, "The time for racial discrimination is over."

He shook up a lot of die-hard segregationists with a speech that did what no governor of Georgia had ever done before.

He correctly pointed out that the whole state "pays a terrible and continuing human and financial price" for bigotry.

His promise of bold new programs and an end to discrimination sets the pace for what we hope will at least be a "New South."

Governor Carter is just one of several new southern governors who seem committed to leading the section out of its terrible heritage of racism.

Governor Holton of Virginia and the new governors of Arkansas, Florida, and South Carolina have also demonstrated that there is a new breed of southern politician.

We'll be watching closely to see that their promises are fulfilled. The new hope among the South's black citizens is a direct result of their ballot power and political strength.

Let's hope the decency and lack of racism expressed by Governor Carter in the heart of the South will find its way into the creative liberals who find racism a fit subject for television comedy.

"All in the Family" Gets Better as Weeks Go By

Norman Mark *Chicago Daily News* February 23, 1971

I've watched All in the Family several times now since its premiere last month, and I'm beginning to change my mind once more about this important new series.

After the first show on Jan. 12, which was funnier than any episode of a situation comedy I had ever seen, I thought the program was in danger of becoming routine fare. The characters in subsequent weeks seemed one-dimensional, and at times there was some flagrant overacting.

What was worse, Archie Bunker (Carroll O'Connor), the series'

All-American bigot hero, and his long-suffering wife Edith (Jean Stapleton) appeared to have no real reason for staying married.

But as the weeks have gone by, I've seen the show improve. The characters are still overly simplified, but we're seeing more of their personalities. And now I can begin to understand why Archie and Edith Bunker stay together as they show more affection toward each other.

In tonight's program (at 8:30 on Channel 2), a young, un-married hippie couple wants to spend the night in Archie's home. They are told, by the ever-bigoted Archie, "This is a Christian home. Get out."

Now whether you are intellectual, liberal, conservative, lower, upper or middle, that is a statement to ponder.

The biggest laugh this week is won, as it often is, by Miss Stapleton. Archie's daughter accuses him and his generation of being afraid of sex. Archie says, "If I was afraid of it, you wouldn't be here. Right, Edith?"

Long Pause. "Right, Edith?"

"I'm tryin' to remember."

All in the Family is a delight. It can and does fight bigotry and stupidity with humor. It is on the cutting edge of TV innovation, and it is slowly unveiling more complexities within its characters.

Furthermore, Archie, who had been treated condescendingly by the writers in the first few weeks, is winning some arguments these days.

And how can you hate anyone who accuses his Polish son-in-law of "coming from a long line of bowling teams"?

"All in the Family": Review

Cleveland Amory *TV Guide*   February 27, 1971

All in the Family is not just the best-written, best-directed and best-acted show on television, it is the best show on television. It is also a landmark show—a complete breakthrough—one which opens up a whole new world for television and has already made the old world seem so dated that we very much doubt that any new program, from here on in, will ever be quite the same again. We realize these are strong statements. But then so is this series. And the remarkable thing about it is that it has done all this by just one simple thing: it has added to the everlasting, everloving, everlaughing, everboring family situation comedy just one secret ingredient—prejudice. There have been documentaries about this, and dramas. But now you have it in prime-time comedy, not only shown up for what it is but also faced, for the first time, by the one force which will surely in the end overcome it—humor.

Norman Lear, who wrote and produced it, deserves the first bow. Second, there's Archie Bunker (Carroll O'Connor). He's the best-written and best-acted character on your screen this year—and this whether he is ranting at one of his wife's long stories ("Edith, will you stifle"), at his daughter's miniskirt ("Every time you sit down in one of them things, the mystery's over") or at anything about his live-in-son-in-law ("He wants to help the underprivileged, let him start with himself"). But don't overlook wife Edith (Jean Stapleton). She can malaprop not only words, but a whole character. And son-in-law Mike (Rob Reiner) is no slouch either. He can even listen funny. Then there's Mike's wife, Gloria (Sally Struthers), and black handy man Lionel (Michael Evans), who is forever putting Archie on. They're all fine—which simply means that so is director John Rich.

In one episode, Mike has written a letter to President Nixon. So, of course, Archie must too. "Dear Mr. President, Your Honor, Sir," he begins. In another, seeking a tough lawyer, he chooses from the Yellow Pages the firm of Rabinowitz, Rabinowitz & Rabinowitz, and over to his house comes the firm's "token Gentile," introduced at the front door by Edith as "Mr. Whitney Fitzroy Eyevee," which is shortly corrected by the lawyer himself to "Mr. Whitney Fitzroy the Fourth." Finally, Archie gets the real McCoy, or rather the real Rabinowitz, only to find that opposing counsel is Clarence V. Marshall, or, as again introduced by Edith, "Clarence the Fifth Marshall." Nothing is sacred here. A nun comes to the door to collect money and Archie takes Edith aside. "Nothing more than half a buck. No matter what they tell you, they spend most of it on gold candlesticks." Another time he is grieved. "What anti-Jewish bias?" he demands to know, "Oh, no, Daddy." says Gloria, "not that again. Even Jesus was a Jew." "Yeah," replies Archie, "but only on his mother's side."

Obviously such a show will give much offense to some and some offense to many—if for no other reason than that it is so different from what we are used to. But you cannot deny that it is funny any more than you can deny that it is true—that it invariably well and often brilliantly holds the mirror up to our human (or is it inhuman?) nature.

Bigotry as a Dirty Joke

John Leonard *Life*   March 18, 1971

All in the Family is a wretched program. Why review a wretched program? Well, why vacuum the living room or fix the septic tank? Every once in a while the reviewer must assume the role of a bottle of Johnston's No-Roach with the spray applicator: let's clean up this culture!

Carroll O'Connor plays the part of your friendly neighborhood bigot, the American workingman as CBS conceives of him, William Bendix with a bad mouth, going on for half an hour every Tuesday night about the spooks and spics and wops and fags. He mugs a lot. Jean Stapleton plays his wife, slightly out of sync, one of those women—like Ruby Keeler—who never seem to belong in the situation in which they find themselves but who try hard, thereby earning from the audience an admiration heavily laced with contempt. Sally Struthers plays their daughter; she's married to Rob Reiner, a slightly long-haired Polack college pinko. Sally and Rob live with Carroll and Jean. They are always having Sunday dinner, the occasion for Mr. O'Connor to spit out his snappy one-liners on the inferiority of alien races, colors and creeds.

Just as most TV commercials are not really insulting to women (they are insulting to *people*), *All in the Family* is not merely insulting to minorities; it is insulting to Mr. O'Connor, Miss Stapleton, Miss Struthers, Mr. Reiner, the American workingman, CBS and everybody who watches the program. Bigotry becomes a form of dirty joke. We are invited to snigger. Invited, hell—we are *instructed* to snigger, like morons in a nursery school, before each episode. Laughter cures, cauterizes, exorcises, even when it's canned.

Take a recent, typical example. Mr. Reiner brings home a long-haired friend whom Mr. O'Connor suspects of being a homosexual. Mr. O'Connor complains about it at his local beer parlor. Mr. O'Connor is made to understand that one of his drinking buddies, a heavily muscled ex-college football star, just may be, well, *that way* too. Mr. O'Connor refuses to believe it. End of program, after much mincing around. Mr. O'Connor always winds up refusing to believe; how else could the sit-com drag its dreary way on to next week?

And what are we supposed to believe? That limp-wristed long-hairs may look like homosexuals but aren't necessarily so disposed, while the short-haired athlete on the next stool lapping up draught beer and shouting at the TV set is suspect? Don't say nasty things about homosexuals, your best friend may be one? Very funny. Cauterizing. Implicit in the sit-com is stasis; it's a condition, not a movement toward or away from revelation. But what *is* the condition of *All in the Family*? Why is it considered to be laughable?

I don't object to this vulgarity because of my ideological delinquencies, my toilet-training, my SAT scores or my Higher Seriousness. I object because the program is a double-edged lie. Cutting one way, the lie tells us that workingmen are mindless buffoons; their opinions, unlike ours, are unrelated to social, psychological or political conditions; their knee-jerk responses to stimuli are so unreal as to be amusing. (See Studs Terkel on *The Great American Dream Machine* for evidence overwhelmingly to the contrary.) Cutting the other way, the lie tells us that Mr. O'Connor's Archie is, anyway, charming. Forgivable. Purely a premise, a *given*, in no way dangerous, certainly incapable of roughing up antiwar demonstrators. A bad mouth, maybe; a sloppy mind, yes; but somewhere anterior to his style of speaking and thinking is an essential decency, or harmlessness, that makes him a figure of fun. Bigotry out loud, like scatology out loud, robs the words of their subterranean power to shock or destroy—another maybe.

But the words to begin with were only approximations of feelings which are in no way defused or defanged by making a sly joke out of them. A double-edged lie and a two-way pandering (we—CBS and the audience—are better than he is; he is ridiculous) . . . just who is the joke on?

Love That Hate

Robert Lewis Shayon
Saturday Review   March 27, 1971

Archie Bunker, the ethnocentric, lower-middle-class American WASP (*All in the Family*, CBS-TV, Tuesday nights), doesn't know that he is a bigot and a sinner who sits in judgment on others. If Archie did know—if he were, even in the smallest degree, self-critical and willing to engage in dialogue about his hostility to all groups but his own (he is also idolatrous, fiercely nationalistic, "My country, right or wrong!")—he would be not only the protagonist of a very funny, smash television situation comedy hit but also a powerful vehicle toward the remedying of prejudice. But Archie doesn't know. Apparently, he is unaware of his ethnocentrism, and it is this blindness to his sin, this supreme confidence in his in-group belief-system, that renders him less socially useful than he might be.

Norman Lear and Bud Yorkin, the program's producers (who modeled their comedy after the tougher-minded BBC occasional series *Till Death Do Us Part*), might well argue that to diminish Archie's extremism would be to rob him of his dramatic interest. Furthermore, their primary job is to entertain; they cannot be expected, in a half-hour television comedy, to erode deep prejudices that have withstood the assaults, over the centuries, of moralists and ethical teachers. The issue is debatable, at least. And yet, it is ever a part of television's fascination that when a potentially instructive piece of amusement appears like a tiny sail on television's vast, silent ocean of reinforcement of ingrained attitudes, speculation cannot be resisted. How would Archie react if someone said to him, "Archie, you're a monolith of ethnocentrism"? Experiments in the alleviation of prejudice have suggested that therapy is most effective in group situations, where prejudices can surface in a non-moralistic context, where no one loses status by admitting prejudice, but where, nevertheless, prejudice is seriously condemned.

This is not Archie's context in *All in the Family*. Archie is loved by his wife, his daughter, and his mod son-in-law. He is a blowhard, but he is never mean. He would not, according to Norman Lear, "throw rocks or join the Ku Klux Klan, but he would ask for signatures on a petition to buy back a house on his block that has been sold to a black family." Some victims of bias might reply that Archie's lovable prejudice is the more insidious, dangerous kind. Each week, Archie is involved harmlessly in a situation that permits him to verbalize freely an abundance of in-group hostilities, using words hitherto forbidden by the Television Code: hebe, coon, spade, wop, kike, polack, etc. Archie wins, Archie loses, but his ethnocentrism is never breached. He awaits next week's lovable encounter with Catholics, Jews, blacks, hippies, commies, et al., with unredeemed lovable hatred.

The novelty is exhilarating. Not since *Laugh-In* or the Smothers brothers' show have people who generally avoid television taken to looking in regularly on a particular program. The fact that the show is done live and is not taped or filmed, before a studio audience whose laughter, though often embarrassed, is natural and not canned; that it has the small-set, small-cast "feel" of television; that its lead time from shooting to airing is only two weeks, thus affording some sense of topicality—all work to make it a unique experience in television viewing. The humor is direct, frank, and explicit (bathroom allusions are common), and most people find it funny (intellectual hardhats laugh, in spite of themselves). Carroll O'Connor (Archie) and Jean Stapleton (his dumb but truth-telling wife) remind many viewers of Jackie Gleason's menage or of George Burns and Gracie Allen.

Viewer response, too, has been unusual. Most critics have waved banners for the series; mail response has been 75 to 80 per cent favorable. Nevertheless, as this is written, CBS has still not decided to renew the series for the fall. Teachers in schools have asked for study guides to help in analyzing the program in class. There, discussion may take up where *All in the Family* leaves off; the dimension of non-accusatory self-critique may be introduced. I would guess that people with hard-core prejudices would not expose themselves to Archie either on or off the air (unfavorable mail bears this conjecture out). CBS cowcatches the show with a statement that the program is designed to demonstrate the absurdity of prejudice. This in itself is a rejection of Archie and his belief-system. Archie himself, listening in real life, would tune out, because, to himself, Archie is not funny but threatening. The belief-systems of most watchers will be congruent with that of the network, and for these viewers the series will serve as attitude reinforcement—not a small service. But if only Archie could reply to the CBS disclaimer, and if only CBS might admit that it too. . . . That would be a dialogue of a higher order, in a more significant family.

III. Critical Reaction:
The Second Season

As I Listened
to Archie Say "Hebe" . . .

Laura Z. Hobson
New York Times   September 12, 1971

I have a most peculiar complaint about the bigotry in the hit TV comedy, "All in the Family." There's not enough of it.

Hebe, spade, spic, coon, Polack—these are the words that its central character Archie Bunker is forever using, plus endless variations, like jungle bunnies, black beauties, the chosen people, yenta, gook, chink, spook and so on. Quite a splashing display of bigotry, but I repeat, nowhere near enough of it.

Let me back up a little. Years ago, after "Gentleman's Agreement," I decided I'd never write about bigotry or prejudice, at least not about the racial or religious kinds. I've stuck to it. No lectures, no articles, no books about discrimination against Jews, against blacks, against whites, against Puerto Ricans. Perhaps I did not want to keep on harping on one theme; perhaps I had nothing to say.

But, after 24 years something happened. A television show that treated bigotry for laughs appeared on the screens of the nation and after a shaky start, when it was way down at the bottom of the Nielsen ratings, it went on to win the Emmy for the best new situation comedy of the year and soon after achieved the glory of the Number One rating of all sitcoms.

The Number One Nielsen, I'm told, means an audience of some 40 million families per week. Forty million families means about 100 million people. Old people, young people, black, white, Protestant, Catholic, Jewish, well-educated, ill-educated, secure, insecure—100 million people every week.

I didn't see the show at its beginnings except for a few minutes of one episode about Archie's horror that a black family had bought a house in his neighborhood. Those few minutes were all I could take so I didn't know the show until after it won the Emmy, and then it was rerun time and I had to make my private little study that way, with an additional pair of kinescopes obligingly shown me at CBS by the Press Relations Department. Thus, though I may have missed one or two of the original 13, I did get to see the majority, with the kinescopes assuring me I had caught two of "the best."

At the start, "All in the Family" drew a few harsh criticisms—of these, more later—but mostly the TV critics and columnists, like the telephoners, all cheered. Cleveland Amory, that historian of the proper and crusader against cruelty to animals, the four-legged kind, gave it perhaps the greatest and most widely read rave, a full page in TV Guide. "Not just the best written, best directed and best acted show on television, it is the best show on television." Tom Mackin, in the Newark Evening News, called it "excruciatingly funny . . . the best situation comedy yet." Norman Dresser, in the Toledo Blade, said the show had "everything . . . honesty, true wit, a bite which is no mushy quasi-love bite, sharp and literate writing and fine acting."

And Jack Gould in this newspaper, and in many other papers that reprinted his column, wrote a follow-up piece some six weeks after the January debut of the show, presumably after plenty of time watching it and for reflection about it, which ended, "Some of Archie's words may chill the spine, but to root out bigotry has defied man's best efforts for generations, and the weapon of laughter just might succeed. The possibility entitles 'All in the Family' to a chance."

Mr. Gould himself did not use any of those words that might chill the spine, did not come right out in hard print with spade and coon and Hebe and spic and Polack. For reasons of his own, he preferred to sum them up as "a string of epithets and slurring remarks that understandably provoke the affected parties."

Of the adverse critics, John Leonard in Life called the show "a wretched program" in which "bigotry becomes a form of dirty joke," and asked, "Why review a wretched program? . . . Well, why fix the septic tank?" Long before Jack Gould's piece, The New York Times ran two other pieces, both adverse, one by Fred Ferretti the morning before the show premiered, and one by Stephanie Harring-ton 12 days later, both of which reveal their authors' disapproval, even disgust. Phrases like "vulgar and silly" and "painfully offensive lines" showed what Miss Harrington felt, and Mr. Ferretti said the bigot-words "don't make one laugh so much as they force self conscious, semi-amused gasps."

The Boston Herald Traveler said, "The same network that fired the Smothers Brothers presents a show crackling with racist remarks ...crude and coarse ... and often offensive." And out in the Los Angeles Sentinel, in what must have been one of the last things he wrote before his sudden death in March, Whitney Young Jr. of the Urban League was even more vigorous. "Gratuitous insults" is what he called those words and remarks, and the show itself "A new low in taste." "It is irresponsible," he wrote, "to air a show like this at at time when our nation is polarized and torn by racism."

That came closest to what I felt, but beyond that I began to be haunted by the notion that there was something else I had to get hold of, for myself if nothing else. Something the critics weren't saying, something nobody seemed to be saying, not even the people I sought out as experts in the field of race relations. As I kept on ploughing through all the reviews, the feeling intensified. I was pulled up often by the phrases "honest show" and "honest laughter" and "a lovable bigot."

This last particularly impressed me. I found it many times in one form or another, the first time in a longish interview by Don Freeman in the San Diego Union and the Cincinnati Enquirer. In it, after contending that reality was the core of his show, Norman Lear, its writer, director, and, with Bud Yorkin, its producer, had said, "My father was what you might call a lovable bigot as Archie is."

A lovable bigot. Your friendly neighborhood bigot. This is an honest show. This is the way it really is. These bouquets cropped up again and again in the reviews and special stories. I must have read them all, for on my desk are no less than 97 clippings from all over the country, the few bad notices right in with the raves and the lets-wait-and-see straddlers, all supplied me by no less a collector than that same Press Relations Department at CBS.

A kind word here about the Press Relations Department at CBS, for, alas, some unkind words about other CBS matters may crop up later. The kind words arose with my first phone call to a vice presi-dent there, about two months after Emmy night, and I began by explaining, "I'm going to write a hostile piece about 'All in the Family' and I wonder if I could bother you with some questions." This perhaps naive way of putting it seemed to endear me to the vice president, for though he later asked to remain anonymous, he couldn't have been more responsive to the questions I asked on the phone or in person, nor more forthcoming about running those kinescopes, at a cost, he said, of about $150 to CBS, nor about delegating various people in his department to collect and send me those 97 clippings and supply me with all sorts of pertinent facts, dates, titles, credits, everything I asked. Except the answer to one question.

On that particular question I got nowhere. It was tied into the special point I was trying to get hold of and day by day it mattered more to me. I asked it of the vice president during a good solid talk in his office and he said he would call Hollywood where the show originated and then call me back, but after he did call me back, I got nowhere. As I began talking to and interviewing all sorts of people, and it began to get around town that I was writing something about the show, a man named Buddy Clarke, who introduced himself as Norman Lear's public relations man, called me and offered me any help he could give. Again I said it would be a hostile piece, and again that was taken in stride, but when I tried my One Question on him, I again got nowhere. He said he would call the Coast and get back to me. A day later he did, and it was the same old story. Nowhere.

But, it seems to me such a natural question, such an inevitable question, if you really let yourself think about this bigotry-for-laughs that's shown to 100 million people each week by a responsible network—so responsible that for a while last winter, an avuncular voice-over assured the listener during the credits that " 'All in the Family' . . . seeks to throw a humorous spotlight on our frailities, prejudices and concerns."

I kept asking that same question outside CBS as I phoned or went to see certain leaders in the field of fighting discrimination and prejudice. Mostly my question startled them—they had never thought to ask it themselves. At the Anti-Defamation League of B'Nai B'Rith, I talked for more than an hour to Benjamin Epstein, its national director, and Oscar Cohen, director of its National Program Division, and was surprised that their organization had taken "no official position" on the show, though several months had gone by since its premiere.

No official position had been taken by the National Conference of Christians and Jews either, another of the nation's best-known and longest-established human-relations organizations. There I talked to Dr. Sterling Brown, its president, following a full hour with Harry A. Robinson, a young vice-president, and neither of them had considered the point my special question raised. By telephone I talked to Dore Schary, recently Mayor Lindsay's Commissioner of Cultural Affairs; he had not seen the show, had heard people say it was funny, and also reacted strongly to the one point I was trying to examine.

I don't know about the NAACP and any official position it may have taken, for despite some six or eight separate efforts over a period of two weeks to get past Roy Wilkin's secretary, to whom I explained what I was calling about, I was never able to get through to Mr. Wilkins himself, even for a telephone interview.

In all these major groups, by the way, the secretaries to whom I talked also surprised me—they all liked the show, thought it was funny. The young vice president, Mr. Robinson, also thought it was funny; he saw Archie Bunker, the blue-collar "hero," as an ill-educated boob who constantly revealed his lower classness by spouting stuff like "misconscrued ideas," "detergent to crime," "I'm motifried" and "not German to the conversation." I asked Mr. Robinson if this might not be an elitist point of view; he himself was indeed superior to Archie Bunker and thus could discount him, but did he think most of the 100 million viewers were college graduates and executives as he was? He willingly conceded that this was a matter he had overlooked.

None of these people at the head of these organizations, of course, nor others at the Catholic Archdiocese, at the Italian-American Civil Rights League, at the PR office of the Commonwealth of Puerto Rico—none of them wondered that I was disturbed at seeing bigotry aired weekly to the nation as a laughable little matter, nor did they disagree that the rebuttal, supposedly built into each show, was pretty feeble. Indeed they agreed that the chiding of Archie by his "liberal" daughter Gloria and her college-student husband, also "liberal" and jobless and living off her family, were merely two more butts for Archie in other kinds of stereotypic prejudice, giving him endless chances to get off nifties about "radical liberal garbage" or "pinko atheistic meathead," as well as "pinko bleedin' heart lawyers" and endless variations of "you dumb Polack." Even his wife Edith, with her stream of dimwitticisms, supplies him with the cue to use his frequent injunction, "Will you stifle, dingbat?" and to hold forth in general on the dopey inferiority of all dingbats, i.e., women.

Somewhere in there among all the phone calls and personal interviews I began to go back to the night I first really tangled with "All in the Family," long before I thought of breaking my 24-year vow. It was the night of May 9, the night of the Emmy Awards, and it involved the word Hebe.

Johnny Carson was the glamorous master of ceremonies that night, with a glamorous audience of TV professionals, actors, writers, directors, producers, the works—and beyond them the national audience looking on. Just after the announcement that "All in the Family" had won the Emmy, and of course in the spirit of the show, Johnny Carson wisecracked, "Norman Lear—a nice guy for a Hebe." The audience roared with laughter.

I suppose Norman Lear laughed too. Would he have laughed, I suddenly wondered, if Johnny Carson had said, "Norman Lear, a nice guy for a kike?"

Unthinkable. Johnny Carson would never never—

I know he wouldn't. Besides, it was never never used in the show. Hebe, yes; chosen people, yes; yenta, yes; yid, yes. But kike? never.

I began to listen for it as I began my little study of the reruns. Never. And sheeny? Never.

Had Norman Lear never realized that what bigots really called Jews was kike or sheeny? That they didn't really go around talking about the chosen people or one of that tribe or yenta? That their own words, the words they actually used, were kike and sheeny? Then why did Norman Lear, in this honest portrayal of the bigot next door, never say either?

And that other word. Where was that one, among the spades and coons and jungle bunnies and black beauties? I was listening to the shows regularly by then, pad and pencil at the ready, jotting down the actual words Archie was so free with, and I never once heard it. But do the bigots of this world really talk about spades moving in next door, or not breaking bread with no jungle bunnies, or signing petitions to keep black beauties from ruining real estate values on the street?

You know the word they use. The one word, the hideous word.

Unthinkable too. Don't even print it. Nigger.

You know and I know and Mr. Lear knows and the anonymous

vice president of the Press Relations Department at CBS knows that Archie Bunker in the flesh would be holding forth about niggers moving in next door, and not breaking bread with no niggers, and getting up a petition for keeping niggers from wrecking real estate values on the street.

Everybody knows it. Then why doesn't this honest show use the real words that real bigots always use?

Is there a little list of Forbidden Words floating around CBS? Is it a little list self-imposed by Mr. Lear himself? Or is it a little list imposed by the Program Practices Department, and the CBS executives in charge of that department?

That was my one big question. Instinctively I knew the answer, but tied into it was that other point: what was that list for? Were the honest producer and the responsible network trying to make bigotry more acceptable? Were they trying to clean it up, deodorize it, make millions of people more comfy about hearing it, indulging in it?

It strikes me that, unconsciously or not, that's just what they were doing. And of course it was the essential trick, to make this show laughable not only to the bigots among that 100 million out there, but also to the "bigotees," the very Hebes and coons and spades and spics and Polacks themselves.

Do you think that any of the nation's blacks would laugh if Archie Bunker constantly said nigger? Do you think many Jews would laugh if he said kike?

I gather that in the first show he did say yid, for nearly every one of the early reviews include that little word, but then something drastic must have happened, for yid was not once said in all the shows I saw myself.

Another missing word was Mafia, though I did catch one remark about a Dago artist painting a ceiling in Rome. Missing also was any name-calling of Catholics. None of that "hotline to the Vatican" and "Pope in the White House" that was so rampant among bigots in the 1960 election, not even any micks and Irish micks.

Strange, all these omissions. But then there are some 20 to 35 million first- and second-generation Italian-Americans in this country, and some 13 million Irish-Americans and, often overlapping, over 48 million Catholics, and if you got them good and sore, as well as nine million Spanish-speaking people and six million Jews and 23 million blacks, where would your Nielsen ratings be?

Don't risk it. Don't tell it like it is. Clean it up, deterge it, bleach it, enzyme it, and you'll have a show about a lovable bigot that everybody except a few pinko atheistic bleedin' hearts will love.

Well, I differ. I don't think you can be a bigot and be lovable; I don't think you can be a black-baiter and lovable, nor an anti-Semite and lovable. And I don't think the millions who watch this show should be conned into thinking that you can be.

And there you have the basis for my peculiar complaint: there's nowhere near enough bigotry in "All in the Family," not by a long sight. How about showing the real thing for a while, before accepting any more praise for honest shows and honest laughter? What about laying it on the line about bigots and then seeing whether CBS switchboards light up with nothing but cheers?

But this is supposed to be a comedy! I know, but a network is supposed to care about the public interest. And one thing that's nearly as nasty as exposing those millions, and their children, week after week to bigotry, is to expose them constantly to hypocrisy.

Particularly since more children than ever will be watching in the new season that starts this week. As I finish this piece, in late August, CBS has just announced a last-minute switch in its schedules. Here in the East the show had been on at 9:30 Tuesday nights; in May, word went out that this would shift in the fall to 10:30 Monday nights, in an effort, some said, to cut away from the younger, more impressionable kids in its vast audience. But now all that has been ditched and the new time—oh, triumph—will be Saturday nights at 8, a time when even the kindergarten set can be in on the laughable business of bigotry.

To be among the first to teach impressionable children that they're not wanted in certain neighborhoods, that there's something that makes people laugh at them and look down on them and call them names, seems to me callous, even cruel. Indeed, to teach other children that it's quite all right to go around saying spade and Hebe and coon and spic—for of course kids always imitate what they see on TV—that seems to me pretty cruel too.

Is there a difference between laughter and cruel laughter? I went back to some unused notes I had made way back at the start when I first felt caught up in this show, and the notes suddenly seemed pertinent. When it comes to writing something like this piece, I'm sort of a nut about doing 10 times more research than I could ever possibly use, talking to 10 times more people, reading 10 times more material. One of the things I did was to re-read a book I hadn't looked at in all the years since college, Henri Bergson's

"Laugher," published 70 years ago.

Right off on page four, Bergson talks of "the absence of feeling which usually accompanies laughter," and speaks of "a momentary anesthesia of the heart." All through the book are lines that are so pertinent they make you flinch. "Comedy can only begin at the point where our neighbor's personality ceases to affect us. It begins, in fact, with a growing callousness. . . . In laughter we always find an unavowed intention to humiliate."

Of course "All in the Family" doesn't mean to do that, nor does CBS. Just now, in the avalanche of spot promotions that herald the new season, they seem to be stepping pretty warily. In one of these promos, Archie puts on his pained face as Edith explains that she sent $3 to OTB because she thought it was for "treating lung disease." In another he tells her that no, the Pentagon Papers weren't what's delivered on people's doorsteps in the morning, and in the third she's worrying about Queen Elizabeth and the Common Market and why couldn't the poor thing afford a really good market.

Nowhere in any of these promos is there one whiff of bigotry. Not one word about Hebes and spics and spades and coons. Was this witer-than-white advertising one more aspect of that Forbidden List nobody had ever yet acknowledged?

That tore it. I picked up the phone and at last made the one call I had been telling myself all along was futile—to California and Norman Lear. The anonymous vice president had long since told him I might call him, had briefed him on the one question I most certainly would ask him, had even given me the phone number I was to use.

Mr. Lear was tied up on another line, his secretary said, and illogically enough, while I waited, I thought about network censors and censorship in general. I am unalterably opposed to all forms of censorship, not only the interior hidden kinds within an organization or a government, but also to any external and public forms, such as pressure on sponsors and libraries and the press. Equally unalterably, I believe in a citizen's right to protest, in peaceful assembly, on lecture platforms, in books and plays and films, and in the newspapers.

Two or three times the secretary came back and apologized for the lenghtening delay and finally she said that Mr. Lear couldn't manage it at all just now and would have to call me back later on.

It was some hours before the call came and when it did, it was not Norman Lear out there in Hollywood, but his PR man, Buddy Clarke, right here in town.

"Norman Lear," he began, "says if you would go out to California, he would be delighted to meet you, run some tapes for you, spend all the time you might want in a personal interview about 'All in the Family' but he feels that this is too sensitive a subject to discuss on the phone."

And that was that. One last time, nowhere.

Or was it?

As I Read
How Laura Saw Archie. . .

Norman Lear *New York Times*   October 10, 1971

In answering Laura Z. Hobson's novella attacking "All in the Family," I'd like first to welcome her back to the fight against prejudice. The world needs every voice that speaks out in this area, and we are proud that we had something to do with the return of Mrs. Hobson's thunder after a 24-year silence.

Now, I have a most peculiar complaint about Mrs. Hobson's complaint. Nigger, kike and sheeny were the words she found missing in "All in the Family," which, according to her, made the show dishonest. But there is another word some bigots use—some liberal bigots. You know the word they use. The one word, the hideous word. Don't even print it.

No, Mrs. Hobson, not nigger. Schwartze.

Mrs. Hobson didn't mind our not using that word. Not, I expect, because she knows Archie Bunker isn't Jewish; she did acknowledge his use of the word yenta. I'll offer another reason later. But first:

According to Mrs. Hobson, when she watched "All in the Family" she sat with pad and pencil at the ready, quickly jotting down many of Archie's words and speeches. But when army bases and Fair Housing Congresses and church groups ask for copies of our shows for use in their interracial programs, or when the Western Electric Company makes the same request for use among its 22,000 employees, you can be sure their intention is not to have people sitting around, pencil in hand, waiting for the epithets to fly. The intention is to have thousands of employees, white and black, Jew and Gentile, laugh together.

"Humor can be a remarkably effective weapon," John J. O'Connor of The Times noted in his review of our show, "which Mrs. Hobson seems intent on ignoring." What, then, is Mrs. Hobson's motive in taking out pad and pencil? Does she feel a sense of proprietorship, of having been the first, and therefore the authority, on the brave new ground of striking-out-at-bigotry? Have we poached on her unconsciously owned territory and must we be driven off by fair means or specious ones?

Mrs. Hobson asks: "Had Norman Lear never realized that what bigots really call Jews was kike and sheeny? . . . Then why did Norman Lear, in his honest portrayal of the bigot next door, never say either?"

Because, Mrs. Hobson, Norman Lear was presenting what to him, out of his knowledge and his life experience, was *his* honest portrayal of the bigot next door.

If kike and sheeny were all that bigots called Jews, why was I so enraged at age 8 that I tackled a kid twice my size because he called me "a dirty Jew"? And at 11, why was I sent to the principal for fighting another kid who all but tore my heart out by calling me a "Christ-killer"? And as a G.I., in Italy, why did I spend a day in the brig for punching a stranger whose voice cut through me like a knife when I heard him discussing "those lousy Hebes"?

If kike and sheeny were the words that bigots really called Jews, as Mrs. Hobson insists, I wasted a lot of tears and some blood in my lifetime on such pleasantries as yid, Hebe and dirty Jew.

The important thing about bigots and their choice of expression, however, is that unless they are conversing with other known bigots, they will always tread very carefully, testing, before coming out directly. For example, I have heard a man laughingly wonder how many of the "chosen people" were at a cocktail party one night. Had he not learned immediately that I was Jewish, he would have felt free to go much further thereafter, I am sure.

Archie Bunker does that. A bigot motivated not by hate, but by fear—fear of change, fear of anything he doesn't understand—he knows that Mike and Gloria will jump his every bigoted remark, which indeed they do, so he tries forever to sneak them by.

Mrs. Hobson, however, feels that Mike and Gloria provide no real rebuttal to Archie. I disagree. Mike is always the one who is making sense. Archie at best will work out some kind of convoluted logic to make a point. But it's always foolish. Totally foolish. The bigger point, however, is that we mustn't expect Mike to convince Archie of anything. A liberal will not change the mind of a bigot that way, not on television and not in real life, so week after week, Mike the liberal doesn't defeat Archie.

We come to the word "nigger." Mrs. Hobson says "All in the Family" is also dishonest for using such words as coon and spade when everyone knows the only word a bigot really uses is nigger. Well, somebody had better correct all the cab drivers I've heard shouting under their breath for "that ———— spade" to move over! or for "them ———— coons" to get off the street!

Speaking of the honest use of words, some bigots say ———— about as often as they draw a breath. I think an Archie Bunker would use that word down at Kelcey's saloon. As a matter of fact, if my only goal was total honesty, I could not do without that word. But here I fess up, I would not use that word on TV for fear of offending too many people. Not so with nigger, kike and sheeny. You don't hear them on "All in the Family"—(a) because I feel they are words from another decade, and (b) they are words that connote real hatred, and Archie, as I mentioned earlier, is not motivated by hatred but by fear.

I am concerned that that answer won't satisfy Mrs. Hobson. "There is nowhere near enough bigotry in 'All in the Family,' not by a long sight!" she exclaims. Friends, "All in the Family" can never satisfy Mrs. Hobson. It can't because I believe I know how Mrs. Hobson likes to see her bigots portrayed in the mass media. I know because her generation has provided dozens of stereotypes for my generation—in movies, books, magazines, radio, etc. I grew up with them.

A bigot is a white man who says "nigger!" to a black man's face, forcing him to move aside so that he may pass, and spitting as he does.

A bigot is a vigilante who lynches a black man, sometimes castrating him first.

A bigot is a white sheriff who rapes a black woman in the back of his squad car.

We've had these bigots through the years—one-dimensional, stereotypes—ad nauseam.

How many of us have ever known a man who has raped a black woman in a squad car? Then how do we relate to him? How do we see a little of ourselves in him? On the other hand, most of us have known people who drop words like spade; and people who with a sly smile have tossed a yenta into the conversational waters to see if it would float. And I have also known people to use that word. The hideous one. Don't print it again.

Schwartze.

More about that in a minute. There is something deeper lurking here. Why do Mrs. Hobson's bigots have to be such outrageous haters to qualify as bigots?

A conversation she had with a Mr. Robinson of the N.A.A.C.P. may shed some light. Mr. Robinson saw Archie as "an ill-educated boob who constantly reveals his lower-classness." Mrs. Hobson suggested that perhaps Robinson, a college graduate and an executive, felt himself superior to Archie and could thus discount him. Mr. Robinson allowed as how that was possible. Then, queried Mrs. Hobson, *what of the other 100 million viewers who were not college grads and execs?* The presumption here is that, unlike Mrs. Hobson, Mr. Robinson, and their upper-middle-class peers, the other 100 million viewers were not capable of feeling superior to Archie and discounting him. Thus Mrs. Hobson raises the age-old specter of the intellectuals' mistrust of the lower middle classes. I submit there is a degree of prejudice in those feelings, Mrs. Hobson.

My hope is that the public won't discount Archie Bunker at all. My hope is that they won't feel so superior to him, so removed from him, that he becomes as much a stereotype as the white man raping the black woman. According to Mrs. Fay Love, who heads a Lutheran affiliated social service agency for children and families in Harrisburg, Pa., there is little danger of that. Viewers there see Archie as "a lovable bigot who helps us all to laugh at ourselves and view our own behavior with new insights."

"Well, I differ," says Mrs. Hobson. "You can't be a bigot and be lovable." Is that so, Mrs. Hobson? And in what vacuum did you grow up? Not a father, brother, uncle, aunt, friend or neighbor who was both lovable and bigoted? In 71 years, was there no one person you absolutely adored, someone you thought lovable, who one day shocked and surprised you with a flash of prejudice you never guessed was there?

A friend of mine had a pal of 15 years' standing. My friend is Jewish and his pal is not. One evening the pal asked my friend quite innocently: "Where were you in the army, Nate? Supply?"

And now about that word. The hideous one. In the publishing

world, at a literary dinner, at a cocktail party, sometime in your lifetime, dear lady, have you never heard the word schwartze pass through the lips of an otherwise respectable, outstanding, humane and even lovable person?

I believe there is a good chance Mrs. Hobson has heard that word. Which brings me to my biggest complaint about Mrs. Hobson's complaint. Why didn't she object to our not using schwartze on "All in the Family" along with nigger, kike and sheeny? She didn't object because she doesn't associate the highly educated, very sophisticated, upper-class individual who uses the word schwartze with a common, lower-class bigot like Archie Bunker. Well, I do. The lower class bigot may hurt the feelings of a hundred people in a lifetime with his racial epithets and perhaps keep one black family out of a white neighborhood. The upper-class gentleman who says schwartze may never hurt the feelings of a black man with his racial epithets, but he just might run a business that employs hundreds of people, none of them black. The thing about bigots, and this includes Archie Bunker, is that *they do not know they are prejudiced*. If prejudice were to disappear at noon tomorrow from the hearts of all the good people in the world, there would be no real problem at all.

I am 22 years your junior, madam, and meaning you no disrespect, if you have not known lovable bigots of different stripes and attitudes, and in varying degrees, we are obviously aging in different wine cellars.

Toward the end of her piece, Mrs. Hobson threw an extra zinger our way concerning the effect she feared "All in the Family" might have on children. I don't wish to get into this at length, except to say I disagree with her in every particular. Life teaches children that "they aren't wanted in certain neighborhoods," and that "there's something that makes people call them names." "All in the Family" simply airs it, brings it out in the open, has people talking about it. And there, in my opinion, is the big effect "All in the Family" can have on children. They will ask questions about the bigotry they see on "All in the Family" and parents will have to answer. Conversation in the home; how bad can that be?

The last thing I'd like to take up is the question of why I did not accept Mrs. Hobson's call when she phoned me from New York. You want the truth? Right from the labonza? I knew the lady was writing a hostile piece. I knew she was along in years. I developed a mental image of Mrs. Hobson with which I had no desire to tangle.

I didn't trust the lady's generation or her sex, which made me some kind of male supremicist and a bigot. Yet there are a few people who will read this and remember I am lovable too.

Can Bigotry Be Funny?

Joseph Morgenstern *Newsweek*   November 29, 1971

Does the weekly litany of racial slurs and epithets on "All in the Family" help cure America's racism by bringing it out in the open, or does it exploit the shock value of those epithets and worsen the situation it's supposed to combat? That's the obligatory question, but there's no easy answer. "All in the Family," which plays to an unimaginably mixed audience, usually manages to mix its own moods and motives within the space of each episode.

The series would be less discomforting if its hero was the flat-out racist lunatic that he was at the beginning of the original version in Britain. Then we'd all agree that he embodied the very worst of our national character, and conclude that anyone in the audience who identified with him was too far gone to be changed one way or another by a TV show. What makes it complicated, though— and ultimately more honest—is that the character has been softened. Archie Bunker is a terribly likable guy, for all his outrageous stupidities. And his popularity coincides with, and probably thrives on, a growing national awareness that the white, Middle American working stiff deserves more sympathy than he's been getting: not for his bigotry, which may be present or absent according to the individual, but for carrying a disproportionate share of America's social and economic burdens.

Nobody knows how to measure the precise impact of a TV show on an audience. Nobody even knows if the audience is paying attention. I watched one episode of "All in the Family" a couple of weeks ago in a middle-class black home where everyone was so busy talking about their own family that they never heard Archie's epithets, let alone reacted to them. For a decade or more we've been debating what TV violence does to children and we're still not sure, so we can hardly be dogmatic about what Archie Bunker does to racism. My own guess is that he has little or no effect on bigots who delight in his candor, or on liberals who delight in his ignorance. For the rest of the audience, the great mass of uncommitted adults and impressionable children, "All in the Family" may have some limited but real instructional value, in addition to its manifest entertainment value. It's not that the show brings nasty words into the open—their shock value helps get the ratings, after all—but that it brings a bigot into the open and shows him, in comic terms, to be a man who puts everything and everyone down because he simply can't cope with the modern world.

The element of comedy is crucial to a discussion of the show's impact. It's an extremely broad, old-fashioned comedy, almost a burlesque that puts the action somewhere between reality and fantasy. Though "All in the Family" pretends to deal with current events, it does so in a clearly pretend way. TV executives and viewers alike may praise the supposed realism of the show, but everything, after all, is relative; most other TV shows have as much bearing on contemporary American life as the Nancy Drew books. And few viewers are likely to confuse "All in the Family" with the 6 o'clock news—though that's admittedly another kind of unreality.

If the show operates somewhere between fantasy and reality, it also hovers between present and past. One of its few constants, apart from Archie's invective, is its nostalgia for a time gone by. "All in the Family" gives this part of itself away gladly at the beginning of each episode with a song that Archie and Edith sing about the good old days. They don't understand what's happening to them, and feel like village idiots in the new global village. They are, in fact, old fogies. Archie is even out of touch with his native tongue. Black militants today call themselves "niggers." Kids call themselves "freaks." The names he hurls around like howitzer shells are being systematically defused by the enemy. As a bigot, Archie is anything but a model of success or power for the audience to emulate.

Whatever his influence on the audience may be, it is tempered by the presence of his wife. Edith is the balance wheel on his erratic behavior, and the only one in the family with an open mind. It's not much of a mind, but it's open and kind. As a juror in a rewrite of "Twelve Angry Men," Edith is open-minded enough to defend the rights of an accused murderer. She's even open-minded enough to tolerate Archie, who lives by the law of the jungle and learns little if anything from experience. In one episode, tender and then startlingly ugly, he realizes he's as terrified of losing his job in the recession as his father was in the Depression. The moment he finds he's safe, though, he stops worrying about co-workers who were laid off, because they can always get other jobs, and in this great country of ours, "them that works eats."

Signs of weakness are inevitably appearing in the series. There's that problem of live audiences sounding like laugh tracks, and also a new didacticism in the writing. Parallels are being constructed, homilies delivered. When Archie makes a dumb crack about a "Chink laundry," Mike lectures him for "putting away an entire people." Archie tells a manifestly dumb joke about a Jewish politician who'll win by a nose, and Mike replies sternly that it's "not only an old joke, it's an anti-Semitic joke." Perhaps "All in the Family" is starting to worry about making itself and its characters crystal clear. Given the show's phenomenal success, it's understandable that the producer, director, writers and cast should try to take stock of their responsibilities to their vast audience. Yet the most responsible thing the show could do is remain irresponsible, continue to be flip and have fun.

And it does have fun—flaws and ill omens notwithstanding—by transforming our preoccupations into comic fantasy. Like so many popular entertainments of the day, "All in the Family" cuts both ways, cuts every which way, turns everything it touches into burlesque. This ambiguity reflects our own uncertainty about what courses of action to take in real life, though it goes down hard with those who like their homilies straight from the shoulder. Two decades ago you could tell where a scriptwriter stood, however flat-footedly he may have stood there. Movies about segregation took a firm stand against segregation. The 1947 movie about anti-Semitism made from Laura Z. Hobson's "Gentleman's Agreement" took a firm stand against anti-Semitism, and Miss Hobson herself, in an article in The New York Times, criticized "All in the Family" for not going far enough with vituperative, not being crystal clear about how ugly and violent a bigot can be.

Her concern is a real one, but her analysis of what words carry the most venom is open to question. It's doubtful today that "sheeny" or "kike" or "nigger" hurt any more or less than "yenta" or "yid" or "coon." They're all outworn. If people have learned nothing else during the last ten years, they've learned that actions hurt harder than words. New epithets like "pig" may hurt plenty and old ones can still hurt too, if they've got enough naked hatred behind them. But there's a conspicuous lack of hatred in Archie, and always that conspicuous old-fashionedness in the man as well as his vocabulary. Will the show, by putting such words into the mouth of a likable character, reactivate them and reintroduce them through the mouths of babes into a culture from which they had been disappearing? Perhaps so, but if they are reactivated by Archie Bunker they won't be the same instruments they once were.

"All in the Family," Miss Hobson said, is "bigotry for laughs." She and other critics of the show have found nothing redeeming in its invective and nothing funny in its minority stereotypes. But which stereotypes do you prefer? The movie version of "Gentleman's Agreement" was awash in them, and they weren't supposed to be funny at all: the upright reporter, the tight Wasp, the Einsteinian Jewish physicist, the all-American mother. At least the stereotypes in "All in the Family" are each identifiable as burlesques and don't pretend to be guides to conduct. To ask that the show speak explicitly and directly to the issue of American racism is to ask more than it could possibly deliver.

How Funny Can Bigotry Be?

John Slawson
Educational Broadcasting Review   April 1972

It has been aptly remarked that the Bunkers in the television creation "All in the Family" will soon replace the Kennedys as America's number one family. Thirty-five million Americans (Laura Hobson says 100 million) are tuning into CBS every Saturday evening at 9 p.m. and laughing loudly, even raucously—fathers, mothers, children and, yes, even those of kindergarten age, for the morrow brings Sunday and a respite from school, so why not let them stay up a little later and be amused.

This program has been heralded as one of television's great breakthroughs. There is hardly a mass magazine that has not featured this highly successful production, and many have given it front-cover display. It has won four Emmy awards. The *Saturday Review* has picked it as the outstanding network series. We are told that "All in the Family" has started to spawn a new cycle of ethnic and racial shows (*Newsweek*, 11/29/71).

Is "All in the Family" just a funny piece? What are the implications, if any, as to its impact upon our attitudes toward members of "other" groups—racial, religious, ethnic, national?

In spite of its galloping popularity, a heated controversy continues around this program, for we still have no way of knowing what effect a television performance has on attitudes and values. It is doubtful whether the nature of the impact is even researchable at this time. Is the program good or is it bad, or is it of no importance in relation to social consequences? There is general agreement, of course, that society's goal is to encourage us to accept our differences of heritage; furthermore, it is imperative that we learn to do so if we are not to contribute to chaos in our diversified social order. However, in spite of the absence of precise tools of measurement, experience in coping with problems of human relations and some generalizations gleaned from the social sciences bearing on allied fields might throw some light on this elusive matter.

At the outset, there is one myth that should be exploded. There is no substantiation for the assumption that unacceptable, aggressive tendencies are drained off as a result of exposure to a television program which portrays overt aggressiveness. Watching violence or crime on television does *not* reduce an inclination to engage in similar behavior. To believe that exposure to a portrayal of violence will sublimate impulses through the harmless process of catharsis has no basis in fact, and is an innocent vestige of views long discarded.

On the contrary, the findings of the 1969 National Commission on Causes and Prevention of Violence (The Eisenhower Commission) point to the conclusion that such exposure tends to *stimulate* violent behavior, rather than divert aggressive impulses to harmless channels. The vast majority of experimental studies support this conclusion. The extent of such relationships, however, has as yet not been established. In other words, presentations of violent and/or criminal behavior on television may actually encourage hostile action by means of stimulation and example.

To be sure, temporary identification with the criminal or aggressor on the screen may be an enjoyable experience and hence constitute a popular pastime. However, this identification may actually increase the inclination for anti-social activity rather than discourage such behavior.

In the case in point, in the fantastically popular program "All in the Family," Archie Bunker indulges in the behavior of a bigot in his actions and expressions toward blacks, Jews, Poles and most other ethnic groups. What Archie says and does is funny, indeed. Although his education is obviously meager, his social outlook extremely limited, and his manner crude, he appears to be a "guy" not difficult to like, especially by members of his social class.

His characterizations—"Spic," "Coon," "Hebe," "dumb Polack,"—and the stereotypes they project come from the head of a middle American family: a practical man who earns a modest livelihood sufficient to support his family in average comfort; a good family man who has a great affection for his daughter; and a true "he man" in relation to his wife, to whom he offers paternalistic protection and for whom he has a conventional, sentimental attachment.

He is a staunch believer in law and order and is patriotic to the extreme. Archie Bunker even financially supports through college his liberal son-in-law Mike—a young man for whom, in all probability, most of Archie's compeers have contempt as an impractical "egghead." It is Mike, the educated, "impractical" liberal, who is the deviate. It is Archie, the bigot, who is the average, "normal" person. Mike vehemently opposes bigotry; Archie staunchly and steadfastly asserts it.

In Archie's vocabulary the crooked lawyer is a Jew. The dumb person is a Pole. The burglar is a black man; also, as the one nearest the jungle, he "hurts less," exhibits "animalistic" prowess in pursuits requiring brawn and savage drive and therefore excels in athletics.

A typical program scene shows a group of neighbors coming to pay its respects to a dead relative of the Bunkers. All are white, with the exception of one black woman neighbor who arrives early. Archie turns to his wife and whispers: "Throw an apron around her and *they* will think she is the maid." Laughter.

Of course the ethnic digs made by Archie Bunker are funny, and of course the millions of viewers laugh. However, these derogatory thrusts, enjoyable as they seem, do not sublimate prejudicial impulses toward the "other" group and thus help relieve suppressed hostility toward it. As a matter of fact, there is every indication that the laughter is a sadistic response, vocally expressed, and symptomatic of submerged hostile attitudes. The laughter is a response to ridicule of an ethnic group. The viewers are not laughing at Archie, but at what this "almost lovable" man is saying. The "belly laugh" here is not one of insight, sensitivity, or recognition of incongruity. (And I wonder how many of us feel guilty when we laugh?)

In the experience of enjoyment of sadistic ridicule as a form of humor, there is apt to be a continuum from the mild to the brutal. It is only a short time ago (1938) that well-dressed Jewish residents of Berlin were forced to scrub the sidewalks of Kurfurstendam on their knees. Standing around were SS guards, Gestapo agents and residents of Berlin, all laughing at this grotesque sight. It is only a short time ago, in the light of history, that the miseries inflicted on blacks—lynching and rape—were also sources of amusement to some.

I can see no constructive purpose served by conveying the impression to millions of Americans that the terms "Spic," "Coon," "Dago" and "Hebe" are acceptable American expressions. Nor do I see the social value of transmitting derogatory images as if they prevail in our land. As already stated, the audience can include children of kindergarten age, and the Eisenhower Commission says: "TV enters powerfully into the learning process of children. . . ."

There is no possibility of a sublimatory effect from "bringing it (bigotry) out into the open" in the manner in which it is done in this presentation. Exposure would be useful only if there were a likelihood of producing *insight* into the problem, and if the aim were towards alleviation and, hopefully, solution. As an illustration of a desirable approach for the examination of a social problem usually avoided on mass media, I cite recent programs on homosexuality (male and female) that have appeared on television. These, for the most part, have been enlightening, hence beneficial. The instructive manner in which the subject is being presented contributes to the realization by the American public that homosexuality is a behavior deviation based on individual choice, not a pathological condition.

Robert Louis Shayon, the perceptive TV-Radio Critic for the *Saturday Review* (March 27, 1970) speaks of dealing with prejudice in the group situation thus: "Experiments in the alleviation of prejudice have suggested that therapy is most effective in group situations, where prejudices can surface in non-moralistic context, where no one loses status by admitting prejudice, but where, nevertheless, prejudice is seriously condemned." This is of course a true and verifiable statement. But as Shayon would no doubt agree, the passive recipients of a program such as "All in the Family" do not have the benefit of a group therapeutic situation, where the catharsis that comes as a result of inter-stimulation and feedback within the

117

group can result in insights into suppressed prejudicial attitudes and feelings. Such a situation also requires a skillful moderator.

"All in the Family" produces no insight into the problem of bigotry. Here there is no clarification of views on prejudice and discrimination. Yet bigotry is a malady, dangerous to humanity, the dynamics of which need to be understood and dealt with seriously. It is a serious matter, and we cannot "joke it away." It has to be dealt with as an obscenity. Problems of race and peace are the two most formidable, most challenging, most crucial of our time, in our own country and the world over. Bigotry is sickness—a psychological or social pathology; it cannot be considered as "behavior freely chosen with no harmful effects on others." We are rightly protective of the physical health of our people to the extent that the Food and Drug Administration bans a drug or labels it harmful even if only a small number of individuals is adversely affected. Why do we not use the same criteria with respect to harmful effects of bigotry?

It is conceivable that the producers of "All in the Family" were of the opinion that bigotry might be dealt a severe blow through *satire*. However, effective satire would require holding up to censure the bigotry of Archie Bunker by means of ridicule, derision and irony. I fear it is instead the member of the ethnic group who is ridiculed and satirized.

It is instructive to note the report in *Newsweek* (11/29/71) that Carroll O'Connor, who portrays Archie Bunker the bigot, confided to his friends that he despises being approached in the street by bigoted fans who congratulate him "for telling the truth for a change."

The program achieves the reverse of what Jonathan Swift accomplished in *Gulliver's Travels*. Even assuming that the producers of "All in the Family" were capable of Jonathan Swift's artistic skill, it is highly probable that it might prove a boomerang with the vast majority of the millions of listeners—and then there are the children, of course, who might easily miss the subtleties of satire.

There are those who maintain that without a cathartic channel for the sublimation of aggression or group hostility, pent-up frustration could blow the lid and produce havoc. However, the danger of these destructive consequences can be allayed not by *sublimation* but by *substitution*.

William James, as far back as 1910, in his classic essay, "Moral

Equivalent of War," proposed that for the love of glory and adventure and the need for pugnacious behavior, which in those days were satisfied in large measure by military combat, there be substituted a different kind of war—"a war against nature." He urged that "an army be enlisted" to accomplish the task of assisting in the mastery of powerful, natural forces as a contribution to the welfare of mankind. At that time this conquest of nature was a priority concern.

Today, much of the impulse for destructive thought and action can be directed to the conquest of social ills produced by man and not be nature—pollution, crime, urban blight, racial strife and the threat of world annihilation.

There is no point in making distinctions between the bigot who is a "lovable person" from the one who is not, as has been suggested. One can presume a "lovable thief," or a "lovable liar," but thieving and lying are pernicious, unacceptable and ugly practices, whether they are found in a "lovable" parent, sibling, spouse or child.

It is interesting to note the observation by the producer himself, Norman Lear, on the "normal" bigot. After referring to the episode when Archie Bunker demonstrates deep compassion (to the point of speechlessness) for his daughter who has suffered a miscarriage, Lear says "A lot of people hate a fact like that moment—they feel it sanctifies the rest of Archie. But that a man who says the things Archie does also happens to adore his daughter is simply a fact of life. I know a lot of Archie Bunkers look at it and maybe don't see he's a fool more than once in four shows. Maybe they cheer and say, 'Right on, Archie!' But what even they have to realize after a while is that he's a man consumed by fear—not hate. What we really have to worry about are not the bigots who burn the crosses and rape black women and castrate black men. God knows, they're animals, but there just aren't that many pure beasts around. What we have to worry about are all the *good* people, who don't hate like that, but *fear*. Somebody once said that if all the bigoted good people of the world were suddenly divested of their prejudice, the problem could be solved and we could take care of the others. . . ."

From a social point of view it is immaterial whether bigotry stems from frustration, insecurity or fear. It can be a consequence of any one of these or a combination of several factors. The result is the same. From a psychological standpoint the treatment may be different, but it is incumbent upon the bigot to rid himself of these fears, frustrations or insecurities by whatever means he can muster. His bigotry cannot be condoned, regardless of how stupid, how inferior, how ignorant or how fearful he might be.

As citizens it is our responsibility to curb the influences that produce bigoted attitudes and discriminatory behavior, but we should not condone their expression even if it be by implication. And this is what "All in the Family" unwittingly does. It has the potential of producing a "halo effect." "It's in our blood. We all seem to have it in one form or another; so what?"

The program is so funny and the script so clever and the actors so superb that, for the millions who seem to enjoy the type of humor the program produces, the ethnic factor as a source of ridicule to produce this result does not really appear to be necessary. I believe Norman Lear, John Rich and their associates ought to try to eliminate the ethnic ridicule motif, and thereby win the plaudits and appreciation of all concerned Americans, regardless of class, who have chosen "to remember the past so that they would not be fated to relive it." This is particularly imperative today when Americans are experiencing unprecedented polarization, confusion, anxiety and even hopelessness.

IV. Audience Reaction: Research Reports

Archie Bunker's Bigotry:
A Study in Selective
Perception and Exposure

Neil Vidmar and Milton Rokeach
Journal of Communication   Winter 1974

The enormously popular CBS television show *All in the Family* centers around Archie Bunker, a conservative, superpatriotic working-class American who browbeats his kind but "dingbat" wife Edith and who is especially adept in the employment of ethnic slurs. His main antagonists are his daughter Gloria and, especially, his son-in-law Mike. Mike and Gloria live with the Bunkers while Mike is finishing college, and the basic theme of the show is the conflict between "lovable bigot" Archie and liberal-minded Mike. Archie rails at Mike for his long hair, Polish ancestry, prolonged state of unemployment, and liberal (if not "Commie") position on sundry issues of the day.

All in the Family, first aired in January 1971, broke rather drastically with the U.S. television traditions of skirting racial and ethnic issues; it also broke all TV viewing records. Writing nine months later in the *New York Times*, novelist Laura Z. Hobson charged that portraying Archie as a lovable bigot actually condones and even encourages bigotry.(5) *All in the Family* producer Norman Lear countered by agreeing with the *New York Times* television critic John J. O'Connor, who had lauded the show on the ground that humor can be a remarkably effective weapon against prejudice. Moreover, Lear said, Mike provides an effective rebuttal to Archie because Mike is "always the one who is making sense" while Archie is always seen by the television audience as the one whose logic is at best a kind of "convoluted logic"; since the program brings

123

bigotry "out in the open and has people talking about it," children "will ask questions about the bigotry . . . and parents will have to answer."(8)

Lear's line of argument thus appears to be twofold: (a) mixing humor with bigotry releases tension, and this catharsis reduces prejudice; (b) poking fun at bigotry and bringing it out in the open gives the viewer insight into his own prejudices, thus helping to reduce them even further. The former argument is, of course, similar to the contention that the portrayal of violence on TV is cathartic and thus reduces aggressive behavior.(6,11)

Following the Hobson-Lear exchange, others have entered the fray with sharply contrasting opinions.(12,17) Sanders, for example, charged that the show appeals to racism and may be teaching impressionable children racial slurs, as evidenced by the fact that fan mail applauds Archie for his prejudice.(14) In sharp contrast, critic Arnold Hano contended that "fifty million Americans are being told, week after week, that it does you no good to be a bigot" and that criticism of the program comes from the "ethnic professionals" and the "so-called intellectual leaders of the community."(3) Actor Carroll O'Connor, who portrays Archie, asserted in a *Playboy* interview that "a lot of people write that we're making them understand their own feelings and their own prejudices."(13) And the Los Angeles chapter of the NAACP, in apparent agreement with the views expressed by Lear, Hano, and O'Connor, presented its 1972 Image Award to *All in the Family* for its contribution to race relations.

For whatever reason, social scientists have thus far not brought their theories and methods to bear on the controversy about the beneficial or harmful effects of *All in the Family*. To date the arguments and counter-arguments that have been made about the show have come from persons in the realms of literature and entertainment rather than in social science. The only exception is an opinion survey conceived and financed by the CBS organization itself, which was conducted during the early weeks following the program's debut.(7) In that study a sample of viewers were interviewed by telephone about their reactions to the program. The results showed that the majority of respondents, including minority group members, enjoyed the program and reported that they were not offended by it. Although CBS was careful to point out that conclusions about attitude change could not be drawn from a single or "one-shot" survey, the report nonetheless implied that most viewers perceived *All in the Family*'s satirical intent—and therefore that its impact would, if anything, be to reduce prejudice.

There is, however, an alternative hypothesis which might explain why the program was enjoyed by the great majority of viewers. Perhaps prejudiced and unprejudiced persons ascribe different meanings to the intent and outcomes of *All in the Family* episodes: nonprejudiced viewers and minority group viewers may perceive and enjoy the show as satire, whereas prejudiced viewers may perceive and enjoy the show as episodes "telling it like it is." Such an hypothesis seems to be supported by the fact that some viewers write letters (to newspaper editors, to CBS officials, and to people associated with the program) which applaud Archie for his racist viewpoint, while others applaud the show for effectively making fun of bigotry.(12)

Our purpose was to provide an empirical basis for determining the relative merits of the opposing contentions about the positive or negative effects of *All in the Family*. The study addressed itself to two hypotheses, which can be identified as the selective perception hypothesis and the selective exposure hypothesis.

The selective perception hypothesis would suggest that viewers differing in degree of prejudice or racism would have different reasons for finding *All in the Family* entertaining, would identify with different characters, and would interpret the outcomes of the weekly episodes differently. A number of studies(1,4,9) have shown that a person's attitudes and values will affect that person's perception or interpretation of social stimuli. Cooper and Jahoda, for example, presented subjects with cartoons that made fun of a prejudiced character named Mr. Biggott. They found that whereas non-prejudiced persons perceived and appreciated the humor in the cartoons, prejudiced subjects distorted their meaning to avoid ridiculing or deprecating Mr. Biggott.(1) Selective perception can similarly come into play with *All in the Family*. To the unprejudiced viewer Archie may be seen as a dumb, bigoted "hardhat," while to a prejudiced person Archie's chief ideological adversary, son-in-law Mike, may be seen as a long-haired, lazy "meathead Polack" who spouts liberal slogans. More succinctly, the selective perception hypothesis would lead us to expect that low prejudiced viewers would be more likely to perceive and enjoy *All in the Family* as a satire on bigotry, while high prejudiced viewers would be more likely to perceive and enjoy *All in the Family* for "telling it like it is." Thus, it can be predicted that high and low prejudiced viewers would enjoy the program to an approximately equal extent but for different reasons: high prejudiced persons would be more likely to enjoy it because they admire Archie, because they see Archie as making better sense than Mike, and because they see Archie as winning in the end. In addition, high prejudiced persons should be less offended by Archie's ethnic slurs and be less likely to see Archie as the person who is being ridiculed.

The selective exposure hypothesis leads us to yet another prediction: low prejudiced and high prejudiced persons will not necessarily watch *All in the Family* to the same extent. A substantial body of literature has indicated that, at least in natural field settings, there is a tendency for persons to expose themselves to social stimuli and situations which are congruent with their prior attitudinal dispositions.(2,10) The CBS survey report, working on the assumption that *All in the Family* is widely viewed as satire, has speculated that it would be low prejudiced persons who would expose themselves to the program more frequently than high prejudiced persons.(7) Thus, Klapper stated that

> *people who view this program presumably feel differently about the topics involved than those who do not. . . . I would venture to guess, for example, that voluntary viewers would be likely to be somewhat more involved in other anti-prejudice activities, even if only in their other media choices.*(7, p.19)

But what if most *All in the Family* viewers do not see it as satire and in fact identify with Archie? In such an event the selective exposure hypothesis would predict that high prejudiced rather than low prejudiced persons would be the more likely to watch the program, because the main character has personal qualities and attitudes which appeal to their own self-image and world outlook.

It is not possible to say in advance which of these competing selective exposure hypotheses is the more tenable, because we cannot say in advance how many viewers will and will not perceive *All in the Family* as satire. But they can be put to an empirical test. Working on the assumption that most viewers will indeed perceive the program as satire, we could predict that *All in the Family* viewers will more likely be persons low in prejudice, identify with Mike over Archie, and disapprove of Archie's use of ethnic and racial slurs. Conversely, working on the assumption that the selective perception hypothesis is correct and therefore that many viewers see Archie as "telling it like it is," we could predict that frequent viewers will more likely be persons high in prejudice, identify with Archie over Mike, and approve (or at least condone) Archie's use of ethnic and racial slurs.

Two groups of respondents were employed—American adolescents and Canadian adults from an area where the program is seen weekly. Both groups were asked about their reactions to *All in the Family* and were, in addition, presented with attitude questions designed to measure their ethnocentrism or prejudice.[1]

The U.S. adolescent sample consisted of 237 students, ranging in age from 14 to 18 years. They attended a senior community high school in a small town in the midwestern United States. Volunteers were solicited during study hours, and virtually all of those solicited agreed to participate. Two-thirds of this group were male, and all were white. The survey was administered as an anonymous written questionnaire.

The initial Canadian sample consisted of 168 adults who were randomly selected from voting lists in London, Ontario. Seventy-seven percent of this sample, 130, agreed to be interviewed; 65 percent were female and 35 percent were male. Half of these respondents were contacted through face-to-face interviews and the other half by telephone. Statistical analyses of differences between the telephone and face-to-face groups showed no differences regarding refusal rate, basic attitudes toward *All in the Family*, or amount of prejudice. Accordingly, we ignored this variable in all further analyses of the Canadian sample.

The survey was basically the same for both the U.S. and Canadian samples, although the ethnocentrism questions were tailored for each culture. Eleven items designed to elicit reactions to *All in the Family* are shown in Table 1. A few additional questions, including a question about frequency of television viewing in general, were also asked.

The measure of ethnocentrism or prejudice for the U.S. adolescents consisted of six questions, each of which had two alter-

[1]This research was supported, in part, by a Faculty of Social Science Grant, University of Western Ontario, and a Canada Council Grant to the first author and by a National Science Foundation Grant to the second author. We are indebted to students in the first author's Current Social Problems course (Summer, 1972) for helping to collect the Canadian data and to Mr. Emil Borgini, Principal of Gillespie Community Unit High School, Gillespie, Illinois, for generously allowing us access to the U.S. adolescents.

Table 1: Percent responses to *All in the Family* item alternatives

	U.S. adolescents (N=237)	Canadian adults (N=133)
1. How often do you watch "All in the Family"?		
every week	13%	24%
almost every week	35	29
only occasionally	32	36
almost never	14	10
never	6	1
2. Is there any reason you don't watch it more often?		
It is offensive	13%	10%
3. Which of the following statements best describes your feelings about the program?		
very enjoyable	53%	38%
enjoyable	34	55
not enjoyable	8	5
very unenjoyable	5	2
4. How funny is the show?		
extremely funny	24%	15%
very funny	39	44
somewhat funny	24	28
only mildly funny	7	9
not funny	6	4
5. Which of the two main characters (Archie or Mike) do you like or admire more?		
admire Archie	62%	66%
6. Archie and Mike often disagree with one another about various issues. In your opinion which of these two men usually makes better sense?		
Archie makes better sense	13%	11%

7. Generally speaking, at the end of program
   does Archie win or lose?

Archie wins	42%	40%

8. Which of the main characters in the show
   is most often made fun of?

Archie	10%	32%
Mike	46	10
Edith	36	58
Gloria	2	0
Lionel	6	- -

9. Archie often refers to members of various
   minority groups as "coloreds, coons, Chinks,"
   etc. Do you see anything wrong in using these
   names for minority groups?

nothing wrong	35%	43%
wrong	33	33
very wrong	32	24

10. In 20 years will your attitudes and values
    be most similar to Archie (or to one of
    the other main characters)?

similar to Archie	23%	- -

11. Has watching the show made you aware
    that you had prejudices you didn't know
    about?

Yes	- -	20%

- -

native responses: (1) Do you think white students and Negro students should go to the same schools or to separate schools? (2) In your opinion, which is more to blame if a person is poor: lack of effort on his own part, or circumstances beyond his control? (3) Do you think Negroes are as intelligent as white people—that is, can they learn things as well if they are given the same education and training? (4) Do you feel there should be strong laws against homosexuals, or do you feel that if two adults want to be homosexuals that is their own business? (5) What factor do you believe most accounts for the failure of minority groups like Negroes, Indians, and Spanish Americans to achieve equality with white people, restrictions imposed by white society, or lack of initiative and hard work? (6) Which of the following statements best describes your feeling toward hippies: they should be forced to get a bath, a haircut, and a job; or they should be allowed to live their lives as they choose? For the Canadian group questions 1 and 5 were replaced with more culturally relevant items, as follows: (1) In your opinion do you think Canadian Indians are so unreliable that they can never be trusted to take care of themselves, or that they are perfectly capable of managing their own affairs? (5) In your opinion, do you think the French Canadians in Quebec should forget about their French culture, including speaking the French language? The responses to the six items in each sample were summed to form a single index, and a median split was used to categorize respondents as high or low in prejudice or ethnocentrism.

Table 1 shows the percentage of persons in each sample who responded to the various item alternatives designed to elicit re-actions to *All in the Family*. The two samples were on the whole quite similar in their responses. Almost everyone had seen the program; most of them enjoyed it (Item 3) and found it funny (Item 4), and only a small percentage found it offensive (Item 2). Table 1 also shows that over 60 percent of the television viewers in both samples liked or admired Archie more than Mike (Item 5) and that 40 percent or more thought it was Archie who usually won at the end of the program (Item 7). A rather small percentage, between 11 and 13 percent, thought Archie made better sense than Mike (Item 6).

Which one of the main characters in the show was most often made fun of (Item 8)? If the show is generally viewed as a satire on bigotry, then Archie should be the person seen most often as the butt of the show's humor. Table 1 indicates, however, that only 10 percent of the U.S. adolescents named Archie as the person most often made fun of; 46 percent of the Americans named Mike and 36 percent named Edith.[2] Similarly, only 32 percent of the Canadian viewers named Archie as the character most often made fun of, while a majority (58 percent) thought Edith was the most ridiculed. Finally, 35 percent of the American sample and 43 percent of the

---

[2]It is worth noting that post-survey remarks by respondents indicated they did not re-member who Lionel was or did not consider him to be a main character in the program.

Canadian sample saw nothing wrong in Archie's use of ethnic and racial slurs (Item 9).

Some of these findings are, of course, quite consistent with the findings obtained by the CBS survey: most viewers enjoyed the program and found it funny, and only a small percentage found it offensive. Other findings, however, indicate a wide range of affective reactions to the show's characters, their behavior, and the outcomes. Considered all together, they suggest, contrary to the CBS report, that all too many viewers did not see the program as a satire on bigotry, had identified with Archie rather than Mike, saw Archie as winning, did not perceive Archie as the character who was the most ridiculed, and, perhaps most disturbing, saw nothing wrong with Archie's use of racial and ethnic slurs.

The *selective perception* hypothesis proposes that the prior attitudes of the viewers would be related to or would predict reactions to the characters and outcomes of *All in the Family* episodes. To test this hypothesis, we split the distribution of attitudinal scores at the median so viewers could be categorized as high or low in prejudice. Then, we compared differences in the reactions of the high and low prejudiced viewers to *All in the Family* by means of the chi-square statistic. Table 2 shows that the high and low prejudiced persons in both the U.S. and Canadian samples were significantly more likely than low prejudiced persons to admire Archie over Mike (Item 5) and to perceive Archie as winning in the end (Item 7). While most respondents did indicate that they saw Mike as making better sense than Archie, we must also note that the high prejudiced American adolescents were significantly more likely than low prejudiced adolescents to perceive Archie as making better sense (Item 6). Findings were in the same direction for the Canadian adult sample, although these fall short of the usually accepted level of statistical significance. Moreover, high prejudiced U.S. adolescents indicated significantly more often than low prejudiced adolescents that their values would be similar to Archie Bunker's 20 years hence (Item 10).[3] Table 3 also indicates that high prejudiced Canadian adults condoned Archie's slurs significantly more often (Item 9), and the U.S. data showed a trend in the same direction. Finally, high prejudiced Canadian viewers saw the show as poking fun at Archie significantly less often than did low prejudiced viewers (Item 8).

---

[3]This question was not asked in the Canadian sample.

Table 2: Differences between high and low prejudice viewers in their reactions to *All in the Family*

Variable	U.S. adolescents			Canadian adults		
	High prej.	Low prej.	p	High prej.	Low prej.	p
3. How enjoyable is it?						
very enjoyable	27%	26%		18%	20%	
enjoyable	19	15	n.s.	29	26	n.s.
not enjoyable	5	3		1	4	
very unenjoyable	4	1		2	0	
4. How funny is it?						
extremely funny	12%	12%		8%	7%	
very funny	17	22		22	22	
somewhat funny	12	12	n.s.	14	14	n.s.
mildly funny	2	5		4	5	
not funny	2	4		2	2	
5. Who do you like or admire?						
Archie	38%	24%		40%	26%	
Mike	18	20	.05	13	21	.05
6. Who makes better sense?						
Archie	10%	3%		8%	3%	
Mike	44	43	.01	43	46	.10
7. Does Archie win?						
Wins	29%	13%		26%	14%	
Loses	25	33	.01	26	34	.05
8. Who is made fun of?						
Archie	4%	6%		11%	21%	
Others	50	40	n.s.	40	28	.05

9. Ethnic slurs?

not wrong	22%	13%		29%	14%	
wrong	18	15	.10	14	19	.01
very wrong	15	17		7	17	

10. Whose values will be similar?

Archie	16%	7%		- -	- -	
Others	39	38	.05	- -	- -	- -

Generally, then, the quantitative data shown in Table 2 tend to support the selective perception hypothesis—namely, that prejudiced persons identify more with Archie, perceive Archie as making better sense than Mike, perceive Archie as winning. We also asked the respondents what they particularly liked or disliked about Archie or Mike. High prejudiced persons spontaneously indicated that they disliked things about Mike significantly more often than about Archie; low prejudiced persons spontaneously indicated that they disliked things about Archie significantly more often than about Mike. But even more interesting are their explanations of why they liked or disliked these characters. People who disliked Archie indicated that he is a bigot, domineering, rigid, loud, and that he mistreats his wife. Persons who liked Archie reported he is down-to-earth, honest, hard-working, predictable, and kind enough to allow his son-in-law and daughter to live with him. Persons who liked Mike reported he is tolerant and stands up for his beliefs; those who disliked him reported he is stupid, narrow-minded, prejudiced against the older generation, rebellious, lazy, and a "banner waver."

Both the quantitative and qualitative analyses supported the selective perception hypothesis. Reactions to the program were varied, and these reactions were related to or a function of prior attitudes. This conclusion is clearly at variance with those who have assumed and have argued that television viewers of *All in the Family* uniformly perceive the program's satirical intent.

The second hypothesis, the *selective exposure* hypothesis, goes further to propose that underlying attitudinal predispositions will cause viewers to watch *All in the Family* to different extents. The CBS report, assuming as it did that the program was more or less uniformly perceived as a satire on bigotry, proceeded to specu-

Table 3: Frequency of viewing *All in the Family* and differences in prejudice, and program reactions

Variable	U.S. adolescents			Canadian adults		
	Freq. view	Infreq. view	p	Freq. view	Infreq. view	p
A. Prejudice						
High	26%	19%		26%	25%	
Low	24	31	.05	25	24	n.s
5. Who do you like or admire?						
Archie	39%	23%		36%	30%	
Mike	11	27	.01	14	20	n.s.
9. Ethnic slurs?						
not wrong	21%	14%		29%	14%	
wrong	17	16	.05	17	16	.01
very wrong	11	21		6	18	

late that the more frequent viewers would be low prejudiced persons. However, if we assume that many viewers do not see it as a satire, it is reasonable to predict just the opposite—namely, that regular viewers of *All in the Family* are more likely to (a) be high prejudiced persons, (b) identify with or admire Archie more than Mike, and (c) condone Archie's use of ethnic and racial slurs. To test these hypotheses, we categorized those viewers who indicated they watched the program every week or almost every week as "frequent viewers" and those who watched it only occasionally, almost never, or never as "infrequent viewers" (see Table 1, item 1 for item alternatives). We then compared these two groups of viewers for ethnocentrism or prejudice, identification with Archie or Mike, and condonment of ethnic and racial slurs.

Although the predicted relationship concerning prejudice was not found for Canadian adults, it was found for the American adolescents: frequent adolescent viewers of *All in the Family* were significantly more likely to be high prejudiced rather than low prejudiced (Table 3). Skeptics might argue that high prejudiced persons watch television generally more often than low prejudiced persons, and are therefore more likely than low prejudiced persons to watch *All in the Family* also. In such an event the significant relationship between prejudice and frequency of watching *All in the Family* would be spurious. To find out, we asked subjects to estimate how many hours of television they watched each day and on the basis of these responses classified them as "frequent" or "infrequent" viewers of television in general. We found no significant relationship between frequency of watching television in general and prejudice ($x^2 = 0.89$, df = 1). We thus seem justified in concluding that high prejudiced adolescents are more prone than less prejudiced adolescents to watch *All in the Family* in particular.

Table 3 also shows that frequent *All in the Family* viewers admired Archie more often than Mike (Item 5)—significantly so, in the Canadian sample. It further shows that frequent watchers in both samples condoned Archie's ethnic slurs significantly more often than infrequent viewers (Item 9). Thus, the data support the selective exposure hypothesis in a direction that seems opposite to that suggested by the CBS report: *All in the Family* seems to be appealing more to the racially and ethnically prejudiced members of society than to the less prejudiced members.

We have attempted to bring social psychological theory and empirical methods to bear on the *All in the Family* controversy. In general, the data seem to support those who have argued that the program is not uniformly seen as satire and those who have argued that it exploits or appeals to bigotry. There are, however, some methodological aspects of the data that need to be discussed.

First, what about the generalizability of the results? The two studies included 370 respondents in the U.S. and Canada; is it valid to generalize from findings thus obtained to over 50 million *All in the Family* viewers? Ideally, of course, more extensive and representative samples would have been desirable. But the basic findings reported here have been replicated with two very different samples, differing in age (adolescents versus adults), nationality (Americans versus Canadians), and method of interviewing (anonymous written questionnaire versus face-to-face and telephone interviews). The fact that the findings were on the whole similar despite such differences increases confidence in our findings.

Second, it should be noted that our study, like the earlier CBS survey, is also a single survey and thus not designed to draw conclusions about the effects of *All in the Family* on attitude change. As Klapper(7) has pointed out, the only true test for attitude change would be an experimental design which has (a) a matched control sample of nonviewers who can be compared to the "experimental" or viewing group and (b) attitude measurements before and after viewing a series of the programs. Despite the fact that the present study is not an experimental study, the findings surely argue against the contention that *All in the Family* has positive effects, as has been claimed by its supporters and admirers. We found that many persons did not see the program as a satire on bigotry and that these persons were more likely to be viewers who scored high on measures of prejudice. Even more important is the finding that high prejudiced persons were likely to watch *All in the Family* more often than low prejudiced persons, to identify more often with Archie Bunker, and to see him winning in the end.[4] All such findings seem to suggest that the program is more likely reinforcing prejudice and racism than combating it.[5]

---

[4]There is tentative evidence that similar psychological dynamics may come into play regarding other television programs as well. *Sanford and Son*, a situation comedy modeled after *All in the Family*, is about a black junk dealer who is prejudiced against whites. On the basis of findings from the present research we speculated that while Sanford is a likable character in many ways, he also exhibits behavior consistent with the common stereotype of Negroes: he is lazy, lives in a junkyard, and throws his beer cans out the front door. On the other hand, his son Lamont is ambitious and hard working. In an exploratory study 97 Canadian adults were asked the following question: Sanford and his son Lamont have different attitudes and life styles; in your opinion which one of these two men is more typical, that is, similar to Negroes in general? Fifty-six percent of the respondents named Sanford, 26 percent named Lamont, and the remaining 18 percent refused to answer on the grounds that it was unfair to stereotype or that they didn't know enough about Negroes. As expected, high prejudiced persons were significantly more likely ($p < .01$) than low prejudiced persons to name Sanford than to name Lamont or refuse to answer. More detailed research is obviously needed, but the finding is intriguing.

[5]Given these findings, a question arises about O'Connor's observation that "a lot of people" have written that the show gives them insight into their own prejudices. Who are these persons and how many are they? The Canadian survey asked a question which hints at a possible answer. Note from Table 1 that in response to a direct probe (Item 1), 20 percent of the interviewees indicated that the show had made them aware of some of their own prejudices. Such a response of course does not mean that they really gained insight or that they all wrote letters communicating that insight, but for the sake of speculation treat the answer at face value. The next question that can be asked is whether these persons were high or low in prejudice and whether they were frequent or infrequent viewers of the program. Of those 27 viewers (20 percent of the sample) reporting insight, 55 percent were low prejudiced viewers and 80 percent were infrequent watchers of the program. The relationship between prejudice and insight was not significant ($x^2 = 0.64$, df = 1), but the data between frequency of viewing and insight were ($x^2 = 8.4$, df = 1, $p < .01$); that is, the less frequent the viewing the more the reported insight. Thus, in both samples

The present findings also seem to cast doubt on Norman Lear's and John O'Connor's contention that by mixing humor with bigotry the show leads to a cathartic reduction of bigotry. If high prejudiced persons do not perceive the program as a satire on bigotry, they will not experience a cathartic reduction in prejudice.

On balance the study seems to support more the critics who have argued that *All in the Family* has harmful effects. Some serious questions have been raised by those critics. Both Hobson(5) and Slawson(16) have asserted that by making Archie a "lovable bigot" the program encourages bigots to excuse and rationalize their own prejudices. Sanders(14) has charged that "already there is evidence that impressionable white children have picked up, and are using, many of the old racial slurs which Archie has resurrected, popularized and made 'acceptable' all over again." Our empirical research suggests that at the very least those charges have a valid psychological base.

References

1. Cooper, E., and M. Jahoda. "The Evasion of Propaganda." *Journal of Psychology*, 1947, *23*, 15-25.
2. Freedman, J. L., and D. O. Sears. "Selective Exposure." In Berkowitz, L. (Ed.). *Advances in Experimental Social Psychology*, Vol. 2. New York: Academic Press, 1965.
3. Hano, A. "Why We Laugh at That Bigot Archie." *Detroit Free Press*, March 19, 1972.
4. Hastorf, A. H., and H. Cantril. "They Saw a Game: A Case Study." *Journal of Abnormal and Social Psychology*, 1954, *49*, 129-134.

---

the data are in a direction opposite to that suggested by O'Connor: the majority of persons reporting insight were low in prejudice and were infrequent watchers of the program. There are three possible interpretations of the finding: (a) the more frequently persons watch the program, the less insightful they become about prejudice, (b) the infrequent, low prejudiced viewers were formerly high prejudiced persons who became less prejudiced as a result of watching *All in the Family*, or (c) infrequent and low prejudiced viewers are more likely to be persons who look for and/or report self-insights into prejudice. The last interpretation seems the most plausible. Because of the very small number of respondents involved in this analysis, one must, however, be cautious in drawing conclusions. Nonetheless, it can be suggested that persons who have written that *All in the Family* gave them insight into their own prejudices were on the whole low in racism or prejudice at the outset.

5. Hobson, L. Z. "As I Listened to Archie Say 'Hebe' . . ." *New York Times*, September 12, 1971.
6. Johnson, R. N. *Aggression in Man and Animals*. Philadelphia: W. B. Saunders, Co., 1972, pp. 152-62.
7. Klapper, J. T. Untitled paper delivered at meeting of The Society for the Study of Social Problems, Denver, Colorado, August 29, 1971.
8. Lear, N. "As I Read How Laura Saw Archie . . ." *New York Times*, October 10, 1971.
9. Manis, M. "Interpretation of Opinion Statements as a Function of Recipient Attitudes and Source Prestige." *Journal of Abnormal and Social Psychology*, 1961, *63*, 82-86.
10. McGuire, W. J. "The Nature of Attitudes and Attitude Change." In G. Lindzey and E. Aronson. *The Handbook of Social Psychology*, 2nd ed., Vol. 3. Reading, Mass: Addison-Wesley, 1969.
11. Murray, J. P. "Television and Violence: Implications of the Surgeon General's Research Program." *American Psychologist*, 1973, *28*, 472-478.
12. *Newsweek*. "TV: Speaking About the Unspeakable." November 29, 1971, 52-60.
13. *Playboy*. "Carroll O'Connor: A Candid Conversation with Archbigot Archie Bunker's Better Half." January 1973.
14. Sanders, C. L. "Is Archie Bunker the Real White America?" *Ebony*, June 1972, 186-192.
15. Skornia, H. J. *Television and Society*. New York: McGraw-Hill, 1965.
16. Slawson, J. "How Funny Can Bigotry Be?" *Educational Broadcasting Review*, April 1972.
17. *Time*. "The Team Behind Archie Bunker & Co." September 25, 1972, 48-58.

"All in the Family":
Racial Attitudes

John C. Brigham and Linda W. Giesbrecht

Journal of Communication   Autumn 1976

Despite strong feelings and much debate about the impact of one of America's favorite TV programs (3, 4, 5, 6, 7, 8), there has been surprisingly little research into the effect of *All in the Family* on the viewer. Indeed, general theorizing as to the effects of hostile humor (such as that provided by Archie Bunker) would allow one to take any of three conflicting positions. A *catharsis* position would predict that viewers will become less racially hostile than they had been prior to viewing the program, since observing decisive, hostile ethnic humor in the program would allow the viewers to release their own hostile tendencies. A *modeling* or social learning position, on the other hand, would predict that ethnic prejudice and hostility would increase as viewers modeled their own attitudes and behaviors after those of Archie, the "lovable" central character. The conflict between these two general viewpoints is currently manifesting itself in the debate over the effect of viewed aggression and violence on the likelihood of subsequent aggression by viewers. Most contemporary research on aggression appears to support the modeling-social learning position, although the situation is complex.

A third position regarding ethnic humor might be called the *constructive learning* approach. It would propose that the expression of Archie's prejudices via derisive ethnic humor allows viewers to recognize the absurdity of such views, both in Archie and in themselves. This recognition, then, could reduce ethnic prejudice and hostility. This is the position taken by many media representatives and by Carroll O'Connor, the actor who plays Archie.

Reactions of minority group members to the program have been mixed. As far as we can determine, not a single black organization has launched any formal protest against *All in the Family*; in fact, the Los Angeles chapter of the NAACP presented its 1972 Image Award to the program for its positive contributions to race relations (9). But not all black spokespersons are so favorable. Psychiatrist Alvin Poussaint, for example, has argued that the program has the detrimental effect of "disarming" the black by getting him to laugh at Archie's racism and bigotry (7). Thomas Pettigrew has told us that in many black families the parents require their children to watch the program as a form of "anticipatory socialization" to give them a good idea of the level of bigotry they are likely to encounter from some whites. This raises the possibility that Archie's overdrawn caricature may come across to black viewers as the *typical* white working man.

In a recent survey involving American adolescents and Canadian adults, all of them white, Vidmar and Rokeach (9) have tried to shed some light on the effects of *All in the Family* on viewers who are members of a majority culture. There was a strong tendency for the highly prejudiced to like and admire Archie, for viewers to feel that he made sense, that his ethnic slurs are not wrong, and that "others," not Archie, were being made fun of on the program. However, differences on these questions were not consistent across both the American and Canadian samples.

Vidmar and Rokeach interpret their findings as supporting the contentions of those who argue that the program appeals to bigotry (3, 6). Furthermore, they argue that their "findings seem to suggest that the program is more likely reinforcing prejudice and racism than combating it" (9, p. 46). However, the impact of these findings is limited by methodological shortcomings, i.e., the fact that Vidmar and Rokeach employed only a short, nonvalidated measure of racial prejudice and used only white subjects within a limited age range. In addition, the somewhat inconsistent nature of their results (cf. 9, Table 2) precludes the possibility of drawing definitive conclusions regarding the effect of the program or the relationship between reactions to the program and racial attitudes.

It was hypothesized, in line with the Vidmar and Rokeach findings, that racial hostility should be strongly related to identification with Archie and to the belief that Archie's opinions about blacks are valid. While it was expected that the overall degree of identification with Archie and endorsement of Archie's racial view would be much lower among blacks than among whites, no predictions were made about likely relationships between blacks' racial attitudes and their responses to these questions. Given the widespread disagreement which exists between observers as to the probable effect of the program, no predictions were made as to the direction and strength of the relationship between viewers' feelings about the effect of the program and their racial attitudes.

Questionnaires were administered to 189 adults, 118 whites and 71 blacks, living in the same city in the Deep South. Introductory psychology students at a predominately white university (N=51), students attending a community college (N=18), members of a local service organization and their wives (N=34), and members of a local women's club (N=15) comprised the group of white respondents. University and community college students were tested in groups and members of the service and women's clubs voluntarily completed the questionnaires during regularly scheduled meetings. The samples widely differed in age from one another; mean ages were 19.3, 25.2, 27.4, and 52.3 respectively.

Students at a predominately black university (N=46) and members of a local church group (N=25) comprised the group of black respondents. University students filled out the questionnaires during a regular class period while members of the church group took the instruments home, filled them out, and returned them at the next meeting of the group. Mean ages of these samples were 21.1 and 25.6 years, respectively.

The questionnaire concerning *All in the Family* contained 18 items dealing with the program and reactions to it, frequency of viewing, identification with the main characters, opinions as to the effect of the program on race relations, and opinions as to the accuracy of Archie's racial views. Question wording was counter-balanced to control for the possibility of response acquiescence set. Participants were asked to respond to each item on a seven-point Likert scale with response categories ranging from 1 ("I disagree strongly") to 7 ("I agree strongly").

Racial attitudes of whites were assessed by means of a short form of the Multifactor Racial Attitude Inventory (MRAI) developed by Cook and his associates (1, 2, 10). This measure has been widely validated by analyzing the responses of criterion groups of whites known to differ widely from each other in their racial attitudes. The present version of the MRAI contained 15 items, each representing a different dimension of whites' racial attitudes. Each question is responded to on a 7-point scale.

Racial attitudes of blacks were assessed using a revised version of the MRAI (labeled the BMRAI) appropriate for black respondents. Eight items dealing with racial policies and self-rated attitudes were identical to those on the original MRAI, while 5 MRAI items originally related to whites' personal reactions to blacks were reversed. Two new items, one dealing with opinions as to the perceived value of the black power movement and the other concerned with the perceived pervasiveness of racial prejudice in whites, were

Table 1: Correlations between expressed racial prejudice of whites and blacks and summary scores regarding reactions to "All in the Family"

	Whites (N = 118)	Blacks (N = 71)
Like and agree with Archie	.58**	.13
See Archie's racial views as valid	.67**	.09
See effect of program as harmful	.24**	.07

**p < .01

added. Item-total correlations for all dimensions of the MRAI and BMRAI indicated a satisfactory degree of internal homogeneity in both measures.

The *All in the Family* questionnaire and the MRAI or BMRAI were combined to form one questionnaire, with the MRAI or BMRAI items occurring last. No names or other means of identification were requested from any of the subjects. In all cases the groups responding to the questionnaire were either all-white or all-black and the questionnaires were administered by same-race experimenters.

In both the white and black samples, there was considerable agreement that Archie's views about blacks were not valid. Analyses of variance were calculated across the 4 white samples and across the 2 black samples to assess the degree of within-race agreement on each of the questions. A considerable amount of within-sample agreement was indicated. Within the white samples, significant differences (p < .05) existed on only two questions: enjoyment of the program and belief about whether the program would cause more harm than good. On both of these items, members of the women's club markedly differed (less enjoyment, belief that the program would cause harm) from the other three samples. Significant differences between the two black samples occurred on 5 of the 18 questions. The church group expressed greater enjoyment of the program, less agreement with Archie and Mike, and less pessimism as to the effect of the program on whites. Although these isolated within-race differences occurred, it should be noted that no significant differences existed within either race with regard to the three summary scores (see Table 1).

Analyses of variance were also calculated across all 6 samples. Significant F ratios were found for 7 of the 18 questions and on one of the three summary scores. As might be expected, blacks showed significantly less liking for, and agreement with, Archie Bunker than did whites. Interestingly, all of the white samples agreed, to a considerably greater extent than did the blacks, that Archie is more prejudiced than the typical white person.

To assess the relationship between reactions to the program and racial attitudes, correlations were calculated between MRAI and BMRAI total score and responses to the various questionnaire items (see Table 1). For whites, racial attitude related significantly to responses for 9 of the 18 individual questions and for all three of the summary scores. High prejudice was strongly (p < .001) related to liking and agreement with Archie and to the belief that Archie's views of blacks were valid. High prejudice was also significantly related to the belief that the overall effect of the program would be harmful, although this relationship was not terribly strong.

As Table 1 indicates, there were few significant relationships between blacks' responses to the questionnaire items and their expressed attitudes toward whites (BMRAI score). The two strongest correlations with individual questions indicated that blacks with negative racial attitudes were more likely to feel that most white Americans agreed with Archie's views and to state that they knew lots of people like Archie. There was a slight tendency for blacks with more positive racial attitudes to report greater enjoyment of the show (r = .22, p < .06). However, negative racial attitudes were not related to views about Archie or about the effect of the show.

However, if one looks at *enjoyment* of the show as the predictor variable, precisely the opposite trend is visible (see Table 2). Within the combined white sample, enjoyment was significantly related (p < .05) to reactions to the show for only 3 of the 17 other questions and one of the three summary scores. Within the combined black sample, on the other hand, enjoyment of the program was significantly related to 8 of the 17 other individual questions, and to all three of the summary scores.

Table 2: Correlations between self-rated enjoyment of "All in the Family" and summary scores denoting reactions to the program and identification with the characters

	Whites (N = 118)	Blacks (N = 71)
Like and agree with Archie	.08	−.23*
See Archie's racial views as valid	−.06	−.34*
See effect of program as harmful	−.29**	−.24*

**p<.01
 *p<.05

Looking only at the summary scores, within both groups there was a significant tendency for persons who greatly enjoyed the show to see its effect as less harmful to racial relations. Within the black sample only, there were also significant tendencies for persons who enjoyed the program most to voice less agreement with Archie and less support for the validity of Archie's views about blacks than did persons who enjoyed the program less.

The results confirm that neither the extent to which individuals enjoyed the program nor the frequency with which they watched it was related strongly to racial attitudes of either whites or blacks. This is in conflict with Vidmar and Rokeach (9), who reported a significant association (p<.05) between frequency of viewing and prejudice for their American sample (although this was not evident in their Canadian sample). In our study no such relationship occurred within either the white or black sample.

Liking for and identification with the main characters was strongly related to racial attitudes within the white sample in the present study. More racially prejudiced whites were much more likely to express agreement with, and liking for, Archie than were less prejudiced whites. A smaller but still significant relationship (in the opposite direction) occurred concerning reactions to Archie's son-in-law, Mike Stivic. Highly prejudiced whites were also much more likely to express agreement with Archie's views about blacks. But liking for, or agreement with, Archie was *not* related significantly to liking for the program as a whole.

Among blacks, on the other hand, racial attitude was not strongly related to reactions to the program. Enjoyment of the program was consistently related to evaluations of specific aspects of the program. Blacks who most enjoyed the program tended to see its overall effect as more beneficial and felt less agreement with Archie and with his views.

Overall, then, enjoying *All in the Family* or watching it frequently did not necessarily mean that the viewer liked Archie or agreed with his views. But, as shown by the correlations between the racial views of the white sample and their liking for Archie and by the responses to the question of whether Archie represented typical white views, the possible effects of the show are more varied and more complex. Assessing the effects of *All in the Family* and of ethnic humor as a whole upon both the viewers of the humor and the ethnic groups who are objects of that humor is a task of critical importance. It has only just begun.

References

1. Brigham, J. C. and L. J. Severy. "An Empirically Derived Grouping of Whites on the Basis of Expressed Attitudes Toward Blacks." *Representative Research in Social Psychology* 4, 1973, pp. 48-55.
2. Brigham, J. C., J. J. Woodmansee, and S. W. Cook. "Dimensions of Verbal Racial Attitudes, Interracial Marriage and Approaches to Racial Equality." *Journal of Social Issues* 32(2), 1976, pp. 9-22.
3. Hobson, L. "Marketed Bigotry." *St. Petersburg Times*, November 22, 1971, 1-D.
4. Klapper, J. T. Untitled paper presented at the Society for the Study of Social Problems, Denver, Colorado, August 29, 1971.
5. Lear, N. "Bunker Booster Parries Attack." *St. Petersburg Times*, November 23, 1971, 1-D.

6. Levy, F. "In Defense of Prejudice. . . ." *The New Republic*, August 5 and 12, 1972, pp. 25-26.

7. Sanders, C. "Nation's New Hero is a Beer-Bellied Bigot with 60 Million Fans." *Ebony*, June 1972, pp. 186-192.

8. Stein, H. F. *"All in the Family* as a Mirror of Contemporary American Culture." *Family Process* 13, 1974, pp. 279-315.

9. Vidmar, N. and M. Rokeach. "Archie Bunker's Bigotry: A Study in Selective Perception and Exposure." *Journal of Communication* 24(2), 1974, pp. 36-47.

10. Woodmansee, J. J. and S. W. Cook. "Dimensions of Verbal Racial Attitudes: Their Identification and Measurement." *Journal of Personality and Social Psychology* 7, 1967, pp. 240-250.

"All in the Family" in Holland

G. Cleveland Wilhoit and Harold de Bock

Journal of Communication   Autumn 1976

Little is known about the cultural effects of exported TV entertainment shown in foreign lands. Our study investigated whether *All in the Family* has attitudinal effects across national or cultural boundaries.

Several research reports dealing with *All in the Family* or the British prototype, *Till Death Us Do Part*, trace the origins of related work to an experiment using anti-prejudice cartoons in the late 1940s. Cooper and Jahoda found that prejudiced subjects "derailed" the cartoon message in various ways to avoid coming to grips with them (3).

Hastorf and Cantril's field study of selective perception of a controversial Princeton-Dartmouth football game in 1951 is a second classic work on selective audience perception. Students from the two schools who participated in the study constructed different pictures of the number of infractions and fairness of play, based on their institutional allegiances (6).

These classic studies suggest that the problem of selective

perception has several dimensions. The football case study focused on the psychological process of actual construction of the reality of an event. The cartoon experiment, on the other hand, pointed up the importance of interpretations placed on messages by their recipients.

There is evidence that beliefs, values, and attitudes are important in the construction of subjective reality (5, 7, 9), but that under some conditions, persons may be receptive to information that is counter to their attitudes. There is also considerable evidence that reinforcement seeking may result in *de facto* selective exposure to supportive messages. However, other motivations, such as entertainment seeking, are also important in message selection (1). Humor in a public affairs message may be one of the factors related to the message's success in getting through to a desired audience (12).

Vidmar and Rokeach's cross-national study of "Archie Bunker's Bigotry" has been widely quoted around the world. Their results, testing a random sample of Canadian adults and a convenience sample of Illinois adolescents, suggested that *All in the Family* reinforces rather than reduces racial prejudice (15). Vidmar and Rokeach interpreted their results as supporting the selective perception hypothesis in the American and Canadian samples. The selective exposure hypothesis—that freqeunt viewers are likely to be persons of high prejudice—was supported only in the Illinois data. No explanation for the divergent findings is apparent in the study.

In 1973, the BBC Audience Research Service studied matched samples of viewers and non-viewers of *Till Death Us Do Part*. The data suggested some selective exposure to the program similar to the findings in the Illinois study of *All in the Family*. Persons who were regular viewers of the program were slightly less likely to be "liberal" in their views on social problems than the matched sample of non-viewers. The writers of the BBC report interpreted the data as supporting the idea of reinforcement of prior attitudes about social topics dealt with in *Till Death Us Do Part* (2).

Most of the studies on problems of selectivity isolate the concepts of exposure, perception, and retention and deal with them one at a time. Our study tackles all three in a longitudinal study of a series of *All in the Family* broadcasts.

The country has a modern television system with 96 percent of the Dutch households having a set (14). In addition, certain social issues—resentment against minority groups such as Surinamers and South Moluccans (4, 16), a growing youth counter-culture in the urban areas, and changing relationships within the family—which are major themes in *All in the Family* are serious contemporary concerns in the Netherlands.

All in the Family was first broadcast in Holland in October, 1972. By the third quarter of 1974, *All in the Family*, broadcast in prime time with Dutch subtitles, had become one of the top programs on Dutch television and was getting considerably higher ratings than other family shows (14).

This study investigated how the Dutch television audience uses an imported program designed for American culture. The major research questions were directed toward the debate about whether the dramatic message of *All in the Family* is affected by selective exposure, perception, and retention.

In previous work on selective perception, two dimensions of perception have been dealt with interchangeably: the denotative properties of messages (the informational aspects of who did what, where, when, and how) and the interpretational components of the communication (the evaluative aspects of purpose, motive and effects). The present research distinguishes the denotative and interpretative dimensions of perception and retention.

Three recurrent themes—Archie's ethnocentrism, his intolerance of divergent life-styles, and his role as an authoritarian husband and father—have pertinence for contemporary Dutch society. Thus it was hypothesized that there would be different *All in the Family* affects, depending on the degree to which persons were ethnocentric, intolerant of divergent lifestyles, or parental authoritarians, in terms of (1) exposure; (2) denotative, interpretative, and projective perception; and (3) denotative, interpretative, and projective retention.

The sample was stratified proportionately by age and education so that the bias of telephone access was minimized. Interviewers were from the part-time interviewing staff of the NOS Audience Research Service. Interviewing was always conducted on Saturdays, following a broadcast of an *All in the Family* episode earlier in the week. Panel mortality was only five percent.[1]

---

[1] The panel was made up of volunteer subjects who were not paid. The sample was also used in general audience research for the Netherlands Broadcasting Foundation. Thus, panel contamination that might have resulted from repeated questioning about *All in the Family* only, was minimized.

Panel sample data were compared to *All in the Family* audience estimates from the official NOS national diary system. Close correspondence between the two sets of data suggested *no panel effect* resulted over time from anticipated questioning about *All in the Family*.

Eight waves of interviewing permitted refined measurement of selective exposure and perception on an episode-by-episode basis and measurement of selective retention in the same study. Selectivity variables were examined by using appropriate events and themes from specific *All in the Family* programs.

Mokken scale analysis was used to develop attitude scales for the independent variables of ethnocentrism, life-style intolerance, and parental authoritarianism (13).

Ethnocentrism scale. Using the dimension of acceptance of various ethnic groups living in housing next to a respondent—based on the assumption that the acute housing shortage in Holland made this dimension of high salience—four attitude objects formed a strong Dutch ethnocentrism scale: Turks, South Moluccans, Surinamers, and Chinese. The test items had this form:

> *Happiness with one's neighborhood is greatly determined by who and what your neighbors are. I would like to know your opinion about a number of housing situations that I will now read to you. Suppose the house next to, or across from you, becomes vacant, and suppose a (Turkish) family moves in; would you mind that very much, mind it somewhat, wouldn't care, or would you like it?*

Questions about these groups were imbedded in a group of questions about other nationalities thought to be well accepted by the Dutch.

Lifestyle intolerance scale. Using the same form as in the ethnocentrism scale, six attitude objects representing different lifestyles formed a strong scale: an unmarried couple, two homosexual males, two homosexual females, two hippies, two feminists, and a group of mentally handicapped persons.

Parental authoritarianism scale. Five items from a Dutch authoritarianism scale (11) formed a moderately strong scale: censorship of reading matter, the form of address required of children, the importance of obedience, the strictness of authority required to maintain respect, and the acceptibility of premarital sex for young persons.

Questionnaire items for the selectivity variables were developed in English and translated into Dutch.

Selective exposure. Self-reported exposure to *All in the Family* was measured after each of the thirteen episodes of the program. Cumulative exposure as reported week by week and exposure patterns for specific episodes were obtained.

Selective perception. Denotative perception questions attempted to get respondents' pictures of *All in the Family* events. Examples of this type of question are: "As usual, Archie and Mike bickered repeatedly in this episode; who do you think started it this time?" and "Who usually starts the bickering, Archie or Mike?"

Interpretational questions were of two kinds. One set of questions measured interpretations of *actual* events (evaluation). A sample question of this type is "When Archie and Lionel were talking in the kitchen, did you consider Archie's arguments reasonable or not so reasonable?"

The other series of questions was directed to interpretations of *hypothetical* events (projection). A sample is "Do you think Mike would reimburse Archie for his room and board if Archie asked for it?"

In addition to these types of questions, a set of adjectival opposites was designed to tap general evaluations of Archie and Mike.

Selective retention. Three weeks after the panel was interviewed about their perceptions of the first episode shown during the time period of the study, the panel members again were asked the same questions from the selective perception part of the questionnaire for that episode.

Uses and gratifications. In the final wave of interviewing "uses and gratifications" questions provided measures of possible intervening variables. Questions covered (a) content seeking and non-content seeking behavior and (b) self-reported need fulfillment in terms of interpersonal relationships, diversion, personal identity, and surveillance (8, 10).

The typical *All in the Family* episode was watched by about 30 percent of the sample during the time of the study. About one-third saw most of the broadcasts and only 25 percent watched none of the thirteen episodes broadcast during the time of the study. More highly educated persons were slightly less likely than respondents from middle and lower education levels to watch *All in the Family*, but this is typical of general television viewing patterns in the Netherlands.

More than 90 percent of the viewers said *All in the Family* dealt with situations that exist in reality in the Netherlands. A little more than half of the viewers thought a substantial number of Dutch families were similar to the Bunkers. Most of the sampled viewers (76 percent) said that *All in the Family* dealt with situations they might be faced with at some time in Holland. Sixty percent felt highly involved when watching the program.

Archie was described as being funny, mean, impolite, unreasonable, and ignorant. Mike was painted in basically the opposite terms. The two characters were both considered funny and not harmful.

These divergent evaluations extended to the characters' role performances as well. Archie was seen as usually causing the trouble in the Bunker family, and Mike was considered usually right in disagreement with Archie. An overwhelming majority of the viewers felt that Archie often made a fool of himself. Mike, too, was seen as sometimes the cause of trouble, and occasionally making a fool of himself.

The two major characters of *All in the Family*, then, appear to have sharply divergent images among the Dutch audience, with the two having only humor and harmlessness in common.

The *selective exposure* hypotheses for parental authoritarianism and life-style intolerance were clearly supported on the simple exposure dimension, with authoritarian and intolerant subjects *less*

Table 1: Exposure to "All in the Family" by average rank using Kruskal-Wallis analysis of variance[a]

	No exposure	Exposure	H	p
Parental authoritarianism	243.95	208.05	5.9393	.0148
Ethnocentrism	204.29	213.19	.4115	.5212
Lifestyle intolerance	235.70	205.66	4.2195	.0400
N	83 (19.3%)	346 (80.7%)		

[a]Percentages are slightly different from those cited in the text because some persons in the panel were not reached at the time measurement of the attitudinal variables occurred.

likely to watch the program. Whether these persons are avoiding the show because it holds up a mirror to themselves is not clear, but reasons given for not watching suggest that substantive, rather than *de facto*, reasons for not watching are dominant. Ethnocentrism was unrelated to simple exposure (see Table 1).

Once exposure to *All in the Family* had occurred during the program season, the extent of viewing had no relationship to either of the independent variables studied. All three of the independent variables were strongly related to extent of *general* television watching. The more ethnocentric, authoritarian, or intolerant the respondent, the greater the frequency of television watching. General viewing behavior, then, appeared to be opposite from the selective exposure pattern for *All in the Family*.

Denotative perception. Events occurring in specific *All in the Family* episodes were perceived similarly by the Dutch sample, regardless of their ethnocentric, authoritarian, or intolerant positions. For example, in the first episode studied, Archie's niece—who was visiting the Bunkers—became friends with Lionel, a young black male living next door to Archie. Early in the episode, Archie and Mike began quarreling. In questioning the panel after that episode, an overwhelming majority of the viewers said that Archie had begun the bickering with Mike in that show. No relationship to ethnocentrism, parental authoritarianism or lifestyle intolerance emerged on this item or on any of the other denotative perception questions asked about succeeding episodes.

When the respondents were asked to generalize about denotative aspects of the entire series, some selectivity emerged (see Table 2). Persons who were highly ethnocentric or intolerant of divergent lifestyles were less willing than persons low on these factors to say Archie was usually responsible for trouble in the Bunker family. And highly intolerant or authoritarian persons were more likely to say that Archie usually had the situation under control in the series. Only panelists who were highly intolerant of other lifestyles were more likely to see Mike as generally initiating the bickering in the series.

On questions about the general role behavior of the main characters in *All in the Family*, then, there was fairly strong evidence that lifestyle intolerance affected perception. Ethnocentrism and parental authoritarianism were related to general denotative perception, but were weaker than the lifestyle variable. A majority of

Table 2: Responses to questions on "All in the Family" by average rank using the Kruskal-Wallis analysis of variance

Does or doesn't Archie usually have the situation under control?

	In control	Not in control	H	p
Parental authoritarianism	153.72	123.75	6.4125	.0113
Ethnocentrism	137.38	124.75	1.3391	.2472
Lifestyle intolerance	150.70	122.64	5.6027	.0179
N	45 (15.7%)	212 (82.5%)		

Who usually begins the bickering?

	Mike	Archie	H	p
Parental authoritarianism	142.70	120.93	1.1673	.2800
Ethnocentrism	129.82	119.52	.2814	.5958
Lifestyle intolerance	160.08	118.42	4.3389	.0373
N	12 (4.94%)	231 (95.06%)		

Do you think "All in the Family" is just entertainment or does the program also have another purpose?

	Entertainment only	A serious purpose	H	p
Parental authoritarianism	150.12	117.67	12.0131	.0005
Ethnocentrism	135.63	122.73	2.2164	.1366
Lifestyle intolerance	143.19	118.32	6.6523	.0099
N	94 (36.43%)	164 (69.57%)		

With whom do you identify most, Archie or Mike?

	Identify with Archie	Identify with Mike	H	p
Parental authoritarianism	126.03	101.84	7.3884	.0066
Ethnocentrism	116.88	103.04	2.8352	.0922
Lifestyle intolerance	128.97	98.90	11.9100	.0006
N	69 (31.65%)	149 (68.35%)		

When Archie and Mike disagree on certain things, who is usually right, Archie or Mike?

	Archie is right	Mike is right	H	p
Parental authoritarianism	154.35	117.02	6.3651	.0116
Ethnocentrism	137.80	116.61	2.2366	.1348
Lifestyle intolerance	157.02	115.11	7.8957	.0050
N	22 (9.17%)	218 (90.83%)		

In general, what do you think of Archie? Is he reasonable or not reasonable?

	Reasonable	Not reasonable	H	p
Parental authoritarianism	166.06	122.96	12.1463	.0005
Ethnocentrism	128.08	126.80	.0124	.9112
Lifestyle intolerance	170.48	119.55	16.1335	.0001
N	39 (15.18%)	218 (84.83%)		

consensus on general denotative perception of the series was apparent, but there was sufficient divergence of perception to support the selective perception hypotheses.

Interpretative perception. Overall *evaluative* interpretation of specific events in *All in the Family* episodes was similar among the viewers, with little evidence of selectivity. On the key dimension of Archie's reasoning, though, perceptions were predictably divergent.

In the episode about the relationship between Archie's black neighbor, Lionel, and Bunker's niece, Linda, Archie took Lionel into the kitchen and attempted to explain to him why he and Linda should not see each other socially. While there was majority agreement among the viewers that Archie's argument was not reasonable, persons who were high on ethnocentrism, lifestyle intolerance, or parental authoritarianism were more likely to see reason in Archie's position.

General interpretative evaluation of the entire program series showed greater evidence of selectivity than did the questions on specific episode interpretation. There was sharp divergence on the perceived objectives of *All in the Family*. Persons high on parental authoritarianism or lifestyle intolerance were more likely to view the program as just entertainment, devoid of serious intent.

In addition, all three independent variables were significantly related to identification with Archie or Mike. About 30 percent of the viewers said they identified most with Archie; they tended to be high on the ethnocentrism, lifestyle intolerance, or parental authoritarianism scales.

An overwhelming majority of the viewers said that Mike was usually right in his disagreements with Archie, but the few who said Archie was usually right tended to be high on parental authoritarianism or lifestyle intolerance but not on ethnocentrism. And, again, the dimensions of reasonableness and sensibleness emerged as characteristics which tended to be attributed to Archie by highly intolerant or authoritarian respondents.

This tendency, however, did not appear to affect the evaluations of Mike. Most of the viewers saw Mike as reasonable and sensible; no significant relationships emerged on any of the independent variables. But, a very small minority, consisting mainly of high authoritarians, tended to see Mike as ignorant and harmful.

The patterns of *selective retention* were similar to the findings on selective perception. No significant shifts occurred in the responses to any of the items.

Denotative retention, as in the data on denotative perception, appeared to be completely unrelated to either of the independent variables. Selective *interpretative retention* appeared on the question of the reasonableness of Archie's argument with Lionel. No projective retention was apparent in the data.

"To have a good laugh" was almost a universal motive for watching the program. "Escape from the day's problems" tended to be cited more frequently by persons high on parental authoritarianism, lifestyle intolerance, or ethnocentrism. This response appeared to fit a general pattern of escapist viewing for these persons.

Key self-reported gratifications from the program—learning from and discussing *All in the Family*—were treated as independent variables for statistical analyses of major perception questions. No significant relationships were found for either learning from or discussing *All in the Family* and the perception items. It appears, then, that the uses and gratification factors are unlikely to be mediators of *All in the Family* perception by the Dutch.

In most previous studies, selective perception has been conceptualized and measured as a single dimension. This study attempted to separate the concept into several dimensions and to test for them on specific program events and generalized program-character attributes. The empirical results suggest that the refinement was fruitful. The selectivity process for *All in the Family* was clearly stronger on generalized attributes than on specific episode events. In addition, evaluative interpretation showed stronger evidence of selectivity than denotative or projective perception.

Our research suggests that Archie is not only funny and personally involving to the Dutch, but he is also *understood*. They seem to understand him when he takes Lionel into the kitchen for a lecture about interracial dating, when he talks politics, or when he disparages Mike. Part of this understanding is a result of expert subtitling done by the Dutch and the widespread understanding of English in Holland. Perhaps more importantly, nonverbal aspects of acting in the show—timing, gesturing, and facial expressions—are superb, enabling Archie's angry ranting and raving to get through without words.

Several previous studies, in both American and British settings, suggested that *All in the Family* was likely to reinforce traditional attitudes of Dutch viewers. In spite of the fact that our research shows some selective perception, which would seem to argue in favor of reinforcement, another interpretation is possible.

In our sample, there was a clear tendency for persons scoring higher on parental authoritarianism or lifestyle intolerance scales to *avoid* watching *All in the Family*. Interpretative perception of specific episodes was fairly homogeneous among the Dutch audience, with limited selectivity occurring on the reasonableness of Archie's arguments and on some generalized attributes of the program. In addition, there was a tendency for those higher on lifestyle intolerance or parental authoritarianism to be *more likely* to say that the program made them uncertain about their own ideas.

Therefore our study suggests that *All in the Family* is not likely to have a reinforcement effect on persons who are high on parental authoritarianism, lifestyle intolerance, or ethnocentrism. The observed selective perception processes do not seem to prevent the basic satirical message from getting through, at least to the Dutch.

References

1. Atkin, Charles. "Instrumental Utilities and Information Seeking." In Peter Clarke (Ed.) *New Models for Mass Communication Research*. Beverly Hills, Cal.: Sage Publications, 1973, pp. 205-242.
2. British Broadcasting Corporation. *"Till Death Us Do Part" As Anti-Prejudice Propaganda*. Audience Research Report, March 1973, pp. 22-23.
3. Cooper, Eunice and Marie Jahoda. "The Evasion of Propaganda: How Prejudiced People Respond to Anti-Prejudice Propaganda." *Journal of Psychology* 23, 1947, pp. 15-25.
4. Drago, Alice. "South-Molucca Lives On in the Netherlands." *International Herald Tribune*, April 26-27, 1975.
5. Guillaumin, Colette. "Changes in Inter-Ethnic 'Attitudes' and the Influence of the Mass Media as Shown by Research in French-Speaking Countries." In *Race as News*. Paris: UNESCO, 1974, pp. 55-90.
6. Hastorf, Albert H. and Hadley Cantril. "They Saw a Game: A Case Study." *Journal of Abnormal and Social Psychology* 49, 1954, pp. 129-134. (Reprinted in Schramm and Roberts, *The Process and Effects of Mass Communication*, pp. 300-312.)
7. Jones, Edward E. and Harold B. Gerard. *Foundations of Social Psychology*. New York: John Wiley, 1967.
8. Katz, Elihu, Hadassah Haas, and Michael Gurevitch. "On the Use of the Mass Media for Important Things." *American Sociological Review* 38, April 1973, pp. 164-181.
9. Klineberg, Otto. "Attitudinal Change with Special Reference to the Mass Media." In *Race As News*. Paris: UNESCO, 1974, pp. 37-54.

10. McQuail, Denis, Jay G. Blumler, and J. R. Brown. "The Television Audience: A Revised Perspective." In D. McQuail (Ed.) *Sociology of Mass Communications*. Middlesex, England: Penguin, 1972, pp. 135-165.

11. Meilof-Oonk, S. *Opinions on Homosexuality: A Study of Images and Attitudes among the Adult Dutch Population*. Amsterdam: Foundation for Social Research on Minority Groups, 1969.

12. Mendelsohn, Harold. "Some Reasons Why Information Campaigns Can Succeed." *Public Opinion Quarterly* 37, Spring 1973, pp. 50-61.

13. Mokken, R. J. *A Theory and Procedure of Scale Analysis*. The Hague: Mouton, 1971; and the Mokken scaling computer program by J. E. Holl of the University of Amsterdam.

14. NOS Audience Data Archive. Netherlands Broadcasting Foundation, Hilversum, the Netherlands.

15. Vidmar, Neil and Milton Rokeach. "Archie Bunker's Bigotry: A Study in Selective Perception and Exposure." *Journal of Communication* 24, Winter 1974, pp. 36-48.

16. Wentholt, Hans. "Oordeel, vooroordeel, veroordelen." NOS Audience Research Service, Internal Report, pp. 50, 72.

The Impact of
"All in the Family" on Children

Timothy P. Meyer
Journal of Broadcasting   Winter 1976

In the early 1970s, "All in the Family" was America's favorite television show. Several episodes drew the largest audiences ever for single shows that are part of a weekly television series. Demographic breakdowns of the show's average weekly audience done by Nielsen indicated that the program was regularly viewed by large numbers of people spanning all age groups, educational levels, and socioeconomic levels. One of the most astonishing figures was the nearly nine million children under the age of twelve viewing "All in the Family" every week (the largest child audience for any regular TV show). This figure is remarkable because the program itself was clearly adult-oriented; the dialogue seemed to be aimed at older, more mature viewers, yet millions of youngsters were also present in the viewing audience. This situation raised a number of interesting questions: (1) Why did children watch "All in the Family"? (2) How much of the plot was correctly understood by children viewing the show? (3) Which of the show's main characters did children most and least admire and why? (4) What types of information was the program conveying to children about standards of adult and family behavior (e.g., morality of characters' behavior, ways to resolve arguments and conflicts, etc.)?

Questions like these seemed worthy of investigation for several reasons. First, the topics, language, and approach used on "All in the Family" were (at least initially) far different than any other situation comedy in television's 25-year history. Heretofore unmentionable topics such as menopause, abortion, menstruation, impotence, "living together," homosexuality, etc., have all received bold treatment; derogatory slang phrases like "Polack, Spic, Black Beauties, Coons, Wops," etc., were also generously used in just about every program. Second, children may be socialized into the adult world far more rapidly than in the past because of this show's treatment of adult topics. "All in the Family" and programs similar to it (e.g., "Maude," "Sanford and Son," "Good Times," and the short-lived "Hot l Baltimore") may well be functioning to inform children at much earlier ages than in the past of behaviors and practices which were previously learned from other sources and at a much later age.

Recognizing that all "children" are not alike, a final question was posed as further morivation for this study: How do different types of children respond to "All in the Family"? Are low-income black children perceiving the show differently than upper-middle class white children? At what age does understanding of the show's content appreciably increase? In what ways do males and females differ in their responses, especially character identification? How does the degree of understanding relate to the kinds of perceptions children have of the program's contents?

"All in the Family" has generated some controversy and research, although both have been primarily directed at the effects of the program on adult attitudes and values. Examples of controversy and speculation over the harmful or beneficial effects of the show on adult viewers' attitudes are represented in the articles by Slawson, Hano, Hobson, and the show's own Norman Lear.[1] Empirical studies have been published recently by Surlin and by Vidmar and Rokeach[2]; both of these studies provide data suggesting that the dominant effects of "All in the Family" on adults is the reinforcement of existing attitudes. In brief, if a viewer already believes what Archie believes, he/she will be further convinced of those beliefs as a result of viewing the show; also, if a viewer rejects Archie's beliefs and attitudes, he/she will be further convinced of this rejection following exposure to the show.

While some evidence of the show's effects on adults has been reported, nothing systematic is known about the program's impact on the perceptions of children. Identifying several major dimensions of the show's impact on children, therefore, was the central purpose of this study.

METHOD

Children (N=320) were interviewed individually after viewing the same selected episode of "All in the Family." The total sample was divided into 12 groups, resulting from the combination of the central factors of concern in the research design: (1) sex; (2) age and grade in school (six to ten years; first/second/third graders); (3) race and socioeconomic background (low-income blacks/upper-income whites), and (4) learning abilities (fast, average, and slow reading ability groups as defined at and by the schools). The black children interviewed were attending an urban, inner-city school, while the white children were attending a suburban elementary school in a clearly upper-income area.

The procedure for the study consisted of showing one complete episode of "All in the Family," including commercials, to small groups of children (five to eight per session). Individual interviews with the children were conducted immediately after the program was over by trained black and white interviewers. Each interview lasted about 30 minutes; the specific questions asked and the responses are presented below. The questionnaire used had been carefully pre-tested on a group of 60 children to assure clarity of question wording and understanding among the children in responding to the questions. Children involved in the pre-test were not used in the final phase of the study.

The episode selected for this study centered around Archie Bunker's attempt to evade paying federal income tax on some money paid to him in cash for "moonlighting" as a taxi driver on weekends. The cab company's owner has his income taxes audited and must get Archie's signature on a sworn statement to verify the wages received as claimed by the cab company owner. Since Archie did not declare this additional income on his own tax form, he realizes that he has violated the tax laws. He proceeds, therefore, to the local Internal Revenue Service (IRS) office to see if he can "make a deal" to avoid paying the additional tax. At the IRS office, Archie finds himself dealing with a black auditor who also happens to be a McGovern supporter. Archie tries several bribes to get out of the taxes, including the offer of a free ride in his taxi and a new set of tires for the IRS agent's car; he further attempts to impress the agent by lying about his also being for McGovern. In the end, of course, Archie ends up having to pay the additional taxes and, subsequently, is annoyed and somewhat bitter about the whole affair.

For several reasons, this episode was appropriate for the study. First, a black character holding a responsible position played a major role. Second, the issue of income tax evasion posed ethical/moral questions, as did Archie's lying and bribery attempts. Third, like many episodes of the show, wife Edith and son-in-law Mike were set off against Archie because they opposed any attempt to avoid doing "what's right" because it was dishonest; this confrontation also had important moral/ethical implications.

RESULTS AND DISCUSSION

The results of this study are divided into three general sections; (1) Character Preferences; (2) Understanding of the Show's Content; (3) Moral/Ethical Judgments of Characters' Behavior. Any differences referred to as "significant" mean that a statistically significant difference was measured at the .05 level or less. Statistical tests included chi-square for cross tabulations (e.g., males vs. females on responses to whether Archie ended up having to pay more tax), analysis of variance for interval data (e.g., degree of like/dislike for each of the characters) and a posteriori comparisons of means via Duncan's Multiple Range Test when F values in the analysis of variance reached the .05 level of significance.

Character Preferences

Given the full range of variables that potentially could affect the like/dislike judgments of the main characters on the show, two basic questions were asked of all children, and responses were then cross-tabulated by each of the following variables: race/socioeconomic status; sex; age/grade (first- vs. second- vs. third-graders); frequency of viewing the show (almost every week vs. once in a while vs. never);[3] and ability grouping in school (school classifications of learning ability by reading tests as below average, average, and above average). Of interest in conjunction with the race variable was like/dislike of the black IRS man in comparison to the white characters. The first questions asked was open-ended: Which person on the show did you like best? least? (reasons why one character was picked over others were also elicited); the second question mentioned each character by name and asked "do you like or dislike [character's name]," followed by "a lot or a little?" The second question allowed for the assessment of the degree of like/dislike for every character. Since all of the variables interacted with both types of like/dislike questions, results are presented with each of the variables separately. The results showed that there were no character preferences consistent across all of the related variables, indicating that like or dislike of characters depended on the sex of the child, race, age/grade, frequency of viewing the show, and learning ability.

The three characters on the show that apparently stood out in children's minds as best liked were Archie (44%), Edith (21%), and Gloria (20%); the other three major characters (Mike, the IRS

Table 1: Variable Levels Affecting Character Preferences*

1. **Archie:** White Male Second-Graders, Slow and Average Ability, Regular and Occasional Viewers
2. **Edith:** Females in the Second- and Third-Grade, Slow and Average Ability
3. **Gloria:** Black Female First-Graders, Non-Viewers, Slow and Fast Ability Groups
4. **Mike:** Black First- and Third-Graders, Fast Ability Group
5. **IRS Man:** Males, Slow Ability Group
6. **Cab Company Owner:** First-Grade, Viewers, Average and Fast Ability Groups

*Characters are numbered according to their order of preference. Race and economic status were combined in this study (see text).

man, and the Cab Company Owner) taken together amounted to only 15%. Only one character other than the "big three" figured into the dislike most picture—the Cab Company Owner.

It is useful to take each of the six characters and summarize their sources of support or liking based on the various research variables which affected children's preferences. The results show the different patterns or types of children who prefered one character over the others (Table I).

Archie emerged as the clearly dominant character in that he was named by the most children as the character liked best (44%) as well as least (25%). Demographically, the types of children who liked or disliked Archie the most were clearly different. Curiously, an examination of the reasons why children liked Archie the most or the least showed that the same major reason was given. The majority of children who named Archie as the character liked most did so because "Archie yells at Edith when she acts so stupid." For the same basic reason, however, other children named Archie as the character liked least. In a similar way, children who liked Archie most said that the funniest thing that happened on the show was "Archie yelling at Edith when she acts so dumb."

After Archie, Edith was the second most often mentioned character as best liked (21%) *and* least liked. The reasons most often given by those who liked Edith best were: "because she was kind, because she was so nice no matter how mad Archie got, because she didn't want Archie to lie," etc. As for reasons why Edith was liked least, most frequently mentioned were: "because she acts so silly or so stupid, or because she acts funny (strange) or runs funny."

Gloria was liked best by almost as many children as Edith; unlike Archie and Edith, however, she was seldom named as the character liked least. Gloria apparently made the most favorable impression on younger black females who named her because "she was so nice, had pretty hair, was so pretty," etc. Nearly all of the responses made references to her attractive appearances or her pleasant way of interacting with the other characters.

Preferences for Mike, the IRS man, and the Cab Company Owner were negligible in comparison. When they were named, however, it was for different reasons and by different types of children. Mike was liked best because "he stood up to Archie when he knew Archie cheated on his income tax"; the IRS man was liked because of his honesty in refusing to accept Archie's bribes; the Cab Company Owner was liked best because he was "right to make Archie say he'd gotten money for driving the cab."

Given the overwhelming preference for Archie, Edith, and Gloria because they were funny, nice, or attractive, it is important to note that moral or ethical standards of behavior as exhibited by Mike, the IRS man, and the Cab Company Owner had little impact on most children's character preferences. The show's emphasis on comedy may well have obscured any moral lessons that could be imparted to children. In brief, doing what is right may be almost totally diminished by being funny, having a nice appearance, being nice, being quiet, etc.

A final aspect of these results worth some discussion was the distinct absence of like/dislike for the major black character as related to the race of the child. Despite the favorable portrayal of the IRS man, black children were no more inclined to identify with him than were white children; in fact, neither black nor white children were much impressed by the black character.

Character attributes other than race influenced character preferences and the amount of like/dislike reported by children. As a viewer variable, sex of the child seemed to be a good predictor of character preference in that male children liked male characters, while females liked female characters best. Thus, while black and white children had distinctly different character preference patterns, the differences were not related to the race of the characters.

Understanding of the Show's Contents

In addition to the identification of children's character preferences, assessing the understanding of the show's content was another major dimension of the program's impact. Five comprehension questions were asked of each child to determine the degree of understanding of what happened on the show. Once again, the results of each of these questions was affected by the child variables of race, sex, age/grade, frequency of viewing, and ability grouping.

The first understanding question asked and the "easiest" to answer correctly was: "Did Archie cheat on his income tax?" Of the total sample, 84% correctly answered "yes"; 16% said "no." The only variable interacting with this question was age/grade; significantly more third graders (90%) than first graders (78%) answered correctly.

The second question was: "Why did Archie offer the income tax man a free taxi ride and a free set of tires for his car?" Only 25% of the total sample understood this large part of the program. Significantly more whites (38%) than blacks (17%) answered correctly; correct understanding also increased significantly as age increased, with only 3% of the first graders, 20% of the second graders, and 53% of the third graders answering correctly.

The third understanding question was: "Did Archie end up having to pay more tax?" Of the total sample, 77% correctly answered "yes" and 23% incorrectly answered "no." Significantly more whites (90%) than blacks (76%) answered correctly; and significantly more second and third graders (82%) answered correctly than did first graders (68%).

The fourth question was: "Was Archie really for Nixon or McGovern?" Of the total sample, 49% correctly answered "Nixon." Significantly more regular viewers (60%) than non-viewers (31%) answered correctly.

The fifth and last understanding question was: "Why did Archie say he was voting for McGovern?" Of the total sample, only 17% gave the correct reason; 83% were incorrect. Significantly more whites (30%) than blacks (8%) answered correctly; significantly more third graders (37%) were correct than second graders (11%) and first graders (4%).

Of the variables potentially affecting understanding of the show's contents, age of the child made a difference on four of the five items; the older the child, the greater the degree of understanding. Race made a difference on three of the five questions, with white children correctly understanding more than black children. On only one question did frequency of viewing affect understanding; and, as expected, frequent viewers understood more than non-viewers. Sex of the child and ability grouping were not related to understanding, a result which is in sharp contrast to the data on character preferences.

One reasonable explanation of why differences in ability groupings did not yield differences in understanding is that groups were formed on the basis of reading ability only. It may be that differences in ability to read print messages do not apply to the ability to "read" audio-visual messages. On all five questions, the slow group was correct as often as the average and fast groups; these findings suggest that ability to understand messages may be limited only to print messages, and that differences disappear when understanding of audio-visual messages is measured.

Moral Ethical Judgments of Program-Related Behavior

The third major dimension of interest in assessing "All in the Family's" impact is the children's moral or ethical judgments of the program-related behavior. Three questions were asked of each child to try and provide some insight into this important dimension.

Question one asked: "Do most people cheat on their income tax?" Overall, 15% said "yes," 82% said "no," and 3% were "unsure." Significantly more black children (23%) than white children (6%) said "yes." No other variable affected responses to this question.

Question two asked: "Is it right or wrong to cheat just a little on your income tax?" This question was asked specifically because Archie argued that it was okay for him to cheat "just a little" on his taxes because everybody else does. Of the total sample, 21% said it was right to cheat just a little, and 79% said it was wrong. Significantly more blacks (26%) than whites (13%) said it was right to cheat just a little (agreeing with Archie's point); significantly more first graders (25%) and second graders (25%) than third graders

(12%) said it was right; significantly more slow ability group children (31%) than average (18%) or fast (17%) group children said it was right.

Since these first two questions were normative in nature, they were asked of an additional group of 80 children who did not otherwise participate in the study; none could recall having seen the program used. Comparing the groups who saw the income tax episode with those who did not showed significant differences among black viewers but not among white. On the first question, 17% of the sample black non-viewers agreed that most people cheat on their income tax; 23% of those viewing the program agreed. On the second question, 15% of the black non-viewers felt it was right to cheat just a little on your income tax, as compared to 26% of the viewers. The difference between viewers and non-viewers was significant, suggesting that for black children who saw the show, the program successfully reinforced Archie's main positions on the propriety of income tax cheating. In brief, their ethical judgments were affected—at least temporarily.

The third and last question on the moral/ethical discussion was "Was it right or wrong for Archie to offer a free taxi ride and a free set of car tires to the income tax man?" Overall, 27% said it was "right," 62% said "wrong," and 11% were "not sure." As with the first two questions, significantly more blacks (36%) than whites (14%) said it was right; significantly more first-graders (34%) than third graders (19%) said it was right; significantly more of the slow ability group (37%) than the fast (23%) said it was right.

Race of the child, as with character preference and understanding, appeared to be the most consistent variable that affected moral/ethical judgments; on all three questions, black children were reliably more likely to feel that most people cheat on their taxes, that it was right to cheat just a little, and right for Archie to offer the bribe to the IRS man to get out of paying his taxes. Clearly, black children in the sample had a different sense of what was right and wrong in comparison to white children. It may be that black children's judgments of right and wrong are influenced by their perceptions of appropriate behavioral standards as practiced by those in the white community, one way of seeing that being their observations of Archie Bunker and "All in the Family."

Age/grade influenced moral judgments in that younger children were reliably more inclined than older children to view cheating on taxes and Archie's bribe attempts as being "right"; in a similar way, children in the slow reading ability group were also more inclined to view cheating and Archie's bribe as appropriate behavior. Younger children appeared to be the most vulnerable to accepting Archie's unethical behavior. While no cause and effect relationship can be ascertained, the relationship between Archie's behavior and younger black children's perceptions of that behavior cannot be denied and becomes a legitimate cause for concern among those who may suspect undesirable effects of "All in the Family."

CONCLUSIONS

Regarding the impact of "All in the Family," this study clearly demonstrated that the program's effects on 6-10 year old children are most certainly not consistent or uniform. Different types of children, bringing different beliefs, attitudes, and values to the viewing of the show as a result of different socialization processes, are affected in distinctly different ways.

As variables affecting the impact of "All in the Family," race and economic status of the child and the child's age seem to be the most powerful discriminators of different responses on all three impact dimensions. Sex of the child and learning ability do not operate significantly on all dimensions; sex discriminates well for character preference, while learning ability seems most strongly related to only moral/ethical judgments.

As an instrument for "learning," the kinds of behaviors depicted on "All in the Family" which are apparently having the greatest impact on most children are *not* the moral/ethical lessons that are the focus of the show; physical appearance of the characters, role stereotypes, comedy behavior, etc. are the ingredients which seem to dominate children's perceptions of the content. This condition seems due largely to most children's inability to fully understand the situations that occur, including motivations for character's behavior and the consequences of that behavior. As a result, aspects other than the complex moral/ethical dimension of situations tend to prevail. Yet, the attraction of nine million children to the program on a regular basis cannot be overlooked even if this attraction is not based on the central themes of the show—Archie trying to survive with his own prejudices and inconsistent behavior. Archie Bunker's way of life is most assuredly not being communicated negatively to most children and even only in the most simplified way for the older children (less than half of the third-graders). This state of affairs points to one of the great paradoxes of commercial television and its reaching large, heterogeneous audiences. Most of the audience for "All in the Family" is adult, and it is adults toward whom the show's content is directed. Because the audience is essentially adult, the show would lose millions of viewers if it changed its focus to children. But, although in a minority, the child audience of nine million still watches the program regularly and is being affected by it in different ways than adults. It seems imperative, therefore, to examine the effects of television programs with a broadly based audience appeal on all segments of the audience, not just the majority of the total audience.

Footnotes

1. J. Slawson, "How Funny Can Bigotry Be?" *Educational Broadcasting Review* 6:79-82 (April 1972); A. Hano, "Can Archie Bunker Give Bigotry a Bad Name?," *New York Times* (March 12, 1972), p. 33; L. Hobson, "As I Listened to Archie Say 'Hebe' . . .," *New York Times* (September 12, 1972); and N. Lear, "As I Read How Laura Saw Archie . . .," *New York Times* (October 10, 1972).
2. S. Surlin, "Bigotry on the Air and in Life: The Archie Bunker Case," *Public Telecommunications Review* 2:34-41 (April 1974); N. Vidmar and M. Rokeach, "Archie Bunker's Bigotry: A Study in Selective Perception and Exposure," *Journal of Communication* 24:36-47 (Winter 1974).
3. Of the total sample, 35% said they watched "almost every week," 50% "once in a while," and 15% had never seen the program prior to viewing the one used in this study; in all, therefore, 85% of the children were regular or occasional viewers of "All in the Family."

Jean Stapleton, Sally Struthers, Norman Lear and Rob Reiner at the installation of the Bunkers' chairs at the Smithsonian Institution, September 1978

All in the Family cast, 1971 (clockwise from bottom, Carroll O'Connor, Jean Stapleton, Rob Reiner, Sally Struthers)

All in the Family cast, 1976

Norman Lear warms up an audience before a taping

The Bunker household: view of the set

Mike and Gloria in their apartment

Archie in his tavern with Stephanie (Danielle Brisebois) and Harry (Jason Wingreen), 1978

The marital bed—another barrier broken by *All in the Family*

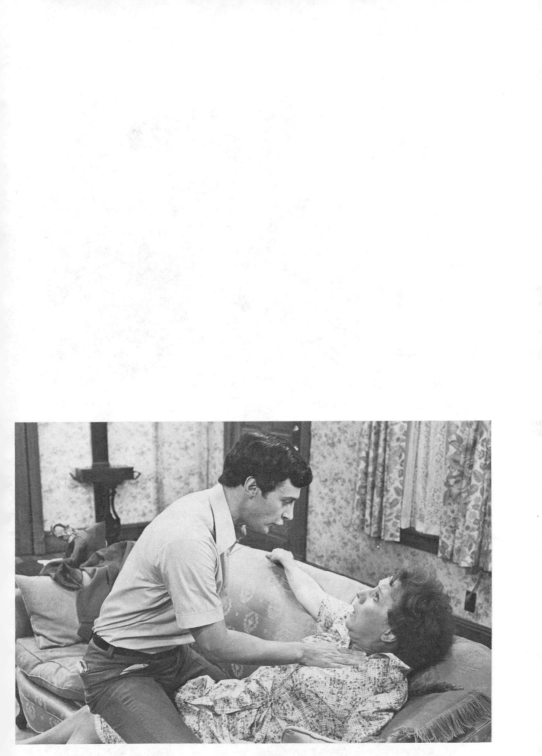

Edith being attacked by rapist (David Dukes), from episode broadcast October 1977.

Archie enjoying a chat with Edith

Archie gives some advice to Stephanie

178

V. Critical Reaction: Later Articles

Bunkerism

Crawford Woods
The New Republic December 22, 1973

The strongest episode thus far? There've been so many.
I won an award for integrating Sammy Davis, no pun
intended, into Archie Bunker's life . . . Edith's menopause
. . . Mike's temporary impotence . . . homosexuality . . .
horsemeat . . . all break-through shows. But, first, entertainment!

I received "All in the Family" on its premiere some three years
ago as a "welcome breath of stale air," and did not suppose it would
have any extraordinary longevity. No more did CBS, which put the
show on tape to cut expenses and aired it in what's known as "Death
Valley," a time slot opposite blockbuster competition where ratings
are neither courted nor expected.

The wonder is that CBS put it on at all, for it was strong stuff
in its day, a sitcom that chose to call a spade a spade, not to mention
a nigger. It had come from under the wing of a BBC series (Bertrand
Russell once said that old philosophies when they die are reborn in
America as discoveries of local professors) which offered British
viewers four years' worth of their social shortcomings. An American
version surfaced in 1969 as a pilot rejected by ABC, was finally taken
by CBS and aired in 1970 in a much-rewritten form. According to
producer-director John Rich, the show almost died on schedule
in its first season, but generally good critical response and an excited

grapevine sent it into reruns where it was discovered in a big way and reborn.

Its success story since then hardly needs retelling. It has become a small, authentic slice of American pie, no time capsule complete without a piece of it. There are book and record spin-offs, Archie Bunker for President bumper strips, and more than a few Archie Bunker for President votes.

Now, three years later, there is little I would change in my original response: "Minus its savage bent, the show would have been a routine sample of what's been cluttering prime time for 20 years— fumbling, lovable Dad, vague sweet Mom, full-of-mischief kids. But here Dad's undercoat of amiable viciousness is revealed, Mom's indirection becomes pathetic, and the kids are offered as a paradigm of our righteous, striving young." But there is something I would add—a dim suspicion that Archie Bunker may not be a healthy hero for our time after all. The notion got no support from Rich—a large and largely unknown force behind the show's success from the beginning—when he was asked if he thought "All in the Family" was as likely to polarize viewers as to unify them:

"Look, it's a 24-minute entertainment, and that's all. I would be foolish to put anything so important on such a little section of our lives. It won't contribute to bigotry, or erase it. It won't change things."

Maybe not. But it's in the nature of TV to alter what it mirrors, to shape the way we live in its reflection, to put a new ripple in the pond. An observation frequently made about "All in the Family" is that the views of Archie Bunker are taken, not as parody, but as a legitimization of *their* views by a sizable part of the audience. How does Rich feel about that?

"I don't know . . . we have no facilities for audience research . . . and as far as I know the research hasn't been done. But I'm always getting letters from Ph.D. candidates asking for scripts."

Although this is one of the most fascinating aspects of the show it is evidently not a fruitful line of inquiry. Like most people concerned with the success of a network product—and the name of the game is delivering audience to advertisers, whether you're talking about "Gunsmoke" or "Civilisation"—Rich, while proud of his program's "breakthroughs," stressed that its core is entertainment. When I asked about the ways major social issues are handled on the show, the producer replied quickly:

"We never start with social issues. Our first job is to be entertaining." Pause. "Of course, there's fallout conversation in the political area."

But how close to the bone? It would seem natural that a man like Archie Bunker would hold strong opinions on social issues, even the less entertaining ones. Impeachment, for example; but Rich says he stays away from that "because events are moving so swiftly." On the other hand, Archie was talking about Watergate even before it snow-balled, and, according to Rich, he's been responsible for some extraordinary, if coincidental, social forecasting: he called a Japanese a Jap before Ehrlichman's lawyer used the word, and meditated on something like a letter bomb before that ugly vogue caught on. In one episode, faced with an empty home oil heater, he snaps out, "Thanks, Arabs." The show was aired the day before the Mideast war erupted.

Technically as well as textually, "All in the Family" is a far more interesting program than most. Rich puts it together during a 16-hour day the way Glenn Gould puts together a Bach recording, splicing the best bits from a quantity of raw material. Each episode is played in front of two audiences, one at 5:30 and one at 8:00, and lines and laughter are used from both. A remark one character made on the first show will get a response from the second if Rich's instinct tells him the second line is best. "We resist the easy laugh for the true laugh." The editing problems are fierce. Internal dialogue edits are frequent, and four cameras are employed instead of the usual three to open new possibilities of pace in a program locked to interiors. The editing by Rich and his able associates is all but invisible.

So is the audience. Nobody knows exactly who watches Archie Bunker—no research!—but it is known how many people do. (Lots.) Nobody knows for sure who's laughing with, and who at, him. Early studio audiences apparently felt some awkwardness about it; Rich notes that they had to be trained to laugh by their developing familiarity with the show. Seventy-six episodes later everybody knows when to break up, and the cast and crew are going strong— "our neuroses are meshing together."

It's a fair prescription for a good series, and compared with the competition "All in the Family" *is* a pretty good series. And it's an American institution, like laughter, bigotry or both. Has Rich special plans for the future of the show? He laughs. "We owe the world 10 episodes—I can't think beyond that. In England, the original had only eight new shows a season. That's civilization."

The Gospel According to Edith Bunker

Edward McNulty
Christian Century   March 27, 1974

The gospel is being discovered in unexpected places these days —in Charles Schulz's "Peanuts," in Mother Goose, James Bond, Andy Capp, *Mad* magazine. If the gospel can be discerned in these unlikely guises, then surely Good News can be found in yet another postcanonical Gospel—the Gospel According to Edith Bunker.

In Norman Lear's TV sitcom "All in the Family," the Good News is uttered not by Archie Bunker, by Mike or Gloria, by Lionel or the new neighbors, but by Edith, who will never be regarded as possessing an overabundance of brains or beauty; a woman disparaged by her husband as a bumbling, fumbling "dingbat." Truly she "hath no form nor comeliness that we should esteem her."

Edith is without pretension. Archie, Mike and Gloria may pretend to be more than they are; they may take off on flights of fancy. But Edith is always there to welcome their return, with the coffee pot on the stove or a full dinner on the table. Often it is one of her innocent remarks that cuts short their flight, bringing them down more surely than the barbs of a cynic. If Archie attempts to pull off some dishonest scheme, it is invariably Edith who blurts out the truth that is his undoing.

Archie chides Mike for allowing Gloria to take a job: "In the old days, the husband worked and the wife stayed at home. Even during the Depression we was proud. Right, Edith?"

Edith: "Yeah . . . and hungry, too!"

Or when Archie is angered by a TV editorial advocating gun control and his son-in-law urges him to call the station and make a rebuttal: "What's the matter? You got cold feet?"

"No, I ain't got cold feet!"

Edith interrupts with: "Oh, yes you do Archie. The other night in bed . . ."

Edith is the "debunker" par excellence, but she is more than that, even as the gospel is more than the deflating of our false pride and illusions. Christ punctured the puffed-up egos of Pharisee and Scribe, lawyer, rich man and disciple. He was truth-bearer, but more than this, he was crossbearer or lovebearer. We see these qualities in Edith, as she greets Archie at the door and hears out his complaints, as she calms down an overwrought Mike, as she comforts Gloria. She is go-between, intercessor or mediator for Archie and whomever he has decided not to talk with—for example, Mr. Jefferson, the black neighbor down the block.

Occasionally Edith succeeds in throwing off her dingbat image, and for a moment we catch a glimpse of a warm, perceptive human being—and we wonder what she might have become had she not married Archie. In one episode, Mike insists that the family, together with Lionel Jefferson, play the game of Group Therapy. Archie refuses to play and stalks off to his tavern. In the living room, things don't go quite to Mike's satisfaction. To his chagrin, each member of the group, prompted by the rules of the game, tells him things he doesn't want to hear: that he's not as open-minded as he thinks, that he has real problems in relating to others. He is especially upset at Lionel's suggestion that he is patronizing and condescending toward blacks. Raging out of control, Mike upsets the game and stomps upstairs. Persuaded to return, he becomes enraged again and rushes out to the kitchen to pout. This time it is Edith who pursues him.

As always, their conversation turns to Archie: "Mom, Archie hates me!"

"No-o-o, Mike, Archie don't hate you."

"Then why does he always say, 'Get away from me, Meathead!' when he comes in the door?"

"Mike, Archie is jealous of you."

"Of *me*?!"

She points out that Mike is young and Archie is growing old: "He'll never be more than what he is now, even though he had dreams once, like you. He ain't gone to college like you. He had to drop out of school to help support his family. He never will go to college. You have your whole future ahead of you, but most of Archie's life is behind him. So you see, he's jealous of you, Mike."

Mike forgets his rage as this unexpected insight sinks in. Presently, Archie returns from the tavern and comes in the door with his usual greeting: "Get away from me, Meathead!" But this time, instead of returning the hostility in kind, Mike throws his arms around Archie and cries out, "It's all right, Archie. I understand!" Fade out slowly on Archie's wide-eyed puzzlement.

As a "little Christ," Edith is Paul's "foolishness of God" incarnate. "Despised and rejected of men," she does not reign even in her own kitchen, but is constantly at the call of an arrogant husband and spoiled children. Occasionally, however, she asserts her humanity, often enough to show that though she might be a fool, she's not a *damned* fool.

Over the course of the series, as the characters are developed, we will see, I suspect, a growing consciousness in Edith. The quality of the writing is high, though I doubt that the writers have any theological intentions. Just as there is no pretension in Edith, there is little to the show itself. Its very theological innocence makes the insights of the show—particularly those of Edith—all the more remarkable.

Edith might think that Plato is a Walt Disney dog, that Aristotle is a Greek shipping magnate, and that Marx is a great comedian, but she possesses something better than factual knowledge: a knowledge of the heart, an insight into the soul.

If Archie shows us Everyman and his foibles, Edith depicts what we can become when integrity and concern overcome our limitations. Critics who have viewed "All in the Family" as a liberal diatribe against conservative rednecks may be missing the point. A theology that comes in half-hour, humorous segments is not Barth or Tillich, but the insights into human nature in each episode ring true. And that, after all, is what the theological quest is all about—the search for truth.

The Media Dramas
of Norman Lear

Michael Arlen *The New Yorker*   March 10, 1975

I have been trying to figure out what is so fascinating about the comedies of Norman Lear. Right now, six of Mr. Lear's shows are being broadcast every week to a prime-time audience: *All in the Family*, *Maude*, *Good Times*, *The Jeffersons*, *Sanford and Son*, and *HOT L BALTIMORE*. The first five programs named are currently among the dozen most popular programs in the nation, while the sixth, and newest, *HOT L BALTIMORE* (the title refers to the Hotel Baltimore, a riffraffy version of *Grand Hotel*), after just six weeks, has received a warm reception, despite a degree of wariness on the part of network-affiliate stations, several of which appear to think that in populating his run-down inn so freely with prostitutes, homosexuals, and other social misfits Mr. Lear may have been pushing his gift for jokey topicality farther than the mass audience will bear. Even so, it's probably a good bet that roughly a hundred and twenty million Americans watch Norman Lear comedies each week—which adds up to a total of roughly five billion viewers every year. Perhaps what is most fascinating about Mr. Lear's œuvre is the dimensions of its success, for he seems to be one of those ordinary but uncommon figures who come along every so often in our mass-entertainment culture and manage to achieve—more or less single-handed and with the appearance of naturalness—what tens of thousands of business geniuses and consumer theoreticians spend half the energies of the Republic vainly striving after; namely, a "feel" for what the public wants before it knows it wants it, and the ability to deliver it.

What is *not* so fascinating about Lear programs is easier to determine. Surprisingly, they are not very funny, for the most part, which is to say that the level of acting—at least, the stage presence of the actors—is generally of a higher order than the humor in each show: the jokes and joke situations. The humor isn't bad, but a surprising amount of it seems contrived and second-rate. "In my building, the roaches are so big that the crunch drowns out the television." And "Deep down, you know, he respects you." "Yes, but I don't want to dive that deep." On the whole, there are few unusual comedy routines in Lear comedies, and there has been virtually no introduction or creation of striking new comedy characters, with the possible exception of Archie Bunker, in *All in the Family*, who was transplanted from the successful BBC series *Till Death Us Do Part*, and, in any case, derives from a mass-entertainment cartoon that stretches back from William Bendix and Wallace Beery to Sancho Panza and Shakespeare's Pistol. And even Bunker, who has most of the best lines in his show, is given an overabundance of easy malapropisms: "Salivation Army," "Let him who is without sin be the rolling stone," "'Pilferers will be prosecuted' means 'Queers stay out of the men's room.'" In fact, much of the feeling of comedy in these Norman Lear programs seems to stem neither from the jokes, nor even from the situations, but from a mainly acoustical atmosphere of hilarity woven into the dialogue by means of the sounds of audience laughter which accompany each program. This laughter, it should be noted, is not the so-called "canned laughter" with which broadcast comedians traditionally augmented their routines. The Lear dramas, as self-proclaimed, are recorded before a "live audience," and so the laughter one hears is at least the sound of real people watching the same program that the home audience watches, albeit some days apart. Even so, while this represents a small advance in the production integrity of mass-entertainment comedy, the presence of this taped laughter as a formal part of a taped show—laughter emanating from the television set, from the same apparent source as the dialogue—is bound to have a defining effect on the viewer. Consider, for example, how one's perceptions of a movie or play can vary according to the responsiveness of the audience; how the presence of certain kinds of insistent audience laughter (such as the "bad laughs" which in many instances accompanied the movie *One Flew Over the Cuckoo's Nest*) can have almost a controlling effect on the rest of the people watching. Moreover, though the laughter which sets the tone for a program such as *All in the Family* derives from a real audience rather than from an old-fashioned "laugh machine," there are now new machines—indeed, a whole new science of acoustics and audio engineering—which make it possible for the laughter to rise and fall and throb ever more subtly and "realistically" behind the dialogue, but in the integrated manner of a rock band's second guitar. Thus, the audience is real, although the producers control its composition as well as the engineering of the sound, with the result that the humor of these most successful American television comedies is seldom witnessed by the viewer unattended by the whoops and giggles, the chuckles and vocal nudges, of this latest electronic institutionalizing of the old theatrical claque.

Also, whereas the level of comedy in the majority of the Norman Lear series is no more (and no less) than routinely professional, with its dependence on gags and grimaces, what often seems more evident than humor is the constant and steady presence of anger. All too frequently, while the persona of the studio audience booms out its merriment in the fashion of a lunatic Greek chorus, the on-screen characters appear to be caught up in a quite separate, verbal ballet of insult and vituperation. Again, Archie Bunker stands as the prototype of the Lear angry-man character. When Bunker first appeared on American screens in 1971, representing the politically and socially threatened silent-majority blue-collar worker, his outbursts on politics and race were taken as quaintly liberating and timely. They also had a specific quality and direction to them: blacks moving into the neighborhood, or being hired at a nearby factory. For some time now, though, Bunker's anger has become random—a random musical note that is methodically sounded by the script as it travels through each half hour. It is an accepted form of stage business. In a recent episode of *All in the Family*, for example, within a space of about fifteen minutes Bunker snarled and mugged such lines as "What's the stink in the oven? What kinda animal you cookin' in there?" (It's a fish.) "So, Irene is a Catholic. That means I gotta pay for *her* mistakes?" (Irene leaves.) "Whadda I care if she leaves. She's not my guest, she's your guest." "C'mon, throw the fish on the table!" "Don't stay in there—c'm here! Move it!" "Listen to this, Commie pinko!" "Let me remind you of something, Meathead!" "Yeah, Dingbat, I'm talkin' to you in English!" "Get in, get in. Just put your keyster in the chair and shut your mouth." If Bunker's anger has settled in as a conventional shtick—like Groucho Marx's walk or Jack Benny's stinginess—it has also been picked up and incorporated into all the other Norman Lear shows, and, for the most part, with the same quality of randomness. On *Sanford and Son*, which was transplanted from *Steptoe and Son*, another BBC series (about two Cockney junk dealers), Fred Sanford is an irascible and bullying black man—often with only the sound track and the vaudeville mugging to tell one that the show is a comedy. In a recent episode, Sanford was waiting for the arrival of his younger sister and her new "mystery" husband. First, he wanted his truck. "Where's our truck?" he asked angrily. "Julio borrowed it," said his son, referring to a Puerto Rican neighbor. Sanford grimaced broadly and slammed his fist on a table. "Now, you gone got *Puerto Rican* all over our truck!" The taped audience erupted in laughter, the joke presumably being that it *was* a joke. The the married sister appeared with her new husband —a white man. The audience giggled apprehensively but delightedly as the husband—a soft, droll figure—sidled warily into the room, unseen by Sanford. Time passed and Sanford still didn't notice him. Then he mistook the man for a taxi driver. Then, finally introduced to and embraced by the new brother-in-law, he went into an elaborate and energetic sequence of grimaces and double takes, crashing about the room in a fury that was again comic mainly in the laughter of the unseen audience. "How come you're lookin that way?" Sanford's sister said to him, feeding the line. "I just got hugged and kissed by a Snow-Whitey," replied Sanford. Afterward, he called the white husband "Mr. Intermarry," "Paleface," "Honky," "Color-Blind," and "The White Tornado," each one to bursts of applause from the tape; indeed, the only purpose or reality of the white husband's existence seemed to be as a butt for Sanford's jokey snarls.

Anger as stage business runs through nearly all Norman Lear's comedies, but it is a curious, modern, undifferentiated anger, which serves to provide the little dramas with a kind of energizing dynamic —sometimes the only dynamic. At the beginning of an episode of *The Jeffersons*, George Jefferson enters his new apartment already angry—vaguely and generally angry. Maude, in *Maude*, appears to be angry at Walter, in one particular instance, for eating too much, but clearly—clearly to the audience—she is just *angry*: it is a state of being, interrupted periodically by stage-business jokes or stage-business sentiment, or sometimes stage-business problems. What is notable here is that anger in a Norman Lear comedy isn't something isolated or set apart—as with, say, Sheridan Whiteside in George S. Kaufman and Moss Hart's *The Man Who Came to Dinner*, or in the traditional routines of "insult comedians." It has become part of the spirit of the occasion, like music in a musical comedy. Also, as with the characters themselves, who, despite their fits of problem-solving and self-awareness, return each week to the same unserial starting point, it is a rage that rarely extends much into the future, or even into the present. An individual outburst of temper may sometimes produce a concrete result, such as the disruption of a dinner, but for the most part these acts of the new anger are strangely actionless, and, in any case, are soon automatically defused and retracted. King Lear's rage has traveled, by way of Sheridan Whiteside's irritability, into the release-rhetoric of the psychotherapist's waiting room.

Modern, psychiatrically inspired or induced ambivalence may, indeed, be the key dramatic principle behind this new genre of popular entertainment. A step is taken, and then a step back. A gesture is made and then withdrawn—blurred into distracting laughter, or somehow forgotten. This seems especially true in the area of topicality—topical themes—which is supposed to be where Mr. Lear's chief contribution to new forms of comedy lies. For it is in Norman Lear comedies that the mass-entertainment public has first been persuaded to deal regularly with serious contemporary social subjects such as racism (*All in the Family*), alcoholism (*Maude*), black middle-class striving (*The Jeffersons*), and black lower-class problems (*Good Times*), and with a hodgepodge of traditionally unacceptable social and sexual situations (*HOT L BALTIMORE*). With or without the help of contemporary trends, what Mr. Lear has done in this regard is no mean achievement. He has taken a lot of the subjects that people privately talked or thought about, in between watching game shows, detective shows, and stand-up comedians, and put *those* subjects into mass-entertainment programming. His shows don't explicitly claim to be constructive or dogmatic, although the writers (and presumably Mr. Lear) are not averse to throwing in periodic doses of social democracy, but they do implicitly claim to be topical.

As things work out, though, it is a curious kind of topicality. The subject seems to be there—for instance, financial problems stemming from the recession, in a recent episode of *Maude*—but the actuality of the subject soon dissolves into the texture of the aforementioned vague anger, or else into a new type of ambivalence, which has been effected by employing fast cutting and the claque sound track. For example, in a recent episode of *HOT L BALTI-MORE* the main drama concerned the breakup of a long-standing homosexual menage involving two hotel tenants—the middle-aged George and Gordon, with George clearly the "wife" in the pair—as a result of George's decision to spend two evenings out of each week studying law. Interestingly, the roles of George and Gordon were cast with a fair amount of sympathy and contemporary realism; at least, the actors and their parts were several cuts above the traditional mass-entertainment depiction of limp-wristed effeminacy a la Billy De Wolfe. The tilt of the drama—rather more a vignette—seemed human, and even serious, but then the mood would suddenly shift, almost in mid-dialogue, into an old-timey gag or a cheap laugh played off the invisible audience. At one point—supposedly a key moment—the youthful and well-intentioned but dopey hotel manager appears on the scene to try to patch things up between the two separating roommates. The scene requires him to shake hands with George. George, quite dignified, extends his hand. The camera cuts to the hotel manager mugging his straight-arrow distaste. Then we see George, playing it seriously. Then back to the hotel manager, alternately rolling his eyes, shuffling his feet, and continuing to mug he-man embarrassment while the sound track variously giggles, sniggers, guffaws, and breathes a chorus-like sigh of relief when the handshake is finally consummated. What seemed unusual about the scene was that the other actors onstage were directed to play it seriously. In other words, the caption on the picture, so to speak, said that we were watching a human, realistic, albeit comedic treatment of a contemporary "social problem," but in fact the figures in the portrait were dissolving into images of our own (and perhaps their creator's) anxieties and ambivalences: into a caricature of the homosexual's role in our society, which the "caption" was attempting to deny. Similarly, in a recent episode of *The Jeffersons* the dramatic vignette concerned a tenants' party in the family's new apartment, in a predominantly white, upper-middle-class building, which George Jefferson had decided to give in order to show off to his neighbors and impress an important white banker with his cultivation. Predictably, the party was a social disaster. A funny "colored maid" went screaming around the room. When an effete, English-type tenant asked for "a Scotch—neat," one of the Jeffersons said, "Don't worry, you'll get a clean glass." George Jefferson had ordered, sight unseen, a grand piano, which none of the family could play, and it was delivered into the middle of the living room, so that everybody tripped over it. And so forth. But none of the people onstage batted an eye. If the real point of the story was that the Jeffersons were pushy, *arriviste*, inept, but unfortunately *there* —in fact, were uppity—it was not a point acknowledged, or even touched upon, except very slightly, by the rest of the cast. There were no haughty looks and contemptuous sneers from the other posh tenants—the way the ritzy people used to look at Charlie Chaplin when he stumbled into the wrong salon. The only way you'd know that the party was an embarrassment was from the sound track, which, with its shrieks and giggles at the awkward moments, keyed the audience: Yes, the Jeffersons *are* uppity. We can't say it too loud, because that would be wrong. In fact, we're going to play it on the level with those other stage tenants, perhaps—Lord knows—encouraging real tenants somewhere to play it on the level with real Jeffersons. But in the meantime let's let our anxieties and ambivalences work up the real drama, and let's have a laugh.

Even so, if what could mainly be said of Norman Lear's comedies was that they were on the cheap side, playing serious topical subjects for easy laughs—with a few jokes and snarls and much professional expertise thrown in—that wouldn't be very new or very interesting, and I don't think it would account for Mr. Lear's enormous success. It may well be that Lear does more with topical humor than comedians and comedy writers before him have done, but topicality isn't his invention, nor is exploiting it a new device, recently discovered. Indeed, American mass-entertainment producers have exploited audience "seriousness" for generations, as with the *Classics*-comics pageantry of Cecil B. De Mille, or with Stanley Kramer's "message" films, or with *The Defenders* on television, or even with the slick good-think of the Smothers Brothers and the political wisecracks of Bob Hope and *Laugh-In*. Topicality doesn't really seem to be what Mr. Lear does best—nor does comedy seem to be his strongest card. After watching a great many of Mr. Lear's six shows this past season, I suspect that what is most fascinating about the works of Norman Lear is that they are our first true "media" dramas.

Consider briefly how American mass-audience comedy has evolved in the past fifty years. For much of this time, comedy—both in print and onstage—was trapped within the joke: the one-liner, the two-liner, the set piece, the funny bit. From these beginnings, with the joke presented as separate or disconnected from ordinary life, came the more expansive—albeit still disconnected—narrative joke or funny story: *Nothing but the Truth*; *Bringing Up Baby*; *Abbott and Costello Meet Frankenstein*. On television, the funny story survives in such now old-fashioned programs as *Hogan's Heroes* and *Gilligan's Island* (as, indeed, vaudeville one-liners still survive with Bob Hope), but, for the most part, during the last generation television—as if it had prenatally digested *The Pickwick Papers* or at least *Life with Father*—has expanded humor from the isolated joke into the so-called family comedy. In *I Love Lucy* and *The Honeymooners* and *The Beverly Hillbillies* and countless other shows, the surface emphasis was still on jokes—Lucy finds a wallet, wins a contest, loses a handbag—but the joke sector of life had been enlarged to include not merely a comedian onstage talking about farmers' daughters but much of ordinary family life, if a rather stylized version of it. Lucy at first was not a real woman, though she had many of the appurtenances of a real woman—modest house, noisy kitchen, gossipy neighbors—but she ended up actually having babies and bringing up children. More recently, Dick Van Dyke and then Mary Tyler Moore expanded the terrain of family comedy further, replacing the home family with the job family, and fashioning, as in the case of the current *Rhoda* and *The Mary Tyler Moore Show*, more or less "real" people to go with the "real" problems and comedy situations. Still, *Mary* and *Rhoda* have remained by and large in the conventional mold of *families* dealing with *family* situations—either home family situations, such as boyfriends or dieting or mothers-in-law, or job family situations, such as office misadventures or employment rivalries.

The comedies of Norman Lear are probably new in that they seem to depend mainly neither on jokes nor on funny stories, nor even on family—although they often given the appearance of depending on all three—but on the new contemporary consciousness of "media." By this I mean that the base of the Lear programs is not so much the family and its problems as it is the commonality that seems to have been created largely by television itself, with its outpouring of casual worldliness and its ability to propel—as with some giant, invisible electric-utility feeder line—vast, undifferentiated quantities of topical information, problem discussions, psychiatric terminology, and surface political and social involvement through the national bloodstream. Thomas Jefferson, it is said, wrestled for a lifetime with the dark, felt concerns of intermarriage and miscegenation, and it is high time that Americans should be able to deal freely and rationally with such historically taboo matters. But lately in the space of a single week, in two Norman Lear shows, the subject of mixed marriage twice breezed blithely by, accompanied by the usual defusing jokes and the laughter of the sound track. Have we come this far so suddenly? In which case, who are *we*? Doubtless we are the same people who, as informed adults and media children, discuss, with all the appearance of passion and involvement, events that have occurred in places we have no knowledge of and had no previous interest in, and with implications we have rarely examined, or tried to connect backward or forward to other events—but events that now sit there and *exist* in the new consciousness in the manner of found objects, tuned into by interested and uninterested parties alike.

Mr. Lear is surely not the first explorer to have stumbled on this pool of media-informed consciousness, but he is the first man, as far as I can tell, to have so formally and so successfully tapped it for the purposes of mass entertainment. It is perhaps not a step higher, but it is a step forward. Ancient drama, one might say, was concerned primarily with the act as act—as the dynamic of drama. Modern drama has gradually interposed motive and guilt as the kinetic forces. Now, maybe, we are treading dizzily into a new phase, where both act and motive have blurred or receded and what we are left with onstage (and onscreen) is the strange dynamic of a ubiquitous, unfeeling, unknowing, discursive collective consciousness. Beginning with the comedies of Norman Lear—as Aristophanes might have been the first to appreciate—we have finally become plugged in to our own Talk Show: connected to nothing except the assumption of being connected to something, which for the time being appears to be our new bond and our new family.

All in the Family

Roger Rosenblatt
The New Republic   May 24, 1975

In this episode of "All in the Family" Edith has sent in a box top that allows her to receive a 25-cent rebate from the manufacturers of the product. Because of a mistake in the company's computer, quarters keep coming by the daily mail. Eventually Edith amasses close to $50 in quarters, despite her protests to the company. She and the children want to return the money. Archie, naturally, wants to keep it. The son-in-law, Mike, tries to phone the company long distance in Buffalo. The company's automatic answering service fails like the computer. Mike rants against the machine age. Archie praises the age.

Edith then receives a sum of money as a death benefit for Archie from the Veterans' Administration. Another machine has failed. Now Archie berates technology while the children taunt him. They suggest that Archie may in fact be dead, and remind him of television's "Twilight Zone." Archie is visibly shaken, particularly by the appearance at the door of the neighborhood undertaker Mr. Whitehead, a mousy man whose great shock of white hair provides the best visual joke of the show. Mr. Whitehead, too, has his technology, and suggests a coffin for Archie with an electric light under the lid. He also suggests the epitaph, "peace with honor."

The Bunkers call at the Veterans' Administration building. Their interview begins with the VA man asking where Archie is buried. The situation is corrected when the VA man discovers an extra puncture in Archie's IBM card. He explains, "every little hole has a meaning all its own." Archie complains that there is no more respect for human dignity, but is relieved to learn that he is alive again. The episode ends on the presumption that he is right.

Death and the Bunkers have been close to each other since the series started. In one story Archie, inadvertently locked in his own basement, drinks himself into a stupor, and believes that he has either crossed the Jordan or the Styx. In another he dreams that he is old and dying, rejected by his children. A few weeks ago he was just missed by a falling crate of machine parts, and temporarily became devout in response to his near tragedy. Archie has epiphanies about death and takes it seriously, as he ought to, because in many ways death is the emblem of his life.

His life occupies a situation comedy, one that remains static from week to week. This type of comedy has no plot; plot is progressive and needs causes for events. Situation is committed to sameness. Plot is connected to growth of character, even when opposed to character as in myth. Situation takes character for granted, and will brook no changes, except when someone "steps out of character" for a joke on himself. Like the comedy of humors, situation presumes that exaggerated consistency is funny. We have no feelings for the people involved, which is the basis of our laughter—even at an episode on death, which is another kind of exaggerated consistency.

Comedy and death are old companions, as Yorick demonstrated, not merely in graveyard and funeral jokes, but in substance. Both are forms of interruption. Both have social stature, and command absolute attention. Neither is fully comprehensible to us, in cause or meaning. Both are forms of criticism and reality, shattering pretense, showing people for what they are. To make a joke of something is to kill it. The terms of comedy are the terms of death: you're a riot, a scream; you break me up; you're killing me.

These terms have a special companionship in "All in the Family" because "All in the Family" was dead on arrival. We knew from the outset that the four main characters always would be impervious to change, that in their particular comedy of humors Edith would shuttle between Bewilderment and Right Instinct, and that the children would play Young Generation forever, permanently settled into lip-service liberalism and the latest freedom vernacular, their every reaction more predictable than Archie assaults. On the surface Archie's humor seems more variable. At times he appears as Hate, Stubbornness, Selfishness or Cowardice, but all of these group under the presiding humor of Death itself, which governs every form of immovability, in Archie and his kin.

Despite the formal stagnation of their lives, the Bunkers reappear every week as if reborn for the week's occasions. They do not learn from past mistakes. They repeat old jokes and epithets. None seems to have much of a memory for former events which might guide their present decisions. Every Saturday they feign surprise to discover how the other thinks, from which surprise, in part, derives our laughter.

By blocking out the past, of course, they block out the future. This sustains them as comedians, like a running gag, but is no joke. In these people we read a jumble of traditional issues such as man versus machine, which they regularly set before us like a buffet chef run amuck. At the same time, by their own behavior, they intimate that life is always to be treated as new business. In the tension between memory and desire lie the Bunkers. Their false innocence intensifies the staleness of their experience. Even the laughter coming "live from Television City in Hollywood" sounds canned.

But the Bunkers do not live in the present, either. Instead of a state of time, they live in a state of mind, specifically Archie's. When the week's problem is announced, the humors gather 'round to offer different perspectives on, for example: What is the meaning of individual honesty in a mechanized world where machines can cheat and be cheated? What are the meanings of death and truth in such a world? These questions appear to be up for grabs, but they are in Archie's control from the start, control that is manifested by childishness and panic. Because Archie always represents the worst response to problems, he bears the focus for possible solutions.

Because no solutions are ever offered or desired on "All in the Family" Archie also always wins the day.

This is the death that the program promotes: the death of motion and enlargement of spirit. Archie's comic consistency is nothing as clean as Avarice or Lust, nothing one can point one's finger to and say "ridiculous." Rather, it is the consistency of serious issues deliberately raised and left to die, the incubator dead rolled from living room to kitchen in a Queens house lined up against its identical neighbor like the vast Queens cemeteries. Archie is Joyce's Mr. Browne, who is everywhere. The death he carries is our amusement at his triumphs.

Is "All in the Family" funny? Sometimes. When Archie reports that the machine parts missed him when he leaned forward to salt his egg, because God's "verse" told him "you need salt on that egg," that is funny. When later in that episode the toilet cover drops on Archie's foot and Mike claims that "God's aim is getting better," that too is funny, at least the way Reiner and O'Connor handle it. But the fun is piecemeal, not connected to a fluid life. It is meant to interfere between surprise and understanding, and then to boing like an overwound watchspring so that once laughing we must start at zero again, and rebuild the situation. Accordingly the laugh we give the Bunkers is disembodied, the laugh laughing not at them but at itself.

Comedy, like death, must embrace the whole life, if it works. It may deny change, but must also acknowledge the possibility of change, of past and future, thereby in its denials suggesting a moral base. The comedy of the Bunkers, which is not of the whole life, which is the blurtings of topical and toilet jokes, rapid fire, scatter-gun, automatic, depending on our habitual courtesy to laugh at familiar things—this comedy is of a different death, a death where life never was. There is nothing intense and nothing to care for. The family are bunkers against our caring.

The final episode of "All in the Family" might pay respects to its intent. Archie could choke yelling Dingbat and collapse in a heap. Edith could go immediately afterward, tripped by a chicken leg. The children could be hit by a sound truck for Cesar Chavez while running for help. Ding-a-ling. Bang. Gone. Then all come forward and take a bow: first Mike, then Gloria, then Edith. We go wild with applause, and stand up shouting as Archie's head fills the screen, big as life, handsome old baby face, scrubbed to a glow and ready to meet his maker. A spotlight traces the skull beneath the skin. How *do* you like your blue-eyed boy, Mr. Death?

Watching
the Sit-coms

Dorothy Rabinowitz *Commentary*   October 1975

Amos n' Andy are long gone, but changing tastes, increased
sophistication, and the jading plenitude that television has provided
over the years seem in no way to have altered the capacity of American audiences to be held in thrall, week after week, by "shows."
The shows Americans have liked the most recently have been staples
of CBS television, the Saturday-night "situation comedies," as
irrelevant a term for these programs as can have been invented. For
it is not for anything as bland as the name implies that the Saturday
night sit-coms have consistenly drawn the highest Nielsen ratings.
Comprising four half-hour segments, *All in the Family, The Jeffersons, The Mary Tyler Moore Show,* and *The Bob Newhart Show,*
the Saturday night sit-coms have more often than not supplied fare
of a kind quite remarkable in the annals of commercial television.
The departure this season of *All in the Family,* the most popular
of them all, from Saturday night to Monday night offers as good an
occasion as any for reflecting on the world of the sit-coms and their
audience.

One begins by taking *All in the Family* (a Lear-Yorkin Production) for what it is, a weekly repository of our most fashionable
pieties. The series is set in a lower-middle-class neighborhood, its
backdrop a lace-curtained, depressed, but impeccable two-story
house of the kind one might find in working-class sections of Queens
or Bay Ridge, Brooklyn. The head of the household, as everyone
knows, is Archie Bunker, a bigot, an enemy of progress and of progressive thinkers of every stripe; a hardhat in short and in fact,
Archie's employment being, vaguely, in the construction line.
Ostensibly a member of the Wasp majority, albeit of its lower classes,
Archie is hostile to blacks, Puerto Ricans, Jews, Catholics, atheists,
homosexuals, and women's liberationists. Not that his crude assaults
on these targets go unopposed, for his household is illuminated
by the presence of a militantly progressive daughter and son-in-
law (the latter, to be sure, something of a sponger and a hothead),
both of whom spring smartly into action whenever Archie opens
his mouth.

An extraordinary number of words have been written about,
and objections entered to, the "bigotry" of *All in the Family.*

Civil-rights leaders have charged that the show disseminates racially and religiously biased attitudes, despite its clearly stated hostility to Archie's prejudices. Women's groups complain about the part of Edith, Archie's wife, a goodhearted but muddle-headed woman whom her husband refers to regularly as "the dingbat," and who accepts the role of loving servant to her husband. Nothing if not aware of these objections, the producers, writers, and directors of *All in the Family* have gone to great lengths to establish *all* of Archie's contentions as bigotry, up to and including his notion that black criminals might be a threat to one's life. Indeed, there is but one figure on whom the show's satire ranges entirely free and unself-conscious, and that figure is Archie himself and, by extension, the hardhat type in general, a target of satire that has inspired more than one progressive sensibility since the days when construction workers fought student radicals in the street, and aligned themselves on the side of the President.

The first aim of this satire, it would appear, is to explode the myth of hardhat virility. Did you think that those strong, inarticulate louts were comfortable with their animal natures? You couldn't be more wrong. Archie's sexual life is limited by inhibition and narrowness, as witness his discomfort when his wife proposes they return to their honeymoon hotel for a twenty-fifth wedding anniversary. Archie is, furthermore, a blusterer and an ignoramus, who can get out no idiom but that it is mangled, no proverb but that it is turned upside down, no word of more than two syllables but that it is mispronounced. (Many of these manglings and mispronunciations are reminiscent indeed of the black-face violence perpetrated on the King's English by Amos n' Andy, back in that unenlightened past which is now to the enlightened an embarrassment to recall: "Wait a minute heah Andy! Whut is you doin? Is you mulsiflyin or re-vidin?") Archie is also a World War II veteran, a factor integral to his status as a reactionary. He has only to narrow his small blue eyes at his peace-marching son-in-law and deliver a prideful reference to "double-yew double-yew two" in order to induce laughter from a studio audience that *knows* how the failures of our past, of our elders, of everything we have become are inextricably linked with the proto-fascist type of the veteran.

Archie is not the only reactionary visible on *All in the Family*. Before their promotion to a series of their own, Archie's black neighbors, the Jeffersons, included in their long-suffering family circle a bigot almost as impossible as Archie, but one whose hatreds were directed against whites. This effort at balance aside, *All in the Family*'s portrayal of blacks has reflected with some precision what the outer limits of comment are thought to be on that subject. The theme of black crime is particularly pertinent. In one episode, Archie confronts two black robbers, as verbal, elegant, and full of graceful effrontery as Archie is gauche and inarticulate. In addition to being cleverer than he (Archie has foolishly put his faith in a gun, while they rely on those typical weapons of the urban criminal, wit and cerebration), they are models of sensitivity—they indulge Edith's off-key singing, force Archie to be nice to her, and generally comport themselves like ambassadors to the Court of St. James. Elsewhere, Norman Lear, the "developer" of *All in the Family*, has developed other avenues for the treatment of this issue, notably in his black-family "spin-offs," whole series created around characters first established in other shows. In the immensely successful *Good Times*, shown on Tuesday evenings, a ghetto family comes to grips with black crime on several occasions, once in an episode during which the lovable teen-ager J.J. is forced to take part in a gang war against his will, and again when a black—and blind—salesman is presented as a bunko artist, an unscrupulous robber of poor ghetto dwellers and, the young militant of the family gives us to understand, of his own people.

"His own people" is the reassuring factor here. Lear's programs endorse the liberal answer to the high rate of black crime, the proposition that blacks are its chief victims. In addition, in all three of Lear's black-family programs—*The Jefferson, Good Times,* and *Sanford and Son*—blacks alone pass judgment on black problems and on black attitudes in general. This enables a modest spirit of self-criticism to seem to prevail on these shows. On *The Jeffersons*, an upwardly-mobile anti-white George Jefferson is balanced off against his wife, Louise, who is sanity and moderation itself. In one episode, George Jefferson and his son Lionel shower contempt upon Louise's elderly uncle, a retired butler whom they berate for having spent his life as an Uncle Tom in a white household and for being, clearly, an activist of the NAACP variety. "Listen, you!" the dignified older man finally roars at Lionel, "I used to spit out six like you before breakfast!" "I worked for many years to get from nigger to Negro, so you'll have to forgive me if it takes me a while to get used to calling myself a black now," the uncle concludes, with hauteur, to shrieks of applause from the audience for this defiance of the new by the old.

For airing sentiments like these, the producer of *All in the Family* has made a not inconsiderable name for himself as an entrepreneur of the controversial. On *All in the Family* alone, such subjects as menopause, miscarriage, and menstruation have all been dealt with, if with the somewhat reverent air that inevitably seems to accompany the principle that all things having to do with our bodies are sacred. Next season, it is promised that *All in the Family* will venture a program on euthanasia. The decision to treat that theme was made, according to a New York *Times* piece, at what was presumably a typical conference between Lear and his story editor. "Can we find a way to do it without copping out?" Lear asks. "Maybe we can have the relatives agree to it and let the audience know they're not sure they made the right decision." It would appear that among "controversial" and pioneering types in the media, of whom Lear is so egregious an example, "no copping out" means that within the format of a show dealing with a morally questionable course of action, the principals decide *for* the action and carry it through; taking the negative side would be equivalent to "copping out." One of the possibilities that Lear and his fellow controversialists seem not ready to contemplate is the notion that moral courage might be more greatly manifested in a decision to defy, or even to ignore, some piece or other of the conventional wisdom.

Yet "controversial" themes have little, if anything, to do with the wide success of *All in the Family*. Its appeal is rooted not in the show's endorsement of liberal values, but, on the contrary, in its vivid, visual demonstration of the abiding attractiveness of the familiar as opposed to the strange, the old virtues as opposed to the new nonsense. The writers who write the show, the actors who act in it, not to say the developer who develops and produces it, are all aware of the rule for success that politicians of every kind, including those in the entertainment business, understand very well—that it is easier to win by reassuring people than by trying to convert them. No matter how much "controversial" material *All in the Family* purveys, or how many progressive positions it endorses—no matter how many women get jobs in the construction firm Archie works for, or how many fine, manly homosexuals are trotted out for Archie's education—it is the fate of all of them to be rendered meaningless by reason of the show's main dramatic energies, which are bent precisely on establishing the irrelevance of the new and the progressive to the life and style of the lovable Bunkers: a life and style, we are given to understand, that are full of decency and worth.

Lear is not the first politician of his age to have read correctly the prevailing winds of the culture and to have perceived the wisdom in following *all* of them, though he may well be the first to have packaged that perception successfully for television. Nor is the package a small achievement, for there have been scenes on *All in the Family* equal to the best that commercial television has had to offer, most of them due to the skill of Carroll O'Connor, who plays Archie with a fidelity that has been the making of the show since its inception in 1971. To see Carroll O'Connor act this part is to have the pleasure of watching knowledge delivered. With his mastery of every inflection, every lift of the eyebrow, of a certain lower-middle-class type, O'Connor succeeds, in the face of all that rings false in Archie's lines, in making that which he knows so well, and which we, watching, know that he knows so well—namely, details—prevail over stereotype and caricature.

In one program, to cite a single instance, Archie learns from his rich, despised, and much envied cousin Russell that Russell, a swinger, betrays his wife regularly. An appalled Archie sits in a bar and listens to Russell's cold-blooded talk about how uninteresting wives are sexually. At home, in a tearful scene, Archie's wife Edith (Jean Stapleton) is hearing the same sort of information concerning Russell from Russell's wife, a woman whose marriage the good-hearted Edith has always admired for its surface glamor. But when the cousins have gone home and Archie and Edith are alone, they cannot bring themselves to talk about what they have found out about the other couple. The camera zeroes in on the mute Archie and Edith, drawn close, suddenly, by an inexplicable current of feeling risen between them; on, particularly, the face of Archie, capably feigning indifference.

It is one of television's better moments, not only because the audience recognizes the truth of this silence—its legitimate observation of the way in which, except perhaps among the sophisticated, each sex still tends to reserve to itself what, for its own good reasons, it is judged the other need not know—or because the observation itself is an appealing one, but also because, in a medium whose chief terror has traditionally been any assay into the subtle, a highly condensed piece of shorthand has been permitted to stand without explication. Audiences have rightly perceived at such moments that in the "new breed" of situation comedy, they are indeed given something not accorded them on traditional programs. In the new programs writers and performers are not so much required to sustain a plot line—as is the case in more traditional shows—as to render social types, to satirize rather than to tell a story. It is required of the audience, in turn, that it know enough to recognize the types, that it follow the actors' shorthand, and that it become, in some measure, their partner and ally—for it is true of any successful satire that it makes its audience a satirist by extension.

The Family of Man:
The Ethnic Joke as Situation Comedy

Arthur Asa Berger   from *The TV-Guided American*

Every situation comedy extant owes fealty to Archie and Edith Bunker and to Mike and Gloria. In one smashing, revolutionary opening half-hour (January, 1971), they destroyed old taboos and liberated television comedy writing.

The nation's critics caught on instantly. The public didn't latch on until the summer reruns, 13 weeks later. The public never let loose. Archie Bunker was a bigot but he was real. The family and neighborhood forces battering him were real. The situations—ranging from female menopause to male impotency, from communism to racism—were unparalleled in television comedy. They were shocking, startling and often uproariously funny.

—DWIGHT NEWTON
San Francisco Sunday
Examiner & Chronicle
October 27, 1974

All in the Family is the most popular television program in America and has been a family favorite here for the past few years, since it was first shown in January, 1971. There is considerable irony in this situation, since the hero of the series, Archie Bunker, is a bigot. A

204

crude, dumb, and ignorant fellow, Bunker is a symbolic hero in the American pantheon of fools and loudmouths, but there is one critical difference between him and previous clowns on American television, and that is that he is not harmless, he has not been sanitized.

All in the Family is really a case study in the demythologizing of the American working classes. In the popular mind, the working-class blue collar worker is seen as a clean-living, honest, hard-working person who is tolerant of his fellowman, God-fearing, perhaps a bit materialistic, but generally speaking a fine figure. This heroic figure, the so-called common man, has traditionally been seen as a reservoir of good sense and an upholder of our democratic values. This is the way the common man is presented in the media, at least.

Curiously enough, this same fantasy of the innate goodness of the common man, a legacy of our past (when the country was filled with nature's noblemen) is kept alive by certain elements of the political left, who have a vested interest in the proletariat as the redeemers of a bourgeois American civilization that has lost its way and is destructive of man's humanity. Jefferson said:

> State a moral case to a ploughman and a professor. The former will decide it as well, and often better than the latter, because he has not been led astray by artificial rules.

We believe that the common man will save us because he is closer to nature and to life. This notion is connected with our egalitarianism and our anti-intellectualism, our fear of institutions and our defining ourselves as "natural" as contrasted to "civilized," a subject I will discuss in greater detail later.

In any case, Archie Bunker does not seem to be very noble, and his description of his fellow Americans seems far removed from what we might expect from the natural democrat. To quote the beginning of a *Newsweek* article, "TV: Speaking About the Unspeakable" (Nov. 29, 1971):

> Archie Bunker, the middle American hero of *All in the Family*, speaks what was utterly unspeakable on television before him. He sees himself menaced by a rising tide of spades, spics, spooks, schwartzes, coons, coloreds, Chinks, Commies and their Commie crapola, jungle bun-

nies, jigs, pinkos, pansies, hebes, yids, black beauties, bleeding hearts, tamale eaters, yentas, atheists, weirdos, dumb Polacks, dingbats, meatheads, fairies, fruits, fags, and four-eyes. These are the words he uses in a medium that usually minces words to the consistency of toddler food.

There seems to be an endless number of people whom Archie hates, and American audiences seem to derive a great deal of pleasure from seeing and hearing Archie vent his wrath upon various scapegoats.

On the basis of this listing it seems obvious that Archie feels threatened by almost everyone around him, and is suffering from a kind of diffuse paranoia. The family of man is myth; everyone is a menace. Now, since the program is bathed in a kind of gruff geniality and since Archie is a fool, we don't take it all as seriously as we might. But many a word said in jest is an honest representation of people's feelings, and we cannot let the comedy completely obscure the aggression beneath it.

Archie is trapped and frustrated; he is locked into a dead-end job, like many Americans, and reacts to this by blaming others for his situation. He was told, like all Americans, that the future was his—if only he had the willpower. And it might have all worked out, were it not for all the Jews and coons and other people corrupting American society.

When you scratch the typical working-class person, and dig beneath the thin veneer of elementary school civics he carries around in his head, you find things to make you shudder. Let me quote, in this respect, from Seymour Martin Lipset's classic, *Political Man*. Discussing the typical lower-class individual, Lipset says:

He is likely to have been exposed to punishment, lack of love, and a general atmosphere of tension and aggression since early childhood—all experiences which tend to produce deep-rooted hostilities expressed by ethnic prejudices, political authoritarianism, and chiliastic transvaluational [pie in the sky when you die] religion. His educational attainment is less than that of men with higher socio-economic status, and his association as a child with others of a similar background not only fails to stimulate his own intellectual interests but also creates an atmosphere which prevents his educational experience from increasing his general social sophistication and his under-standing of different groups and ideas. Leaving school rather early, he is surrounded on the job by others with a similarly restricted cultural, educational, and family background.

If you think of it, *All in the Family* can be looked upon as a kind of ethnic joke that has been expanded into a situation comedy. In the case of *All in the Family*, the fact that Archie's son-in-law is Polish facilitates the whole matter, for in the program Mike Stivic actually is (to people sympathetic with Archie) a "Polish joke."

Ethnic humor has been around for a long time! Since the first man noticed he was different from the second, and ethnocentrism first appeared, ethnic jokes must have been popular. The Greeks had ethnic jokes about the uncouth Romans, the Romans had ethnic jokes about the uncouth barbarians, and the Chinese probably had ethnic jokes about everybody. Jokes feed on differences and dis-tinctions, and if one of the functions of ethnic jokes is to ridicule others, another function (and one which we are seldom aware of) is to maintain a sense of one's ethnicity, and with it, identity.

America, as a nation of immigrants—each with different cus-toms and traditions and values—is, par excellence, a breeding house of ethnic jokes. The jokes help *release aggression without guilt*, and as such, have no doubt been instrumental in facilitating the relatively stable mixing of different ethnic groups in America.

We realize, of course, that America is not a mixing or melting pot. Rather, different groups have lived side-by-side, often with an uneasy toleration (at best) of one another. Telling jokes about other ethnic groups is a good way to let off steam; verbal aggression becomes a substitute for physical aggression. It is cheaper and the results are almost guaranteed.

Ethnic humor, as a manifestation of ethnocentrism, is generally built upon stereotypes—vague and usually absurd notions people have about other people, frequently picked up from the mass media, but also learned from family, school, and social experiences. The jokes tend to reinforce the stereotypes in the minds of the teller, even though he realizes they are absurd and incorrect. This is because we generally believe there is a core of truth to stereotypes, even though they may not be nice.

There is a question as to whether ethnic humor is, in fact, ethnic—that is, whether it is aimed at the ethnicity (and distinctive qualities) of groups or their socio-economic status. It may very well be, for example, that the jokes about Polaks, Wops, Yids, Micks, and others, may *really* be attacks on their lower-class life styles and not ethnic peculiarities. Perhaps Americans associate dirtiness, cowardice, uncouth behavior, vulgarity, and other distasteful qualities, with classes beneath them, and just single out different nationalities to represent assigned vices.

Ethnic jokes may represent the opposite of ascribed status; they are *ascribed deflation*, which gain currency because the jokes are comic and release aggression in a fairly economical and harmless way. This deflation may be the key to comedy, for as Hobbes says in *The Leviathan*:

> The passion of laughter is nothing else but sudden glory arising from a sudden conception of some eminency in ourselves by comparison with the infirmity of others, or with our own formerly.

We take comfort in the relative deprivation of status that we inflict upon others. This would lead us to believe that there is an element of status anxiety involved in ethnic jokes—both in the kinds told about others and the kinds ethnic groups tell about themselves.

This explains the significance of a figure like Archie Bunker, the supposedly "lovable bigot." He is full of ethnic prejudices and bigotry, but because he is dumb and a clown figure (he makes all kinds of malapropisms and logical errors), we don't seem to take his bigotry seriously and can find him funny, and in some way endearing. The reason some people reject ethnic jokes is because the aggression in them is too overt; when that happens, and the aggressive content is not adequately masked, the joke falls flat and our superego, no longer tricked, comes into action and pricks our conscience.

With Archie Bunker we get a double payoff, so to speak. We are able to enjoy the ethnic humor, in one sense, and condemn it in another. And by making Archie Bunker ridiculous (or by telling infantile Polish and other ethnic joke-riddles) we minimize the aggressive aspect of this humor. It is as if to say, "But don't take this seriously, please!"—which happens to be the truth. The point is that we can get the forbidden pleasure of aggression against ethnic groups and the pleasure of aggression against the aggressor, and so get twice as much pleasure for our money—or time spent—and we come out smelling like the proverbial rose. Or do we?

One of the most controversial aspects of the program involves the effects of *All in the Family* upon the American public. The producer of the program argues that it pokes fun at bigotry and brings it out into the open, where it can be observed and condemned. Those who attack the program say that having Archie a lovable bigot actually serves to reinforce prejudice and condone bigotry. Until recently the social scientists had not become involved with the argument, but a recent issue of the *Journal of Communication* carried a compelling article on the matter. Entitled "Archie Bunker's Bigotry: A Study in Selective Perception and Exposure," authors Neil Vidmar and Milton Rokeach reported the results of a survey in America and Canada. Shortly after the program began, CBS made a telephone survey of viewer opinion of the program. This survey reported that most of the viewers perceived the program's satirical intents so its impact would be to reduce prejudice.

Vidmar and Rokeach are not certain such is the case:

There is, however, an alternative hypothesis which might explain why the program was enjoyed by the great majority of viewers. Perhaps prejudiced and unprejudiced persons ascribe different meanings to the intent and outcomes of *All in the Family* episodes: nonprejudiced viewers and minority group viewers may perceive and enjoy the show as satire, whereas prejudiced viewers may perceive and enjoy the show as episodes "telling it like it is." Such a hypothesis seems to be supported by the fact that some viewers write letters (to newspaper editors, to CBS officials, and to people associated with the program) which applaud Archie for his racist viewpoint, while others applaud the show for effectively making fun of bigotry.

Different people view the program in different ways; both bigots and nonbigots see the show as supporting their particular points of view. As a result of an empirical survey the authors concluded, finally, that the program is harmful:

On balance the study seems to support more the critics who have argued that *All in the Family* has harmful effects. Some serious questions have been raised by these critics. Both Hobson and Slawson have asserted that by making Archie a "lovable bigot" the program encourages bigots to excuse and rationalize their own prejudices. Sanders has charged that "already there is evidence that impressionistic white children have picked up and are using, many of the old racial slurs which Archie has resurrected, popularized and made 'acceptable' all over again." Our empirical research suggests that at the very least those charges have a valid psychological base.

It is not hard to agree with the authors if you know anything about satire, for large numbers of people are unable to recognize that someting is being satirized. Young children don't see the satirical intent of *Batman*, and unsophisticated sensibilities cannot recognize the satire in *All in the Family*. Whatever the case, though, it is obvious that large numbers of people are deriving pleasure (of varying sorts) from the program.

It is interesting to compare *All in the Family* with the program which it is modelled upon, *Till Death Us Do Part*. This program was originated in England in 1966, by the British Broadcasting Corporation, and it has not only spawned *All in the Family* in America, but a legion of similar programs in other countries.

There are similarities between the two programs but also considerable differences.

Till Death Us Do Part has been the most popular English television comedy of the past few years—and certainly one of the most popular television programs of this period. It is now in its fourth series and still going strong, though some of the critics have suggested that it may have outlived its usefulness and no longer is as funny or remarkable as it once was. I can't judge the merits of these criticisms because I have not seen the other three series, but even my limited viewing of the most recent episodes is enough for me to grasp that it is a remarkable program.

What we find is a genuine *grotesque*, Alf Garnett, who fights endlessly with his wife, another grotesque (but a much more human-ized one than Alf), his daughter and son-in-law, and all the forces of liberalism in England—such as the Labour Party, his pet hate.

The title of the show is most ambivalent. It has something to do with the marriage contract and with marriage conflict. There is a little world of people who share a small, run-down apartment and who fight to the death, a blood feud between members of the same family who enjoy it all, who can't avoid the cutting remark or the practical joke, who love and hate each other a great deal.

Alf Garnett is, like Archie Bunker, "a working-class authoritarian." He is a bigot, a racist who has contempt for Jews, Negroes, colored people, and members of the Labour Party, whom he calls "bloody wogs." He, himself, is a study in contradiction—a working-class Troy, who can't understand what the members of the Conservative Party are talking about, but whose habits of deference carry him on. He digs the fancy types who would find him absolutely loathsome, and he wears a homburg to complement his cheap National Health Service glasses.

He is a grotesque, whose grotesquery mirrors the distortions in the society in which he finds himself. He fascinates, perhaps because he forces us, in some strange way, to see ourselves. Monsters like Alf, full of rage and fury, reflect all of us—how we would like to be able to insult people, to "vent our spleen" at people we don't like, to be irrational and luxuriate in malicious and absurd hatred. Alf is pure feeling in a country full of up-tight people with monstrous superegos, who cannot let themselves go and express their feelings, whether generous or not. There is a great deal of tension in the air in England over the matter of aggression (which explains why darts and the hunt are so popular), and in this carefully preserved sea of nervous tranquility old Alf Garnett is thrashing about, screaming bloody murder, a brilliant antihero who has the luxury of being able to hate—and, as a corollary, being able to feel. *In a country full of repressed hysterics, Alf Garnett is the ego-ideal of millions.*

They don't know this, of course. And he pays a price—he is a fool, nobody takes him seriously, people laugh at him. Actually he provides a number of gratifications for his followers. As I suggested above, he speaks for their secret souls, which would like to be free to admit their hatred (at times, at least) of people. But we get a double payoff from him, as well as Archie. In addition to getting, vicariously, the forbidden pleasure of aggression against ethnic groups and political parties we don't like through Alf, we then get the added pleasure of feeling legitimate aggression against Alf, the aggressor. He gives us good value for money.

What, we may ask, is the source of Alf's energy? What fuels his rage? I can only offer a guess, but I sense it is the result of frustration, the result of his being a petty and powerless figure, locked like his confrere into a dead-end job with no sense of the future. It is a consequence of *stasis*—there is no tomorrow for Alf in the sense that tomorrow will be no different from today. He is perfectly secure within the confines of his little world, which helps explain why he is so open and obvious. He is at the bottom of the totem pole and doesn't have to worry about offending anyone and losing face.

And yet, underneath the rage, underneath the hate lavished on Wogs and the Labour Party and the whole intellectual elite of liberal or radical persuasion, there is a diffuse sense of terror in old Alf. He is stuck in his own Hell (which, as Sartre said, is "other people"), and he cannot justify his life, or English politics, except by finding scapegoats, sacrificial victims who have invaded the paradise that was England and prevented the policies of the Conservative Party from working. (The tragedy of the working people in America is that too many of them hate and not enough of them vote. Alf, at least, I suspect is not caught in that bind.)

Alan Coren of *The Times* has recognized this static quality in the show and criticized it:

> Nothing happens. The great creation remains locked in his East End parlour, loggerheaded with his monster family, and waits for some news to break upon which his now familiar spleen can be predictably vented.

He concludes that "Alf has become a bore," and suggests that Johnny Speight, who writes the show, "must make him do, not just let him be." I would not agree, for the genius of the fool is in being and not doing. The creation of contrived situations would diminish and dilute Alf's personality. Situation comedy rests on the triumph of situation over individuality and personality; anyone, placed in certain situations, becomes comic. A great character like Alf must *be* comic and not be made comic.

The humor in the program is essentially verbal and is based on insults, revelation of ignorance, facetiousness, sarcasm, and repartee. Dandy Nichols, who plays the wife (and who is a much stronger figure than her American counterpart) is a superb actress and is a perfect foil for Alf. She is a master of the disdainful glance and the nasty repartee. In one program which was based on a practical joke—the idea that his wife had not made his evening meal—there was the following conversation. Alf complained about not liking cheese sandwiches.

ALF: "I'm not a bloody mouse!"
WIFE: "I wish you were . . . I'd set a trap for you."

There was also a scene in which Alf tried to get a word in edgewise some six or eight times, but each time he said "Look . . ." his wife interrupted him and rambled on.

The acting is generally quite superb and it helps to carry the program. It also is very topical and manages to focus upon some critical event in the political scene each week as it rolls along. Oil, the three-day week, for example, are all grist for its militancy. We cannot be sure that the best lack all conviction, but in Alf Garnett, we can have good reason to suspect that the worst are full of passionate intensity.

It is obvious that *All in the Family* is much softer and weaker than *Till Death Us Do Part*. It is much more sanitized, and Archie, while a bigot, is shown as a much more easygoing and friendly figure. All of the characters in the American version are diluted, and in this respect they mirror something of considerable consequence.

In an egalitarian country like America, there is an immense and subtle pressure exerted upon people to conform, to be ordinary, to be "nice guys," and in consequence we find that the model American personality lacks what might be called definition. The parameters are very narrow, and anyone who dares to develop a strong personality and identity risks being considered deviant, strange, and un-American, somehow. For to be an American is to be absorbed in the great anonymity of this country, to be like everyone else, to have an anonymous personality. Archie (*arch* is defined in the dictionary as "extreme, most fully embodying the qualities of his or its kind"; *bunker*, "full of bunk, nonsense") does not really have an individuated self. He is merely a strange combination of "nice-guy and bigot," but though he is a study in contradiction in qualities, there is nothing much else there. He is a personification of an abstraction—the law of contradiction.

Somebody has said that men adopt ideologies to shield themselves from the painful fact that their lives are minor events in the ongoing universe. But to grasp an ideology requires a certain kind of consciousness, and this seems to be beyond Archie Bunker's capacity. He is a pipsqueak with petty hatreds and ignorant prejudices. He is the American common man.

VI. Behind The Scenes

Seven Days with "All in the Family": Case Study of the Taped TV Drama

James E. Lynch
Journal of Broadcasting   Summer 1973

It began Wednesday, August 9, 1972, in the offices of Tandem Productions on the second floor of CBS Television City in Hollywood. The time was 6:00 p.m. and in 30 minutes John Rich, producer of "All in the Family" was scheduled to begin trial editing of a "Family" episode from the previous week.

Editing did not begin on schedule. Rich was conferring with writers about a future show; the CBS-TV production supervisor interrupted with a last-minute studio facilities change; and the director of the current week's episode (which had begun dry rehearsals that morning) wanted Rich's advice in handling a knotty staging problem. It was 7:00 p.m. before we left the Tandem Production office.

One of the final steps in the production process is trial editing. Here seven hours of camera blocking, two show tapings and a so-called "pickup" period move toward a finished 24-minute program. To assist in the process, Tandem Productions employs the services of Hal Collins, a former Milton Berle comedy writer turned videotape editor, who has his studio and living quarters above a garage in a modest neighborhood near CBS Television City. The setup has a "Rube Goldberg" look with three Sony ½-inch tape recorders, four television monitors, a maze of buttons, and the speed and precision of Collins. Sony designed and built the complex to Collins's specifications. According to Rich, it is the most efficient and effective means of trial editing available.

There was a problem this particular evening. At the outset, it was found that the dress and air tapes dubbed from CBS machines had audio distortion. Apparently an earlier feed into the Sony machine had been patched incorrectly. A call to the CBS editing center arranged an immediate redubbing. Collins's assistant took a ½-inch Sony recorder back to CBS while Rich, Collins, and associate director Bob LaHendro tried to work with the audio distorted tapes. Several headaches later, they decided to wait for new tapes before continuing the editing process.

Redubbed tapes arrived at 8:15 p.m. and editing began again. Using an air show as master, the tape was run from the top. LaHendro worked from a script, Rich relied on memory, and Collins operated the machines. When a trouble spot arrived, the tape was stopped and played back. Precise starting and ending points for the sequence were noted, using a time counter (super-imposed across the monitor picture) that showed hour, minute, second, and frame.[1] The same sequence in the dress tape was switched on the line monitor and, if a pickup (repeat of a scene after dress and air) was taped, it too was shown so the director could choose between the two. Once a decision was made, beginning and ending times of the proposed edit were listed on a master editing script. The air tape was then rolled again until another problem appeared. Sequences were often run a number of times on all three tapes until agreement was reached on the best version. Rich indicated that in final electronic editing, a ½-hour episode averages 50 to 60 edits.[2] So many things can go wrong in a taping—a line missed or read wrong, one actor blocking another, poor pacing in a scene, an arm or partial head appearing in a shot that calls for a clean view of another actor, etc. Finding the trouble spot is easy. Difficulty lies in replacing the faulty shot or sequence with a better one from either dress or pickup so that action flows smoothly. For instance, a hand might be raised halfway in an air tape and shoulder high in the dress. The trick is to find a precise point when the position of the arm is similar in both tapes. This involves running tapes back and forth several times until a trial edit can be made. One such edit could take 10 or 15 minutes.

Trial editing is an important preliminary step to electronic editing at CBS. The flexibility of machinery in Hal Collins's apartment-studio makes it possible for a director to lay out a concise videotape editing blueprint. Through instant switching and matching, he can select the best moments from three different tapes and set precise timings for editing on Thursday. The associate director, using a marked script that includes the proposed edits, then works closely with CBS editor Marco Zappia to prepare a final air tape.

Rich recalled that early in the 1971-1972 season he, as director, had to fight technical hurdles to impose a cinematic, composite tape-editing technique at CBS. "I was introduced to the videotape room," Rich said, "where I thought I would be able to repair anything that had gone wrong during the live performances. I was told that the equipment was not capable of doing what I wanted. For example, you couldn't stop frame to get an exact cut. The process seemed to be more suited to the needs of variety or musical shows than to the requirements of finely tuned comedy that depended so heavily on words. With my neurotic drive not to settle for anything but the best," he added, "I challenged the fine editors, Marco Zappia and Jim Steiner, to prove that they and the machines couldn't do it. They not only accepted the challenge, they proved they could do more than I had expected and soon we were accomplishing extremely fine edits—within words, sometimes—and pull-ups and double edits."[3]

When editing is completed, the tape is viewed by both producer and executive producer. They may accept the final cut or decide to make further changes. The associate director then smoothes out sound levels and "sweetens" applause, laughter, and sound effects.[4] Total editing time runs 12 to 15 hours (4 to 5 hours of trial editing; 6 to 7 hours of electronic editing at CBS; and 2 to 3 hours for "sweetening"). The operation is slow, demanding, precise, and frustrating. But, the results reflect a clean, smooth production without destroying the feeling that it is all happening live at that moment.

The entire production process for an episode of "All in the Family" takes seven days, but editing of one show on the sixth and seventh days overlaps the first two days of dry rehearsals for another. A regular weekly rehearsal and tape schedule follows this pattern:

Wednesday   Reh. Hall—C-2

Read and discuss script for next week	10:30 a.m.— 3:00 p.m.
Read and discuss script for this week	11:00 a.m.— 3:00 p.m.
Lunch (served in rehearsal hall)	1:00 p.m.— 2:00 p.m.
Begin rough staging	3:00 p.m.— 6:30 p.m.
Director to editing (last week's show)	6:30 p.m.

Thursday	Reh. Hall—C-2
Continue staging	9:00 a.m.— 1:00 p.m.
Lunch	1:00 p.m.— 2:00 p.m.
Continue staging	2:00 p.m.— 7:00 p.m.

Friday	Reh. Hall—C-2
Rehearse w/props	8:30 a.m.— 1:00 p.m.
Lunch	1:00 p.m.— 2:00 p.m.
Rehearse	2:00 p.m.— 3:30 p.m.
Line Rehearsal	3:30 p.m.— 4:30 p.m.
Run thru	4:30 p.m.— 5:30 p.m.
Notes w/cast	5:30 p.m.

Monday	Studio #31
Dry block in set w/all props	9:30 a.m.— 11:00 a.m.
Engineering set-up (E.S.U.)	10:00 a.m.— 11:00 a.m.
FAX rehearsal (camera blocking)	11:00 a.m.— 1:00 p.m.
Lunch	1:00 p.m.— 2:00 p.m.
FAX rehearsal (camera blocking)	2:00 p.m.— 4:30 p.m.
Run thru w/complete wardrobe	4:30 p.m.— 5:00 p.m.
Dismiss crew. Director notes w/cast	5:00 p.m.

Tuesday	Studio #31
Director notes with cast	1:00 p.m.— 2:00 p.m.
Engineering set-up (E.S.U.)	1:30 p.m.— 2:30 p.m.
FAX rehearsal (continue camera blocking)	2:30 p.m.— 4:30 p.m.
Break for cast notes, make up and wardrobe	4:30 p.m.— 5:30 p.m.
2 VTR/FAX (Dress) w/audience	5:30 p.m.— 6:30 p.m.
Meal break. Notes to actors	6:30 p.m.— 7:30 p.m.
Video tape check in	7:30 p.m.— 8:00 p.m.
2 VTR/FAX (Air) w/audience	8:00 p.m.— 9:00 p.m.
Pick ups	9:00 p.m.— 10:30 p.m.

August 9 to 15, however, was far from a regular week. To begin with, Carroll O'Connor (Archie Bunker) called Rich's home early on Thursday, August 10, to say that he was ill and could not make the second day of dry rehearsals. A question immediately arose: Did O'Connor have a one-day virus or would it be necessary to cancel the entire production for that week? Rich decided to cut Thursday, add Saturday, and await further word from O'Connor. The director and remaining actors in the cast were notified of the schedule change.

At this point it should be said that production process is somewhat different from program process. If one considers the time it takes to create an idea, develop it into script form, and carry the show through to a finished 24-minutes tape ready for airing on Saturday night over CBS-TV,[5] the period is much longer than seven days. In the case of "All in the Family," program process can be two to three weeks or two to three months, depending on the time needed to develop a shooting script. During the 1972-1973 year, program ideas for the most part were solicited from outside writers. A one-page proposal is sufficient for the production group (Norman Lear, John Rich, and three staff writers) to decide if the idea has promise. Many are thrown out because they either have been done before or fail to fit requirements of the show. Some are just bad ideas that could not be used on any television series. If a proposal has merit, the writer is called in for a conference and Tandem Productions is committed to story credit and a minimum fee of $508. Sometimes a writer is dropped right there and another idea is considered; or he may be called a second time and asked to develop a screenplay. Once that is done, the writer must be given screen credit and a fee ranging from $2,000 to $3,500 (depending on the writer's reputation). Rarely, if ever, does Tandem go with a script from an outside writer, as submitted. Staff writers, in consultation with Norman Lear and Rich, generally rewrite the material a number of times before it is ready for the seven-day production process. And, even during the process, extensive changes are made by the producer, director, and executive producer right up to the final taping at 8:00 p.m. on Tuesday night.

Apparently, the key to a successful "All in the Family" script is executive producer Norman Lear, who spurs writers, producer, and director to come up with just the right words to fit both situation and characters in the program. It is he who draws on long writing experience and intimate knowledge of Archie, his family, and their reactions to forces outside the Bunker household. "Norman is a superlative writer with a sensitive ear for realistic dialogue," says Rich. "He remains the difference between a good script and an excellent one."

The first three days in the production process are called the "discovery" period, so named to designate a time when actors and director are exploring a script for its full potential. In the opening session on Wednesday, two scripts are read and discussed (the current week and the next). Regular cast members, principal supporting actors, director, and production assistant sit around a table and thrash out what will or will not play. There is even discussion as to whether or not an entire script will play.

A rough timing is taken early in the discussion, and then the script is read line by line until someone questions or challenges. The director tries to keep an open mind on any interpretation of line or situation. Subtly, sometimes aggressively, he forces actors to think, contribute and defend.

"Discovery" occupies all of the first day until around 4:00 p.m., when staging begins. The director has no preconceived ideas about blocking; he lets it come out bit by bit. Actors are kept moving but are urged to remain open as possible in order to facilitate better shooting patterns for all cameras.

Staging continues on Thursday and Friday (in the current episode, it was Friday and Saturday because of O'Connor's illness on Thursday) in much the same way with a step-by-step process, whereby each scene is carefully blocked and then rerun for consolidation. Changes come about all three days; nothing is permanently set; no pressure is put on actors to learn lines. Around 3:30 p.m. on the third day, there is a line rehearsal to straighten out all changes up to that point. Finally, a run-through of the entire show is scheduled to consolidate movement and dialogue. The associate director, stage manager, props, lighting, writers and network people are brought in to watch. It is the first time anyone other than actors, director and production assistant is permitted in the rehearsal hall. This is a policy laid down by John Rich during the 1971-1972 season. "The reasons are simple," he says, "actors must be given a chance to fail, fumble, and discover in these early rehearsals without press, relatives, agents or other visitors looking on. Also, there is a tendency to be 'on' for an audience and to assume the role of 'star.' Out of this comes tension, loss of concentration, and failure to explore every facet of the script material. Besides, in the first two days (our most intense 'discovery' period) actors are not ready to give a performance for anyone."

After the run-through on the third day, there is a session with cast members to discuss notes taken by the director. Actors are released about 6:30 p.m. The associate director finishes marking his script so that it coincides with the director's copy; staging, props, costume, and lighting people confer with the director in preparation for camera blocking in Studio 31 Monday morning. If all has gone well to this point, two days of systematic camera rehearsal on Monday and Tuesday should lead to successful tapings Tuesday night.

This particular episode, however, did not follow the regular production process schedule. Carroll O'Connor was ill at rehearsal on Wednesday, August 9, confined to bed on Thursday, August 10, and back in rehearsal Friday, August 11. A lost day on Thursday meant that final staging and run-through would extend through Saturday. The director was at a disadvantage. He was working with a cast, whose principal performer was sub-par physically; the tempo of the production was disturbed by a delay midway in the dry rehearsal period; and most importantly, the preparation time between the end of dry rehearsals and the start of camera blocking was sliced in half.

Action now moved to Studio 31 in CBS Television City. Dry blocking in the set with all properties began at 9:00 a.m. on Monday, August 14. Actors including the regulars, Archie, Edith, Mike, and Gloria, and those performing supporting roles were joined by the director and production assistant. Cast members were working in the set for the first time (all dry rehearsals previous to that were in a barren rehearsal hall with folding chairs simulating furniture, props and entrances/exits). It was necessary to run the action and accustom actors to playing positions, movement, and use of props within the actual set area. It was also a time for the director to check out his preplanned shots, in preparation for camera blocking.

At 10:00 a.m. technical personnel began their engineering set up while dry blocking continued in the set area. Cameras were aligned, microphones attached to booms, intercommunication lines between control room and studio floor tested. In all, 14 technicians were involved—a technical director (T.D.), 4 cameramen, 2 camera cable pullers, 2 audio boom operators, 2 boom pushers, an audio man, a sound effects person, and a video control operator.

In the control room associate director Bob LaHendro was giving shots to the four cameramen. No numbering system was used; he merely described the shots in sequence and designated cameras. Cameramen, in turn, drew up their own shot sheets. Terminology was brief and to the point. "2 is Archie, 4 is Edith, 1 is a cross 2-shot, 2 gets Archie and picture, 2 loosen Archie and picture, 1 is a wide shot, etc." When all shots in Act One (first 12 minutes of the script) were set, the associate director added, "Stay loose, we may find that some of the shots do not work. I'll see you later for Act Two."

Camera blocking got underway at 11:15 a.m. The director was delayed on the studio floor ironing out last-minute problems with the cast. Once in the control room, a slow, tedious, but necessary process begins. The director, flanked by a technical director, associate director, and production assistant, proceeds in stop-and-go fashion, to set each shot as action progresses on the floor. Two further elements are necessary—effective communication from the control room to the floor, and control of blocking by the director. Under the CBS associate director system, director and associate director have lines to cameramen and stage manager; technical director and audio can talk to cameramen and microphone boom operators. In the early stages of blocking, it is imperative that the director be in contact with cameramen to set and adjust shots while an associate director releases cameras and moves them to their next shots. Once composition is decided, the associate director takes over more and more, setting shots, moving cameras and leaving the way clear for a director to view shots as they are set and to call them "on the air." The technical director, with a marked script indicating what camera (1, 2, 3, or 4) is taken when, responds to an arm motion or a click of the fingers by the director and electronically switches a camera on the line. It is team effort all the way.

Camera blocking, like the staging of actor movement in dry rehearsals, follows an established pattern. The script is broken down into two acts (24 minutes of playing time). On the first day (Monday) an attempt is made to set all shots in Act One; rerun the act without stopping to consolidate; return to the shot-setting process for Act Two; rerun the act; and end the day with a complete run-through of the show. Most of Tuesday is spent smoothing out rough spots from the day before. If time permits, another run-through of the entire episode is scheduled prior to a dress tape (which is done between 5:30 and 6:30 p.m.). Following a dinner break, cast and technical crew return for an air tape at 8:00 p.m. Both performances are given before live audiences. The final step in camera blocking are the pickups or retaping of any scenes that had errors in both the dress and air tapes.

The director managed to set all his shots and get a full run-through of the show on Monday, but he was not satisfied with either the progress of the actors or the visual interpretation of the show. Most troubles centered around three complicated sequences. The story line of the episode involved a racial encounter between Archie and his black neighbor, Lionel. Archie's niece, Linda, is visiting the Bunkers, she dates Lionel, and at a party a picture is taken showing them sitting on a sofa with Lionel's arm around Linda. While Archie is out of the house, Lionel comes to pick up Linda for another date and gives her the picture. She leaves it with Edith who absentmindedly places it on the table next to Archie's chair. Archie returns and after a series of attempts by Edith to hide the picture, he discovers it and explodes. In a fast-paced second act Archie confronts Henry Jefferson (Lionel's uncle) and Lionel himself with the Linda-Lionel situation. The payoff comes when Archie tries to set Lionel straight about "whites and coloreds." Lionel rebels and tells Archie to "put a lid on it." Linda sides with Lionel and turns against her uncle. In the end, Archie is squelched.

The problem scenes were the Edith-Archie sequence toward the end of Act One when the picture is hidden by Edith and finally discovered by Archie; an Archie-Lionel conversation in the Bunker kitchen; and a verbal battle between Archie and Lionel's uncle, Henry Jefferson. All were fast-moving in dialogue and/or action, and each relied heavily on perfect coordination between camera and actor. There was not enough time that first day to make the scenes run smoothly.

After the rehearsal on Monday, the director and producer met to discuss the progress of the show. A final run-through had been spotty, and the question arose as to whether there was enough time to get the episode in shape for dress and air tapings Tuesday night. It was also observed that the director had been ill during most of the rehearsal period on Monday. With these limiting factors in mind and knowing schedule and budget limitations did not permit a delay or postponement, the director asked if it was possible for Rich (the producer) to take over the production and carry it through the final taping. Rich had directed all 37 episodes of "All in the Family" in the 1971-1972 season. He was familiar with the script, had sat in on some of the dry rehearsals, and was present during parts of camera blocking on Monday. An agreement was reached. Rich would join the show Tuesday and continue camera blocking through the air tape and pickup period.

The first step in the changeover process was script preparation. Rich and the associate director carefully reviewed previous shot patterns and agreed on several changes that might smooth out troubled spots in both acts. Newly marked scripts incorporating Monday's work and the suggested changes were prepared Monday night and early Tuesday morning.

Just before noon on Tuesday, Rich and the director met with members of the cast. They explained the directing change, asked for cooperation, and moved on to the control room. Bob LaHendro, associate director, notified technical personnel and gave shot changes to the four cameramen. Rich arrived shortly afterward to begin camera blocking. Instead of going immediately to the sequences that needed reworking, Rich elected to start from the top of the script, so that he might see the production as a whole. Shots were set, action began, actors were stopped, further shots were set and action continued. It was stop and go all through Act One until 2:30 p.m. Rich challenged cameramen to get just the right shot, urged actors to try difficult moves one more time, and listened to suggestions made by the associate director. His concentration was intense. Even actors "horsing around" in the set failed to distrub him. Despite time limitations, Rich had precious minutes to repeat sequences with bothersome camera moves. His object was smoothness, but he also wanted camermen to feel secure. In the case of actors, he never hesitated to change staging or dialogue to better facilitate camera shots. However, cast members were never forced to do anything that was uncomfortable for them.

Much time was spent blocking action and shots around a key sequence at the end of Act One when the picture of Lionel and Linda is first hidden from Archie's view, and then discovered by him. Visually we must see the picture when Archie doesn't and worry with Edith as she desperately tries to keep him from seeing it. All steps along the way have to be carefully set—a shot showing the picture in the foreground on a table next to Archie's chair, with Archie talking on the telephone in the background; attempts by Edith to hide the picture; and a closeup on Archie's face when he finally sees the picture. After discovery Archie was supposed to jump up, come around the chair and grab the picture. He suggested that Archie get up, move around the chair, stalk the picture like you would a tiger and then pounce on it. Rich liked what he saw and incorporated the change. Act One was completed.

After a short break, camera blocking of Act Two began. Everything went smoothly until the entrance of Henry Jefferson, Lionel's uncle. The problem was to cover Archie's move to the door, his exchange with Jefferson, the move by both of them back into the room, and a quick thrust of photos by Archie and Jefferson as they shout, "I want to know what youse people are gonna do about this!" Movement and dialogue were fast paced and cameras had to adjust quickly to cover the action. It took two or three run-throughs to perfect the sequence.

At 3:10 p.m. (with 10 more script pages to go) an unplanned event stopped the rehearsal completely. CBS brass had decided to visit the "All in the Family" set. Arriving in a mini-truck were programming executives, John Schneider, Bob Wood, and Perry Lafferty with the new CBS president, Arthur Taylor. Taylor was introduced to actors and production staff. Public relations was served, but a precious 15 minutes of camera rehearsal got lost in the process.

It was back to the script and two more critical spots in the show. One was the climatic scene in the kitchen with Archie and Lionel, after Lionel brings Linda home from the dance; the other involved a "crowded" sequence at the end of the episode. Each presented a difficult camera problem. In the kitchen, cameras 1 and 2 had to be positioned so as to provide clear over-the-shoulder or cross shots of Archie and Lionel as they have their heart-to-heart talk about race relations. Archie reminds Lionel that "the whites ought to stay with the whites, and the coloreds ought to stay with the colareds." Lionel takes it all in, rises, and stings Archie with, "We've been friends and we can go on being friends, but I don't want to hear any more of that race jive anymore . . . in other words . . . put a lid on it, Archie!" The shot problem was cleared up by breaking camera 1 from the main set to the kitchen early enough and then quickly moving camera 2 into place. More importantly, Rich also used the time to talk with Archie and Lionel about the scene and why it was not playing right. The discussion paid dividends in both dress and air tapes. Each time, Lionel's final line to Archie got applause from the studio audience.

The "crowded" exit scene with Archie, Jefferson, Linda, Lionel, and Edith presented a different problem. Staging was such that actors were covering each other and not allowing enough space for good reaction closeups. Slight repositioning of cameras and actors did the trick, but it was 4:15 p.m. before the entire show was completed. Ten minutes later, the tag scene after the final commercial and before the credits, was done. No time remained for a run through before the dress tape, scheduled at 5:45. Actors broke for dinner and cameramen came to the control room for shot changes made during the last two hours of rehearsal. There was also an attempt to rearrange the technical crew's schedule to include a dress tape, dinner break, air tape and one and a half hours of "pick-up" time.

At 5:30 Rich was back in the control room checking last-minute shots with the associate director and looking over notes taken by the production assistant. A full studio audience had been admitted for the dress tape. Technicians were beginning to check out cameras, microphones, and intercom. The audio man, video control operator, technical director and associate director were in place. While cameramen were getting their final briefing from the associate director, Rich moved out to join executive producer Norman Lear for the audience warmup. Actors were introduced to the audience by Lear and a question-answer period was in progress. By 6:00 p.m. the warmup was finished, and Rich returned to the control room. Suddenly, it was quiet. The associate director gave a "standby" and Rich said, "Up on 2."

The dress ended at 6:30. It was rocky in spots but received a good audience reaction. There were several missed shots, a dropped line or two, and some faulty moves by the actors. Rich was not too pleased but the show played well. Cutting was precise and it appeared to be in rhythm with the action. Under pressure, both actors and technical crew had performed well.

The task, however, was not yet completed. As the audience filed out of the studio, a decision was made to continue on, clean up rough spots in the dress, break for one hour at 7:30, and be ready for an air tape around 8:45. Two scenes were especially bothersome. One involved the movement of Mike (Rob Reiner) at the beginning of Act Two. During the dress he was seen in the background of camera shots covering an Archie-Edith-Gloria scene. The sequence was run several times until an exact spot was found for Mike. A position was marked by the stage manager. Another stumbling block occurred midway in Act One when Linda and Lionel leave for the dance. Linda had thrown off the timing of a shot sequence by starting down the stairs late and arriving at the wrong place. Rich, sensing the pressure under which a young, inexperienced actress was working, reran the scene until Linda's confidence returned. She was letter-perfect in the air tape. Polishing continued until 7:20 but not before an exit by Jefferson and an entrance by Linda late in Act Two were cleared up. Again, it was a matter of timing. Rich changed one line and suggested that Jefferson start his move earlier. A run-through smoothed out the action.

Norman Lear, who had watched the dress from the control room, joined Rich for a conference with the actors. The purpose here was to make last-minute line changes conditioned by audience reaction to the dress and to further discuss overall pacing of the show. Lear left at 8:30 to begin an audience warmup for the air tape (different audiences are admitted for dress and tape); Rich joined him a few minutes later. Back in the control room there was a final meeting of cameramen with the associate director to iron out shot difficulties in Act Two.

The air tape was better technically but actors were down in their performances, especially in Act One. By page 12 there were seven obvious pickups. Rich remarked to the production assistant, "We should re-do all of Act One. It will help in editing tomorrow night."

As soon as the air audience left, cast and crew moved into the "pickup" period where scenes and parts of scenes were redone to correct minor errors in dialogue, actor movement, and camera shots. One factor that helped actors improve their performances in the pickup period was the immediate tape playback capability in the studio. The director would call for a replay of a scene in the dress or air tape, show the actor his mistake, and then retape the scene.

At 11:30 p.m. studio work was completed. Actors and crew were released. It was an end to a 15-hour day. "The show can be a good one," Rich said, "with the material we have to work with in editing. There were some nice moments, like the final discovery of the picture by Archie, Lionel's big scene in the kitchen, and that last exit." Trial editing would begin tomorrow night at 6:00 p.m. in Hal Collins's studio above the garage, followed by electronic editing and "sweetening" at CBS on Thursday.

Footnotes

1. Not only does the counter measure length of segments to be cut in the air tape, it also provides exact timings on dress and pickup tapes for the beginning and ending of portions to be inserted into the master tape.
2. "Award Winner: John Rich," *Action* (Directors Guild of America), May-June, 1972, p. 15.
3. Ibid.

4. No canned laughter, applause, or sound are added to the show. "Sweetening" means adjusting levels of audience reaction taken from soundtracks on both dress and air tapes.
5. There are 24 minutes of program and 5 minutes of commercials, open and close, and credits.

VII. The "Real" Archie Bunker

What the
Neighbors Think

Newsweek   November 29, 1971

What will the neighbors think? That is a question that perennially haunts Archie Bunker. Clearly, Archie and his family loom a lot larger than life, but the show's creators have taken considerable pains to reproduce a physical and social setting that evokes hundreds of thousands of American homes. To find out what people who might indeed be Archie Bunker's neighbors think about him—and how they react to the show—*Newsweek* sent reporter Ann Ray Martin to the Richmond Hill section in New York City's middle-class Borough of Queens. Her report:

Driving past the rows of attached houses in Richmond Hill, an outsider almost expects to hear the strains of "Those Were the Days" wafting out of every living-room window on the block. The neighborhood, like the setting for "All in the Family," is predominantly German, Irish and Italian. With its small, fenced-in front yard and brick stoop, the home of Joseph and Catherine Eccles at 94-27 115th Street is a warmer, more attractive replica of the Bunker homestead, right down to the lace-covered table and the paternal armchair that—like Archie's—is off limits to everyone but 55-year-old Joseph Eccles.

The Eccles family has its reservations about some of Archie's attitudes. "I don't like the way he talks to his wife," says Eccles. "And there are other things too. Let's take the way he goes after the colored. Now, I'm conservative on most things, but I'm liberal about that. I'd be glad to work alongside them or live alongside them, and I would vote for a colored." But by and large, Archie Bunker fits right in with the Eccles family. "I think he's pretty accurate for the most part," says Eccles. "He typifies the way we think. We'd discuss things on a higher level but, yes, Archie worries and talks about the same things we do."

As with many members of "All in the Family's" audience, the subject of race dies hard in the Eccles house. Volunteers 9-year-old Edward: "There are eleven colored children in the neighborhood—I just counted in my head." "That'll do, Edward," cautions his father. "You'll speak when spoken to." Like Archie, Joseph Eccles is one father who knows best—and isn't afraid to say so. "This is *not* a democratic household," declares Eccles. "When the final say is in, *I* get my way."

The head of the family, an assistant service and maintenance manager for a large company, sympathizes with Archie in other ways. "I do agree with Archie about the Vietnam war," he says. "I think we should have an honorable conclusion to it. And I'm with him on China; I sure wouldn't mind reading that the Red Chinese had been kicked out of the U.N." The older Eccles son, 20-year-old Joseph Jr., a student at Queens College, has something in common with Archie's son-in-law, Mike. "Sometimes when Dad and I argue," he says, "I think Dad is like Archie." And although Kitty Eccles, 49, would never stand still for being called a dingbat, she does see something of herself in Edith Bunker. "I don't iden-tify with Edith, no, but I sympathize with her," she explains. "Like Edith," adds Joseph Jr., "Mom is the mediator between Dad and me, or Dad and my sisters Maureen and Cathy."

All the members of the family agree that the character of Archie Bunker is deliberately overdrawn. "I think Archie is an exaggeration; comedy *has* to be exaggerated," says Mrs. Eccles. But the family also thinks that the show does a lot of good. "I firmly believe that this show, 'All in the Family,' can help people live with each other," says Joseph Sr. "We need to be able to look at things with more humor." And after sitting through another chapter of "All in the Family" on the evening I visited them, young Joseph noted: "Tonight Archie used the word 'Mick.' I'm Irish, but that don't bother me. I have Jewish friends who don't get bothered by the words he uses about Jews. My best friends are some Italian guys and a Spanish guy. I call them 'guinea' and 'spic,' and they call me a Mick. We can get away with it because we're friends."

The Eccleses have been watching "All in the Family" since last spring, enjoying it more every week. "There are so many favorite episodes—we love them all," says Eccles. At the heart of this affinity for Archie is the family's conviction that Archie is blessedly normal. "Nearly every picture or TV show has some glamorous character," says Joseph Eccles. "I think a couple more shows with *real* people is what's needed. I feel Archie does speak for people who have worked hard, tried to live right, to live by the rules. And now society's trying to change the rules. Where does that leave us?"

It's All in This Family, Too

Marshall Frady *Life*   December 13, 1971

On a recent Saturday evening in the Oregon lumber town of Klamath Falls, Louie Leroy Pastega—a bullish 63-year-old neighborhood grocer—sank into his moss-green easy chair and refired his frayed cigar butt. He grunted with anticipation as, on the screen of his color TV set, *All in the Family* commenced the 1971 season with its tinny piano duet between Archie and Edith. It was an anticipation common throughout Klamath Falls, where *All in the Family* has attracted a nearly unanimous viewership. Louie Pastega and his family themselves remarkably reflect in myriad ways the Bunkers.

Clad now in a baggy short-sleeve shirt open at the neck, Louie —member of the Elks, the Moose, the Sons of Italy—listened as Archie Bunker blared at his son-in-law, "Will you vacate that chair, meathead?" Louie emitted a low, groaning, "Heh-heh-heh," while his feet, which were propped atop four cushions on an ottoman, briefly waggled in delight. "See, he's the boss," Louie croaked to his family seated around him. With a gold front tooth glinting in his grin and an extravagant winking of both his small pale eyes, he said, "The boss—like me, huh?" Louie lifted an empty candy tin from a bookshelf beside him and, removing his cigar, delivered into the tin a neat quick spurt, then twitched his cigar back in his mouth.

Somewhat more thoughtful, he allowed to no one in particular, "Yeah, I tell you, I wish there were more Archie Bunkers. You just can't change their ways, that's all. Like me, they're asking me to go along with all these new ways today, but I can't see it. Me and Archie—it's too late for us."

Since its startling premiere on CBS last January, *All in the Family* has enacted with a gutteral authenticity almost all the antagonisms that have closed in on the American household in the late '60s—the generational divide, the new politics, the new moralities. Archie Bunker, head of the TV family, is a lumpish, casually invincible bigot in white socks. He brandishes his well-chewed stogie like a stumpy conjuring wand of inexhaustible malarkey as he dispenses such insults as "There's one thing Archie Bunker ain't ever gonna do, and that's break bread with any jungle bunnies." Archie's wife, Edith, now and then allows herself such timorously rueful assertions as, referring to their black neighbors, "Archie ain't unclenched his teeth since the day they moved in." Edith and the Bunker daughter, Gloria, act more or less as buffers between Archie and his live-in son-in-law, Mike. A graduate student and rampant new-culture advocate, Mike is forever luring Archie into blurtings like "Listen, we didn't come from no monkeys, you atheistic pinko meathead."

Ever since *All in the Family* first appeared, its critics have complained that the show is a coy, mercenary exploitation that counterfeits a truly vicious and grim matter in American society as something cute and trivial. Some of the show's popularity, no doubt, owes to that secret glee of seeing the unmentionable scrawled on a public wall. But there is a very large question about how cheerfully it strikes blacks to see such indecencies as "jungle-bunnies" made amusing at all.

Nevertheless, *All in the Family* usually renders its weekly cosmic melees with a boldness and intimacy which is a quantum leap beyond anything else shown regularly on television. For that reason, apparently, the show has connected in a way no family series ever has. As one lady explained, "It's like going home again, only this time I can laugh." Many of the testimonials are precise and absolute. Louie Pastega's 35-year-old son Richard, himself a new-culture guerrilla, recently observed: "My father *is* Archie Bunker."

At the foot of a weedy windblown yellow slope lightly strewn with flimsy squat dwellings, sits Pastega's Market, a pink cinderblock building guarded by a single Mobil gasoline pump. A kind of neighborhood commissary open "10 to 10, 7 days a week," a musky cache of Honey Bee yams and pickled pork feet and Rainer's beer and Huberd's shoe grease, the store has been in the Pastega family for 48 years. The current Pastegas have their living quarters in the back, up two steps and through a door behind the meat counter.

There, as Louie Pastega was watching the first show of the new season, he reposed in a room that was uncannily like an enlarged mirroring not only of the modest parlor on the screen before him but of the diversities and alienations in the Bunker household itself. Around him, antimacassars daintily webbed the arms of knubby-fabric chairs, and the lamp tables bristled with miniature bowling trophies. Atop the television's bulky cabinet, there was a dense gallery of framed family photographs. Among them was one of the younger son, Robert, dressed in his knife-blade-neat khaki uniform of the Redding, Calif. police; and a portrait of the older son, Richard, when he was a chastely barbered high-school teacher, posing in a black suit and horn-rim glasses, thin and angular as a stork.

Now sitting on a sofa beside his father as they watched the Bunkers, Richard was wearing rumpled, faded jeans, a nimbus of unpent electrically sizzling black hair around his head, peering over his circular wire-frame glasses as he absently plucked and twined his dark scribbling of a beard.

His transfiguration, Richard claims, was brought about by his own students—"They radicalized me"—and some two years ago Richard repudiated the system. He then began a pilgrimage through the outermost landscapes of the new consciousness, a pilgrimage that ended in a blind gulch in San Francisco. "It's over with in the cities," Richard now says. "I realized that if things are really going to happen in this country, they've got to happen back in the little places like Klamath Falls."

He came back home last January and began publishing a home-made underground weekly newspaper called *Breakdown*. With a free circulation of some 5,000 sustained by local advertising, the paper has introduced Klamath Falls to such heady issues as birth control, the iniquity of Vietnamization, forebodings about the pending nuclear test on Amchitka Island, and corporate ecological vandalism. The paper also introduced readers to an ad for contraceptives, which got *Breakdown* tossed out of 12 stores. "The ad was talking about how great lovemaking is," says Richard, "so now I know what this town is really touchy about. Not Vietnam."

If Richard has disconcerted much of Klamath Falls, his return home as a new-left evangel traumatized his family. Louie's wife, Jennie, recalls, "Louie wondered if he could ever go back to the Elks Club again." Not only did Richard scandalize relatives by tutoring a cousin in how to get a conscientious-objector clearance but, with Richard putting his newspaper together in a room behind the store, there began to pass back and forth through the market— before the incredulous gazes of the elder Pastegas at the counter— processionals of barefooted biblical-haired youths in regalia of amulets and Apache headsashes.

"Since I came back," Richard admits, "the only difference between us and the Bunker family is we do a lot more screaming. This is an Italian family, and it just doesn't make any difference how old you are: they still believe in hitting you out--not physically, but every other way, believe me."

Richard's metamorphosis has been particularly trying for Jennie. A finely crafted woman, with sugar-white hair and luminous brown eyes, Jennie confesses she has been suffering lately from random stunning headaches. "My husband and Richard, they just don't understand each other," she says, "and I'm caught in the middle. It's been awfully hard on Louie."

Indeed, the Pastegas encompass, within their own household, almost the entire national spectrum of estrangements and aliena- tions, the point-blank antitheses, that would seem to be dismantling the American family. "We've got it all," Jennie continues, "just about everything and everybody—all the way from Richard, the radical, to his dad, who's Archie Bunker in the flesh. Then there's Robert, the policeman. And when my two boys get together--what a hassle!"

But there was only gingerly hassling when Robert recently visited the Pastegas with his wife, Margaret Ann. A lean, tense, grave figure, spare and deliberate of word and gesture, Robert chose to be a policeman "because of the challenge. It gives you a great deal of satisfaction, you know, when you catch somebody." But throughout dinner the conversation was studiously light and idle.

Finally, Robert, without glancing up from his plate, ventured to Richard, "I looked through *Breakdown* a little bit—some of it is all right. But some things—like about George Jackson at Soledad Prison, I just don't believe he was killed the way you have it written in there. I believe the guards' story."

Richard softly snapped, "Well, you tell me how he could have hidden a pistol in his hair--"

Louie looked up and barked hoarsely, "You ever seen their hair? Huh? The way they're all wearing it these days?"

Jennie laughed thinly. "Yeah—it looks exactly like Richard's."

The next afternoon, Louie Pastega gazed out of the small curtained window over the kitchen sink, his hands plunged deep in his sagging trousers and reflected, "Hell, when I was growing up, you knew what a man looked like. But today—I don't know what the kids are doing, they've gone bananas. Richard, he reminds me of a guy 70 years old with that hair. I just don't know how I went wrong with him. I offered him this place six months ago, but he told me he didn't want to be tied down like we are. What I don't understand, my son sits there and ridicules me, but I live what I think is a normal life. I'm not the richest man in town, but I don't have to take my hat off to nobody, either. But Richard, he tells me we ruined him. And I guess we did—we gave him too much. Going through the Depression, that put a fear in us and we wanted our kids to have more than we did, never to have to worry like we did. But it was bad—bad, bad. We gave them too much. And now, they're coming back at us, like Richard."

Despite the exuberance in Klamath Falls for *All in the Family*, life in the Oregon town could not, at first glance, seem more remote from that in Queens, N.Y., where the Bunkers reside. Nestled along lakes in a low lap between dark fir forest to the west and scrubby chapparal wastes to the east, Klamath Falls is a community of some 43,000 people occupied principally with ranching, lumbering and railroading.

Though Indians today make up just 2.84% of the county's population, they constitute about the only visible minority in Klamath Falls. As one local resident put it, "The Indians are the niggers of the Northwest." A local media executive said, "We got our Modoc Indians here, you see, and soon as those Modocs get a little rum-rum in their tum-tums, baby, look out."

One Saturday afternoon not long ago, as a visitor was about to enter an aqua-painted cement-block tavern, two hulking whites suddenly barged out the door before him, one of them advising the stranger, "Goddam place in there is goddam full of Indians," while he shoved his companion farther out into the dirt parking lot: "C'mon, c'*mon*, now, Moose—I'm getting you out of here before you kill one of 'em."

But considerably more befuddling is the fact that, though blacks amount only to a virtually indiscernible .94% of the county's population, listening to the Saturday afternoon commentaries in taverns and poolrooms one might suppose one was somewhere in Queens, Chicago, or even Bessemer, Ala. "Fal-*coons*, Lin-*coons*," snorted one waitress as she swabbed the counter before a roosting row of railroad workers. "When you 'spose they gonna start making a car for *white* folks." One customer replied, "Hell, I know what you mean. Five years ago, I didn't feel this way—but with all the stuff that's been going on, I'm fed up. I'm not putting up with it from them anymore." Louie Pastega, who was among the 10% of Klamath County voters who voted for Wallace in 1968, genially confides, "What I really think, now, is we shouldn't of ever turned 'em loose in the first place. I know it can't be changed back now, but everybody was just better off the way it was 150 years ago."

Almost as microscopic as the settlement of blacks in Klamath Falls has been the vagrant infiltration of new-culture disciples into town—"the longhairs," as they are commonly denoted. But however small their numbers, the community maintains a ferocious vigilance toward their ideas.

What these improbably testy humors in Klamath Falls disclose, perhaps, is that we have at last become one country—one continental community of irascibilities, rancors, suspicions, piques and harassments—whether leafy small-town or mammoth-city apartments. It becomes, then, not quite so surprising that *All in the Family* has found a constituency in an isolated little town in Oregon, whose inhabitants identify with the Bunkers as if they were next-door neighbors—or, more precisely, themselves.

Some of the local ebullience over the show lends currency to the misgivings of certain critics that Archie stimulates the bigotries of the common workingman. "What's great about that show," one railroad switchman reported to a friend, "is that it *is* biased. What I mean is, it's just like you feel inside yourself. You think it, but ole Archie, he *says* it, by damn."

But on the whole, one senses from the sentiments in Klamath Falls that the show has actually worked to ventilate long-pent fumes of resentment and mistrust. And there seems a general recognition of an interesting fact about Archie Bunker. As one lady suggested to her husband one evening at the Pelican Bar, "I don't really think Archie's too bright. I think Archie's prejudiced, but he doesn't know it." "Yeah," grinned her husband, a windburned road-department worker wearing a suede jacket, "and I say exactly the same things, don't I, honey?"

Speculations and ruminations about the Bunkers have become a preoccupation around town. One recent afternoon, some workers at the Jeld-Wen Lumber Yard retired after their shifts to the massive circular bar of the Waldorf Cafe. "Well, I don't know how I'd react, for instance, if a Negro came over for dinner some night," offered Monte Duell, a 34-year-old father of three. "I don't really think I'd mind, but my wife—she's the one who'd say no. But I don't think you'd razzberry a man who's a guest in your house, like Archie did that time. I think they enjoy making Archie look a little bit foolish. I don't think he *really* means what he says about people."

Despite the fact that they share the same roof, Richard Pastega and his parents could be inhabiting two separate universes in Klamath Falls. In a bizarre adjacency, on the other side of the wall from the Pastega's sedate living room is the workroom where Richard puts together his newspaper—a dishevelment of copy sheets littered across a plywood board, with a miniature Vietcong flag pinned to an upside-down American flag on one wall, along with posters of Zapata and Chief Red Shirt and one panoramic psychedelic foldout from *Earth Magazine* of a three-faced bronze-limbed nude. Whenever a townsman arrives at the store to inquire about placing an ad, says Richard, "Mother calls me out to the front. She doesn't want anybody to see what's happened back here."

Richard often distributes his paper around town with the help of a collection of young teen-age boys who are generally ragged-maned, somewhat ragamuffin in garb, frequently barefooted and ceaselessly flicking cigarettes with immensely solemn nonchalance. On the whole, as this party proceeds around town—flurrying in and out of such locales as Linda's Beauty Chalet, Low Cost Super-market, Freeman's Saddlery—it presents the apparition of a wily Fagin trailing behind him a gaggle of Artful Dodgers. Richard's own manner during these weekly tours tends to give his operation more the character of furtive hit-and-run raids: he will plunge through the door to plop his papers wordlessly on the nearest counter and swoop back out before anyone's really realized he's appeared. "I just don't enjoy confrontations particularly," he acknowledges.

As far as Klamath Falls seems from Queens, does Los Angeles seem from Klamath Falls. There, on a recent afternoon, Norman Lear, *All in the Family*'s producer who conceived the show from a similar series in Britain, insisted mildly, "I really didn't think a lot about what this show was going to mean to American households, really. I just thought, when I saw the British show, '*Damn*, that's a funny idea—a funny, funny idea.' To think about its teaching lessons would be a pretty futile, ridiculous approach." But eventually, Lear began talking about the episode from last season when Archie returns one evening from work to find his daughter Gloria has suffered a miscarriage. He stampedes upstairs to sit by her bed, bumbling phrases for several minutes until Gloria finally asks, "You want to say something, Daddy?" He wheezes, "Unhh-Unh—I, uh—I," and she says quietly, "You love me." He only nods his head, staring at her helplessly and she says, "I love you too, Daddy." Lear now says, "A lot of people hate a fact like that moment—they feel it sanctifies the rest of Archie. But that a man who says the things Archie does also happens to adore his daughter is simply a fact of life. I know a lot of Archie Bunkers look at it and maybe don't see he's a fool more than once in four shows. Maybe they cheer and say, 'Right on, Archie!' But what even they have to realize after a while is that he's a man consumed by fear—not hate. What we really have to worry about are not the bigots who burn the crosses and rape black women and castrate black men. God knows, they're animals, but there just aren't that many pure beasts around. What we have to worry about are all the *good* people, who don't hate like that, but *fear*. Somebody once said that if all the bigoted good people of the world were suddenly divested of their prejudice, the problem could be solved and we could take care of the others. . . ."

Several afternoons later, in Klamath Falls, Louie Pastega rummaged up for an out-of-town visitor the meager hoard of pale smoggy snapshots of his past—dim glimpses of a strapping, smirking youth in bib-coveralls, standing with a rigid formality behind the same counter 40 years before. Then he produced a few yellowed newspaper clippings—"And here's one, this is when I won the blood donor's contest for the Moose." Finally, he pulled out a small beribboned medallion, dulled now and dowdy as a Spanish-American War service decoration, which was inscribed: Louie Pastega, Dead Lift, 535 lbs., 1949." Louie croaked jubilantly, "You know, I was 40 years old when I did that. It was during a holiday celebration of some kind down on Main Street. Back at that time, I was considered the strongest man in town. Course, I never thought much about it back then, but I could have won a whole boxful of medals like this one. Now that I'm 63 years old, I wish sometimes I had more of those medals. You know, last year was the first time I was old—just, I started getting awfully tired all of a sudden. Isn't it funny how a guy changes, hunh? I mean, they used to see me coming, boy, and get off the road. But now—funny how everything changes."

That afternoon, he and Richard rode with friends up to a high weedy bluff and Louie stood for a long time beside the car looking out over the distant scattering of the town and finally he mumbled through his cigar, "God, I used to take a girl to the top of this hill, you know it? I guess I ain't been up here since at least 1950." He paused, withdrew his cigar to spit to one side, then clamped it back in his mouth and said, "I got a great ole gal—whole secret of life is a good woman like that. She did too much for all three of us. She never did like to go out much, but I was a great one for dancing, so we'd go to the lodge every week. Boy, when we were going to those dances, I didn't miss a one. But for some reason, we even stopped doing that about a year ago. It's all passing away, all right. Coming up here like this again, you realize how you can get in such a rut: I'm at the store, then I go uptown maybe for a couple hours and play cards, then I go back home. Meanwhile, it's all passing away. I don't get along with my kids, we just don't *talk* together anymore; even Robert hardly ever calls."

Richard later observed, "You know, actually my father and I talk now more than we have in some time. He's changing, or maybe I am, I don't know."

Indeed, nine months after Richard's return from San Francisco, the Pastegas seemed to have passed beyond the angry blind heats of those first few weeks, and to have arrived at a certain quiescence of tenuous understandings, a tentative rediscovering of each other. Somehow, moving in profoundly different directions, it's as if Richard and his father have nevertheless arrived at a momentary proximity, like the briefly brushing fields of gravity of two alien planets swirling past each other. Louie likes now and then, when there are customers in the store, to pick up a copy of *Breakdown* with a theatrical flourish, and then loudly bay, "Let's see, now, I'm gonna read about the new generation—the one that's going down the drain—" But after a moment, he will add, with a wry glint in his eyes, "Course, 90% of it is probably true. It's just that 90% of us wouldn't say it. See my ad here? I got to help sponsor the paper in some way, hunh?"

But more often than not, these somewhat grudging indulgences are only enunciated in the presence of other people, obliquely. Frequently, they are fretted by lingering crackles of snappishness.

Recently, the elder Pastegas rode with Richard for the first time during his round of deliveries, and after several stops, Louie pronounced from the back seat with a kind of casual amazement, "My God, Richard, what a job you picked to do. To go through all this for no reward." Richard, glaring for a few seconds through the windshield, finally hissed, "It's better than working in a grocery store." Louie mumbled, "I don't know. Be better off if you had a grocery store . . ." For awhile he merely gazed out of the window, and at last offered in a somewhat softer voice, "Well, one guy at the store, I gave it to him and he threw it back at me, and I picked it up and threw it back at him and said, 'Take the cockeyed thing and read it, there's nothing in there but the truth—' " But Richard— still sunk in that abrupt unappeasable aggrievement of sons toward their fathers which is finally beyond all accounting or rationality— muttered tautly, "How come you businessmen are such liars?" Louie howled, "Whaddaya mean? I only did it 'cause it was *you*, *your* paper. I never liked the goddam thing—you know that."

Later, back at the store, Jennie reflected, "Sure, some people come in here and see the paper and say, 'What the hell is this Communist thing doing on the counter?' But just as many come in and tell me, 'You mean, it's your son who's putting out this paper? Well, you tell him he can't give it up—it's the best thing that's ever happened to Klamath Falls.' " She proposed then with a small uncertain proud smile; "I still don't like it. But you know, it *does* take bravery, I think, to just go out and start up something like this. Richard's paper is the first thing that's ever happened in Klamath Falls to talk about."

She was sitting at the dinette table in the kitchen, her hands folded before her, only a few minutes away from starting supper. Pondering a short moment, she continued, "You know, maybe Richard came back here, changed the way he is now, to make us more tolerant of people. You know how society does things to you— you have your friends, and you always think what they'll say about something. You know how people automatically think if someone has long hair, that means they're dirty. Well, labeling somebody dirty just because they have long hair is just like labeling you a Wop or Dago. And that's one thing at least that Louie and I know about, from our own time."

The truth is, the Pastegas still approach an acceptance of Richard's transformation on the rather dire terms, as Jennie put it, of "say your son was born crippled or retarded, you'd accept that, wouldn't you?" Like the Bunkers, Jennie acknowledges, "We're just common everyday people. We're not any kind of a model family." But the Bunkers—who have become a kind of alter ego for numberless American families—remain marooned each Saturday night at that obstreperous starting point where the Pastegas found themselves shortly after Richard's return home. The difference is the Pastegas since last January slowly and doggedly have grown— in curiosity, in understanding, in a sense of each other's actual distresses. And this, in turn, could cultivate tolerances which might eventually extend beyond their own front stoops. The Pastegas present sturdy intimations that the most seemingly impossible, intractable, irreconcilable divisions and conflicts staggering countless American households cannot only be endured but accommodated —so long as there holds fast a certain vital center: that same center which stubbornly holds, despite all beleaguerments, both the Bunker and Pastega families together in an equilibrium of unspoken need and mutual indispensability. It is what drew Richard back home. As he explained it: "There was nowhere else I belonged."

Through Queens
with Pad and Pencil

Rowland Barber *TV Guide*   August 30, 1975

"From Television City, in Hollywood . . . *'Boy, the way Glen Miller played . . . Songs that made the Hit Parade . . . Guys like us, we had it made . . . Those were the days! . . .'* " As we drive down off the eastern end of the bridge, into the borough of Queens, my head rings with the voices of Edith and Archie Bunker, singing their way into another episode of *All in the Family*.

Ahead of us lies the sprawling urban savanna of New York City's biggest borough, ranging from the industrial clot of Long Island City out to the shaded Tudor duchy of Forest Hills and beyond, to the reaches of LaGuardia Field, John F. Kennedy International Airport, and the space reserved for World's Fairs in Flushing Meadow. The borough's arteries—boulevards and expressways—are shouldered with bastionlike apartment houses, trans-American-modular shopping centers, mortuaries and catering spas. Set back

245

from the main drags, in neighborhoods with names like Richmond Hill, Jackson Heights, Middle Village, Glendale, Hollis and Woodside, lies what's left of primeval Queens: here a block, there a checkerboard swatch, of wooden row houses. Detached, semidetached, neat as fish bones.

One of them, one of the hundred-thousand of them, could be the house of the Bunkers. My mission: to pinpoint one such row house and meet the family that lives in it, and see how much they're like Archie and Edith and Gloria and Mike. I will find out if they feel any special kinship to the Bunker household and way of life—if, indeed, they ever watch *All in the Family*, and know who the Bunkers are.

So on this overcast morning, we drive over the Queensboro Bridge. The driver is my old friend Guido, proprietor of Guido's Corner Bar in Greenwich Village and Past Exalted Ruler of the Elks Lodge No. 1. If anything can be found in New York City, Guido will find it. I am also banking on the theory that one good Elk leads to another.

Thus our first stop is the Elks clubhouse in Queens Boulevard, where I explain my quest to Bill, who tends the bar adjacent to the gym and steam room. Bill points us in the direction of Joe's house in Woodside. Joe is outside watering his roses. He listens, then hails his brother-in-law Mickey. Mickey knows "just the block you're looking for." After he consults with his nephew Charley, we are led to 41st Drive and the home of the Rawald family.

Forty-first Drive is Bunkerland incarnate, to the last semidetached, peaked-roof, brick-stooped, wood-frame row house. Family cars parked bumper to bumper, average vintage 1971. Here and there the fruit of hard-scrabble landscaping: a tough little privet, a lonely hydrangea, a pot of geraniums. Just as gallant, the stabs at personalizing the dittoed house fronts: painted clapboard, asbestos shingling, simulated fieldstone; window boxes, doorjamb sconces, minishrines to Our Lady.

I push the bell, expecting, I suppose, to hear the *tump-tump-tump* of Edith's bovine trot and the muffled bleat of the dingbat, "Oh, *my*! Who could *that* be?" Instead, a moment of silence, and then the door opens and Tillie Rawald greets us: a compact, well-rounded lady in her mid-40s, fluffy nimbus of ash-blonde hair, alert eyes behind modish white-framed glasses. After being told why I am here, she asks us in.

I am not prepared for what's inside. Case of video shock. The look of the Bunkers is not here. No bleak, curtainless stairway window, no bald radiator, or hall tree, or varnished woodwork, or threadbare rugs, or rock maple and overstuffed furniture by Grand Rapids out of a 1935 tourist cabin. Instead: a fully appointed living room, nifty as a display in a trading-stamp redemption catalog, dominated by wall-to-wall, deep-pile, burgundy carpeting.

"Sorry my husband Paul's not here," says Tillie. "Every Saturday he does the family grocery shopping. He's terrific at it. Right down the list, one-two-three, no impulse buying like when I get in a market." I find it hard to summon up a vision of Archie Bunker pushing a shopping cart from Ajax to zucchini, comparing prices and thumping melons for ripeness. It becomes apparent that I have to discard all my preconceptions about real-life counterparts, at once.

The biggest difference, I am to find, is involvement. The one universal objection in Queens to the character of Archie Bunker is his sloth, which is not regarded as a comical defect. A house painter with whom I strike up a conversation on Woodside Avenue, under the tracks of the IRT, says: "That guy sings about the good old days when 'everybody pulled his weight,' then he plops *his* weight down in the easy chair and pops a can of beer and watches TV. Sure, we all watch TV around here, but there's always something else goin' on, and Woodside is a place where everybody pitches in."

The focal point of the Rawalds' involvement is St. Sebastian's Church. St. Sebastian's is a large parish (5000 families), and its aegis shelters a myriad of activities. Swimming, baseball and basketball leagues. The Golden Gloves. Drama club, teen club, the Boys' Brigade, the Girls' Brigade. Preschool Classes and Marriage Encounter Weekends. Bazaars and bingo. Pride and joy of the parish is the huge Parish Center, with its gym, Olympic-size pool, and meeting rooms.

"We all pitched in to build the Center," says Tillie Rawald, "and now we all pitch in to run it. And it's paid off. We always know where our kids are."

Tillie bowls on Tuesday nights, "helps run the bingo for the church" once a month, is a Library Mother, and in between serves on "all kinds of committees, for this, that, the other thing."

Ricky, her oldest son, just 22, is married and already owns his own business, a German-Italian delicatessen. He bowls with his father in the Catholic War Veterans Post League. Regina, 17, is busy this summer at the Center, where she's a lifeguard and a secretary, and will enter Hunter College in the fall. Ron, 15, is working in his brother's deli during his vacation. Robert, 9 this August, is having a summer of baseball—while earning extra money by making deliveries for the neighborhood Avon Lady.

We are sitting in the kitchen, over coffee. The paneled kitchen holds a remarkable collection of built-ins, appliances and gadgets—the newest of which is a Mr. Coffee. "You've seen Joe DiMaggio selling these on TV? Well, my husband went through grade school with Whitey Ford, and of course Whitey played for the Yankees too. . . ."

"We believe in action around here," Tillie then says. "You remember the Kitty Genovese case over there in Kew Gardens a few years back? Where all her neighbors watched her being attacked and killed and nobody lifted a finger? It would never happen in Woodside. Last year my son Ricky chased a thief down Roosevelt Boulevard, and caught him. People here care.

"Yes, we had a drug scene, like any place else. Until three-four years ago. A girl OD'd and died in a storefront clubhouse. All the families got together and called a meeting with the police and demanded action. We put in a task force, parents and police, and we wiped the neighborhood clean. Now it's safe on the streets at night here.

"You don't see Edith and Archie Bunker ever involved like that, even though they're supposed to live in the same kind of neighborhood. What I guess you'd call blue-collar, lower middle class. My husband works for the post office. Men along the street here are like firemen, policeman, truck drivers, repairmen."

I ask her if she watches *All in the Family* regularly. "Oh, sure," she says. "The kids and I. Paul, not so much. I think it's a funny show. But we don't know anybody around here like the Bunkers. The Bunkers seem to be years behind the times, the way their house is furnished and all."

She laughs, as she pours more coffee. "Now I've told you how busy I am, with church affairs and keeping this house clean and food on the table, I have to confess that I'm a TV nut. See this little set behind me? That's my black-and-white, soap-opera set. Our other two TVs are color. I never miss *General Hospital* or *One Life to Live*. I get a kick out of *The $10,000 Pyramid*, *Gambit* and *Password*. If the 4:30 movie doesn't look good, I'll watch *Mike Douglas*."

Robert comes in from his baseball game ("I got a double and

we won, 5-3!") and Ron comes home on a break from the deli. They concur with their mother on the household's favorite night-time shows: *Police Woman, Petrocelli, Marcus Welby, M.D., M*A*S*H, Good Times* and *Chico and the Man*, besides *All in the Family*.

"Except for my Dad," says Ron. "He doesn't watch so much. His big thing is reading and doing the crossword puzzles." "I'm sorry Paul's not here," Tillie adds. "When he's late back from shopping on Saturday, it means he's stopped off at the Post." "The Post?" "Catholic War Veterans Post, over on 61st Street. That's his club, his home away from home." She says it without a hint of censure.

I met Mr. Rawald on my next visit to Woodside. Paul is a slight, wiry, dark-haired man with a deep voice, whose speech is punctuated by a soft, nervous giggle. It's like a running apology—but he has nothing to be apologetic about. He will soon be 48, hopes to retire when he's 55, after 35 years with the post office. He has worked hard to support his family, at the stamp window, as station manager, and moonlighting evenings, weekends and on vacation time; and he and Tillie have raised an exemplary family. The work ethic is supreme among the Rawalds, and nobody—from little Robert on up—complains about it, and nobody seems to have any trouble "getting his head together."

Rawald joined the Navy at the end of World War II. "Spent the whole hitch hanging over the side of a destroyer escort, seasick. When I got out I looked for a job in a print shop—I went to the New York School of Printing in Manhattan, although I grew up out here in Astoria. But it was the old story. Couldn't get in the union. So I answered an ad for temporary post-office clerk—and that's been my career. Tillie and I met five years later at a dance in Richmond Hill. Whitey Ford had given me a couple of free tickets, but I didn't have a date. I got to talking to this cute girl from Ozone Park, Tillie Ambrosio, and she didn't have a date either. We danced—and that was it."

I told Paul I understood he was not much of a television fan. "Before I got married," he said, "I was a TV nut. But not any more. Except for news and sports, it's an idiot box to me. I think *All in the Family* is boring.

"That Archie Bunker—he's a recluse. Lives in that damn chair. How can he be so uninvolved? Know what my easy chair is? The first step on the living room stairs. That's where I watch the news from, and read my paper. I just don't feel comfortable being comfortable. Too much to be done."

Paul Rawald ticked off the political issues he and Archie agree or disagree on. "I'm a conservative too," he said. "On the Democratic side. But we went for Nixon around here in 1972, like everywhere else.

"Now there's one thing Bunker and I see eye to eye on. I am also strictly a law-and-order man. I got to admit there are a few TV shows I like. The cop shows. *The Rookies*, I guess, is my favorite. Cop shows are very, very big up and down this block.

"I think Bunker goes overboard on the racial thing. I believe in live and let live whether it's Jewish people or colored or whatever. There's a mixed-marriage couple lives down the corner. We don't bother them, they don't bother us. Old Man Wiley, around the corner, he's black but he's lived here like 50 years, ever since they built these row houses. You may have noticed the private academy over on 58th Street. They're all black students, but they're from your higher-class, colored families in the City.

"The public school buses in black kids. But we don't have any busing problem, because our kids go to St. Sebastian's. There are some new elements moving into the neighborhood. Lot of Oriental couples, some Puerto Ricans, and for some reason Greeks and East Indians. It's hard to make any acquaintances on account of the language barrier. But any of them's certainly welcome in the church, if they're Catholic. We now have a Spanish Mass in the chapel every Sunday.

"One thing I understand about Archie Bunker is his having to moonlight once in a while as a cabdriver. A family in Queens just can't make it on the income from one job. For seven, eight years I drove cab too, at night. For a while I worked nights in letter shops. Got a job once driving new garbage trucks to Philadelphia, another time Army trucks from Staten Island to Philly.

"Tell you one bone I have to pick with Bunker—that's him always knocking his son-in-law Mike's going to college. The number-one thing in my life, as a father, is the kids' welfare and education." Paul paused, and giggled, then said, "Well, tell you the truth, I'll take part of that back. If my daughter brought home a lazy husband like that Mike who only went to school and didn't work to support her, I'd throw the both of them out of the house."

Rawald finished his beer and said, apologetically, that it was time for him to go to the lanes. Wednesday night. Before he went upstairs to get his bowling shoes, he said: "Now, you ask me to look at that show as a critic and I'll tell you exactly what's wrong with it. There's no storm door on the Bunker house. Archie comes home all bundled up in his hat and lumberjack on a winter day, and he has to open only the one front door to get in the house. I'd hate to have his heating bills!"

On that last day I dropped by Shelley's, one of the two traditional watering places of the neighborhood (the other being Donovan's Pub, across from the church). There I met Ed Fowley, the owner of Shelley's, a man everybody had said you had to meet if you wanted to know Woodside. Fowley, a slight, soft-spoken bachelor, has been the moving force behind the Youth Program and the Boys' Brigade. At the moment he is zeroing in on Woodside's program for the Bicentennial celebration. "The history of Woodside will be told," he said, "in murals the high-school kids are painting, and in a giant patchwork quilt made by the ladies of the Lutheran Church. We're going to put in new sidewalks out front here, and trees, and cement tubs for flowers.

"Well," Ed Fowley said, "I'll tell you the kind of place Woodside is. It's a place where once a week the sisters of St. Sebastian's go out ringing doorbells, door to door, looking for the needy, or old people who might be lonely." Turning to me, he added: "I'm glad you got to know the Rawalds. Nice people, aren't they? What's nicest about them is they're typical."

As my train rattled out of Bunkerland toward the City, I tried to put all my impressions in order. It was good, I decided, that Archie Bunker was in so many ways atypical of the place he had been cast in. It spoke well for the real people of Queens, and it spoke well for the creators of the show, who had brought a true original to life.

Then I got to wondering how Archie would be celebrating his country's 200th birthday. Probably buy himself a miniature flag for his hatband—at half-price, on July 5th.

VIII. The Meaning of "All in the Family"

A Symposium

In early 1979, the editor of this book asked a group of TV critics and television industry leaders, as well as some of those who were responsible for creating All in the Family, *to comment on the significance of the series to themselves personally, to the television medium, or to the larger society. Their responses follow.*

I see no evidence that the Judeo/Christian ethic has helped over all the centuries to diffuse—let alone eliminate—mankind's appetite for prejudice, bigotry, or its indifference to human suffering. Therefore, I am always startled to learn that there are some few who believe "All in the Family" has managed to matter in that troubled area. While I would be proud to believe it true, there seems to be no tangible evidence.

By the same token, there is every indication that "All in the Family" has not served to strengthen the attitudes held by viewers who share Archie's prejudice. In nine years we have received hundreds of letters from individuals who wrote to say: "Right on, Archie!" But without exception, every one of them went on to say, one way or another, ". . . but why do you always make Archie a horse's ass by the end of every episode?" The Producers' point of view was never misunderstood.

We have only been able to perceive a definite effect when we have addressed specific issues. When we did a show in which Edith was afraid she had breast cancer, the response across the country was measurable. Women by the thousands called local chapters of The American Cancer Society. Rape prevention centers were, in whatever states they exist, contacted by thousands of women when "All in the Family" dealt with that subject, too. We have seen similar responses to episodes that dealt with mental retardation, obesity, heart disease, etc.

To get back to the question of whether we have helped to change attitudes, however, I feel we are like a group of people standing at the perimeter of a lake throwing pebbles into the water. The physicists tell us that each pebble makes the level of the water rise. We cannot see the water rising; we cannot hear it or feel it. Yet the physicists tell us that with each pebble that body of water is being affected. To carry the metaphor further, if the pebbles we have been throwing into the lake of social awareness have mattered at all, we don't see it. But we are terribly happy to know that some people do.

Norman Lear

The personal rewards and professional impact of "All in the Family" on my life and career are unequivocal. Because of the moral conscience that permeates the series it has seemed to me more than just another acting assignment. I feel privileged to have been part of a mass entertainment piece that has touched the social awareness of Americans. After our second year on the air a Protestant minister told me that "All in the Family" had done more in one half hour to uncover the nature of bigotry than he could accomplish in a year of preaching.

I remember when I first read the pilot script I was struck by its content and honesty. These were real characters relating to each other in an authentic way. This was exciting. I said to myself "This on television! How unique!" I believe that this, too, is a key to our success. A foundation of truth, of probability, is always the basis of successful dramatic realism. As we approach each week's episode we ask ourselves, "Is this probable? Could Edith, Archie, Gloria, Mike really experience this situation?"

Another factor which has always prevailed in the preparation of "All in the Family" is artistic freedom. On the very first day

Norman Lear established an atmosphere in which we could all comment, accept, reject, contribute to the script. For nine years this method has been cultivated by John Rich, our first director, subsequent producers and writers, as well as our current director, Paul Bogart. As an actor this approach has caused me to stretch, expand and grow. Encouragement and approval by all concerned have also contributed to my growth.

Another important ingredient to our success is the remarkable creativity and talent of my colleagues, Carroll O'Connor, Rob Reiner and Sally Struthers. Also, the mutual respect which enriched our ensemble was conducive to excellence.

I have often been asked why I have not grown tired and bored with my role on "All in the Family." I believe that playing a different situation each week and developing the character through the years helped to keep it alive for me. Another important reason was the studio audience. Until this season we performed each show twice before two different audiences thus closely approximating the theatre experience when the audience nourishes the actor, expanding comic moments and dictating delicate timing.

In retrospect "All in the Family" may become the most challenging and fulfilling experience of my acting career.

Jean Stapleton

I'll never know what significance *All in the Family* had for the public, but for me it meant exposure to eight years of the best possible training an actor can receive. I was literally growing up while Gloria was growing up on the show. Being in this "Family" I was exposed to a completely different world than the real family I came from. I'm proud to say I never experienced any bigotry, prejudice, or injustice in my own family, but this made me a very sheltered little girl. *All in the Family* gave me my social awareness. I learned about the failings and foibles of the human race, why they exist, and how to deal with them. It started out as a casting call in 1970 and wound up as an addition to the Smithsonian Institution in 1978. What more can I say?

Sally Struthers

It is very rare to be connected with a piece of theater that works on so many levels—that not only entertains the audience, but informs them, makes them cry, makes them think. *All in the Family* dealt with some important subjects; it portrayed real people; it made people laugh. It did just about everything that a piece of theater could do.

In addition, we who worked on the show were allowed tremendous creative latitude. Everybody had a say in the scripts, in the ways in which the shows were presented, in what the shows had to say. One day, Herb Gardner, the playwright, happened to come to one of our rehearsals and stayed for a note session afterwards. During the note session, he witnessed the director, the actors, the writers, and the producers pitching in to make the show better, changing lines, fixing the script, cutting scenes out, talking about what needed to be edited, what needed to be stressed, what needed to be unstressed. Everyone was working toward the common good, toward making the best possible show. Gardner couldn't believe it, because he said, "You people have creative communism here." That *was* what we had throughout all the years of the show. From that standpoint, working on *All in the Family* was an incredibly rewarding creative experience.

Rob Reiner

From the very beginning, I always felt that the show, if it were successful, would make both a psychological as well as a sociological change in the viewing habits of the American public. In my opinion, the show did just that.

It is impossible for any family in America to watch "All in the Family" when it deals with a controversial issue, turn the television set off, and not enter into some healthy conversation. It quickly closed the generation gap! Parents were able to communicate, for the first time, with their children in difficult subjects that normally weren't discussed in the living room. The program brought out the deepest of passions in many of the viewers allowing them to truly become involved with a television program.

For me "All in the Family" not only changed the habits of the viewers at home, but it also changed the thinking of the creative community. For the first time television writers began to deal with subjects of social significance and through comedy "All in the Family" was able to show the foibles and weaknesses of the American people. It held up a mirror for the viewer to look at; he in turn delved introspectively within himself in a positive manner. We're all better for this experience!

Bud Yorkin
Producer-Director

The pleasure of directing "All in the Family" lay in several places: the strong talents of the cast, the positive characters they had created, and the singular autonomy we developed in which we were free to examine whatever human behavior the script opened up to us.

With that autonomy we were able to explore subjects orginarily considered un-funny and to take the time to involve the audience in that exploration, to not fear the occasional absence of laughter, and in the end to make people laugh with us nevertheless, sometimes as they wept.

AITF rattled the bones of the "situation comedy" formula which wanted never to offend or provoke but instead to bend life to serve jokes. AITF killed jokes if they bent the truth and instead built humor based on how we are; it gave its audience "character comedy" which is what good drama and good popular theatre are all about.

Paul Bogart
Director

"Breakthrough," "pioneering," "significant," "phenomenon" are just a few of the words that have been used to describe the arrival and success of "All in the Family." Those are descriptive words that do not explain what really happened.

In simplest terms, AITF represented an effort by television to treat in a comedic fashion major societal issues of topical interest and concern. The success of the series demonstrated that the concept worked—for CBS, for broadcasters and, most important, for the viewing audience. It offered a new genre in television programming that was welcomed by a broad cross-section of the American public, and served as a precursor of other topical series, specials and movies on all three networks.

Success was not without problems. There are many viewers who respond in an unthinking, emotional way to AITF, ignoring the full plot to focus on a line or two. Example: Archie's use of the expletive "God damn" brought a flood of mail that ignored Edith's lecture and her forbidding Archie ever to use profanity again in her home. Example: The continuing complaints about Archie's references to Mike's Polish heritage, complaints that always ignore Archie's use of such epithets as the defensive mechanism of an uneducated man who saw himself threatened by his much smarter, college-educated son-in-law.

We do not believe that AITF increased the use of profanity in the American home any more than we believe that AITF gave rise to Polish jokes. Indeed, we do not believe that AITF changed American mores or our way of life. We do believe, however, that AITF helped change American television, and CBS is proud to have been the catalyst in that change.

Gene F. Jankowski
President
CBS/Broadcast Group

"All in the Family" shattered well-established beliefs and myths cherished by the television networks—credos they gave substance out of sheer ignorance. Networks held for years that the public did not want shows dealing with problems; that they did not want any material delving into social areas, with social significance; that no comedy would be accepted if the husband were not some kind of a dolt, the wife a sort of zero whose delight was in dominating that dolt and her kids. A bigot! No way the audience would accept that, the networks would say.

"Family" proved all those myths to be just that. It also proved the audience is far ahead of the networks in terms of taste and quality. Its irreverence and breakthrough of traditional standards and concepts was just what the people had been waiting for. But it must be done with quality and taste, as the many carbon copies of "Family" which have failed have illustrated.

Hollywood TV producers of comedy series welcomed "Family" and its success because it enabled them, in turn, to produce their shows with a more realistic and adult look at life, something forbidden until the success of "Family." The show has bite, satire, sort of a nonchalant and carefree look at life in comedic terms. It has delved into some very real and identifiable problems within the context of comedy, and in so doing has proved that the public does not seek utter escapism on TV, that perhaps there is a hunger for something better, one this show satisfies as few do.

Dave Kaufman
TV Editor
Daily Variety
(Hollywood)

"All in the Family" did much more than change the face of television comedy. It opened it up to the real world.

Before "All in the Family" went on the air, successful family comedies were played out in a world where all the problems were little ones and all the endings were happy. A parade of bumbling fathers, competent mothers and adorable children passed through the American television scene, with the subject matter of each series as well-scrubbed and antiseptic as its characters.

"All in the Family" marked the first time that television comedy tried to treat the world as it really is. It is a tribute to the brilliance of the cast and the scripting that subjects from bigotry to rape could be presented in a comedy context, without either trivializing the subject or overwhelming the comedy.

The explosive success of "All in the Family" meant that television comedy would never be the same again. The unreality of "happy people with happy problems" was forever over. Writers and producers with something to say found they could say it in a comedy format. What "The Defenders" did for drama on television, "All in the Family" did for comedy.

Today, on all three networks, situation comedies can deal with public issues and national concerns. That is the most important legacy of "All in the Family."

Fred Silverman
President
NBC

"All in the Family" is not merely a good television show. "All in the Family" is not merely a great television show. "All in the Family" is great populist art. In its blend of exaggeration, truth and humor, it is a worthy link to the tradition and legacy of Mark Twain. And, like Twain, its masterful storytelling has brought to huge audiences comments on social injustice and universal values with vastly more impact than a year's supply of sermons and lectures by well-meaning do-gooders and professional soul-savers.

What is utterly startling about "All in the Family" is, in the end, its consistency of quality over such a long period of weekly shows. There has never been a better American television series. And to turn out a weekly series in which bad episodes seem to be outlawed means, quite obviously, there has been an attention to essentials, and to details, that one would be hard-put to match in any area of the entertainment field.

"All in the Family" marked the start of a revolution in U.S. television. By taking subjects and language long taboo in broadcasting, and bringing them out into the open, it helped TV maintain a certain credibility in the modern world rather than letting it slip more and more into a tradition-bound mortuary light years behind the other arts. In short, "All in the Family" brought a new freedom to the airwaves, a freedom that has been violated in taste by tasteless entrepreneurs—but which was necessary at all costs so that serious contemporary artists could present themselves and their work, whether in humor or drama, after a period of repressive TV banality. We always pay a little dearly for freedom, but it is worth the price.

There are those who say that "All in the Family" has had its cake and eaten it too—meaning that its portrayal of bigotry has been palatable to bigots as well as the rest of the audience, and that its commercial success and artistic success are therefore somewhat tainted. But those who say such nonsense do injustice to the basic intelligence of the American people. In Archie Bunker, we have seen not only a bigot, but a bigot who is caught up in the changing social scene that threatens to make him a relic, that confuses him because his political heroes have become suspect, to say the least, and because, from his casual daily encounters to the vast issues of war and patriotism and ethics, he has become truly perplexed and has backed off a little and, thus, perhaps has changed somewhat for the better—for the good of all of us, including those who have a bit or a lot of Archie in them.

Finally, "All in the Family" is just one hell of a theatrical achievement. In entertaining, it never fails to say something. And in saying something, it never fails to entertain. As the show's enlightened young grownups, Rob Reiner and Sally Struthers were brilliant even in the shadow of extraordinary performances by Carroll O'Connor as Archie and Jean Stapleton as his wife Edith. Stapleton's portrayal of a not-too-bright but loonily incisive and wonderfully decent woman has won her a place in show business annals. But towering above all is O'Connor, whose Archie is one of the genuinely unforgettable characters in American entertainment history. We know the producers, the directors, the writers and all the others without whom "All in the Family" would not have succeeded. But to millions of people each week, it is Archie who is the prime source of the show, and O'Connor has projected with unceasing momentum a maddeningly uproarious portrait of a certain kind of Americana, every bit as pertinent and true to our time as Huck Finn and Tom Sawyer were to theirs. Huck and Tom survive to this day intact, and there is no doubt in my mind that Archie Bunker will himself survive for years to come—perhaps becoming a little quaint to viewers who will wonder what all the fuss was over the social comment, but who will understand a little better what we once were.

And when the time comes when the social comment is perhaps obsolete, people will still laugh at "All in the Family," and that is its ultimate triumph: It is a work that succeeds on all levels through the gift of that which we always need to keep us afloat—humor.

Rick Du Brow
Entertainment Editor
Los Angeles Herald Examiner

"All in the Family's" audience not only included the small segment of the population who understood the content as a sophisticated incisive examination of prejudice and hate stemming from the competitiveness of the American economic system, but it also included the very large segment of the population who are the produce of that system and who found justification and rationalization of their own prejudices, biases and stupidity in Archie Bunker.

This program was (and more than ever, still is) *the* acceptable outlet for prejudices and stupidity that heretofore was not verbalized in public places. The program was not intended to elicit this response in the public, but it certainly was exploited—which is okay with me —for if one is to live under this system, one should use it (exploit it) for personal gain, because the system dictates, "I got mine and to hell with everyone else."

This "honesty" about selfishness is revered in the rich, and envied and emulated by the very people who are the product of this selfishness, the poor.

Fascism, exploited with biting, brilliant humor (or even in well done hard police action) is the most viable visual product to the vast mass audience of the low income class, especially in a free medium; ergo, the success of "All in the Family."

Paul L. Klein
Former Executive Vice President
NBC

Trivia-engulfed television critics ever hunger for a program worth criticizing. "All in the Family" qualified from Day One. Controversial, unsettling, provocative, laced with shocking dialogue. The premise of a situation comedy constructed around a shallow brained ignoramus was revolutionary to the American viewing experience. Production was tops. No one could short the portrayals of bellicose bigot Archie Bunker, that dingbat Edith, offspring Gloria and meathead son-in-law Mike.

Meanwhile, out there in TV land, the series quickly made waves all the way from ghetto to academe. It delighted the bigot in that Archie's outlook reinforced his own views. It delighted bigot-haters in that Archie always got his comeuppance (like the robber in the cops and robbers shows). Others doted on how Archie mangled the language; Mrs. Malaprop revisited. It attracted social reformers in that Archie was a superb target to crusade against. A likable bigot? Intolerable. Off with his head!

Yet these were but peripheral reactions among limited blocs of viewers. The Great American Mass loved Archie dearly and mainly because he was entertaining. He was funny. He induced chuckles. He induced bellylaughs. He was different. He actually aroused human emotions; even at times, the human intellect. Scenes between Archie and Edith and their marvelously sustained reactions were works of comedic art.

Archie proved to be uncommonly durable. Long before the novelty of bigotry wore thin, Archie was coping with social themes never before hung on a comedy series—nudity, alcoholism, drugs, racism, menopause, tax evasion, homosexuality, inflation, impotency, rape, death, robbery, etc., etc. In these weekly confrontations, Archie, Edith, Gloria and Mike made their greatest contributions to the television industry. Their pioneering became profoundly significant.

In the television years 1948-1970 B.B. (Before Bunker), situation comedy skirted contemporary social themes as though they were poison. The industry traditionally churned out plastic family life comedies, pratfall comedies, bucolic comedies, fantasy comedies. Archie changed that. Archie took the taboos out of the television closet. He broke down barriers. And the new freedoms spread. First to his own spinoffs—"Maude," "Good Times," "The Jeffersons,"— and to his stablemate show, "Sanford and Son." Archie's success encouraged "M*A*S*H" to tackle topics beyond its previous norm. The Archie influence even permeated serious television, leading to bolder approaches in made-for-TV movies. The significance and importance of being Archie would be reflected in contemporary themes adopted by new youth oriented comedies that subsequently would overtake and surpass Archie in public popularity. Archie even opened the way and conditioned prime time viewers to accept subject matter that has helped make "60 Minutes" television's most looked-at documentary series. Nearly every "All in the Family" episode was in itself a documentary theme, having far greater impact on the Great American Mass than those ponderous, hour-long formal documentaries of yesteryear.

Archie Bunker, through weekly confrontation with latter day crises, contributed enormously to the broadening of America's social awareness. He educated, he informed, he challenged, he angered, he astounded—and above all, he entertained. He was the right hero for the right medium at the right hour in an ebb flow of television programming. It was a pleasure to sit in at his birth, see him develop, see him knock down uptight mores, see him become— in retrospect—television's renaissance man.

Dwight Newton
Critic Emeritus
San Francisco Examiner

Norman Lear and Fred Silverman, on a technical level, broke ground in the "tape TV comedy form." Hard comedy, strong laughs, and with an attending audience for approval, looked for and found laughs and American points of view that were not available to the American TV audience before this concept.

On a creative level, Norman and Silverman moved television forward in the Lenny Bruce tradition of comedy: if it makes people laugh, it's funny—and it doesn't seem to hurt anybody.

There were negatives. Lots of the audience wanted what was said and done to be not said and done. Yes, it was being done but why say it, why show it? That "keep you head in the sand" attitude leaves no room for progress: more than that, creates a negative atmosphere for our young people who are aware and wonder why the "establishment" turns its back. In brief, it presented entertainment in a more truthful manner and gave respect to the medium that had lost it.

It made the rest of us Comedy Producers sit up and take notice. It split the men from the boys. If we had something better and more to say, the door was open.

Every small step forward is a giant step. Norman Lear and Fred Silverman took their step and with belief, and patience, and sheer "c'mon, why not?"—opened a new level (which was coming sooner or later) to the minds of the "Vast Wasteland" that certainly is "vast" but no longer such a "wasteland."

> *James Komack*
> President
> Komack Co.

"All in the Family" was, I think, a direct outgrowth of the turmoil of the late '60s, the concern over Vietnam and, later, the national guilt over Watergate.

I doubt that anyone realized how ready the nation was for its frank and relevant satire. I remember Carroll O'Connor telling me on the very day the first "All in the Family" went on the air that he thought CBS would run three or four of them, to save face, then pay off the company and performers and forget it. CBS put on extra operators on the switchboards in anticipation of a barrage of protesting calls, which never came. Other people in the comedy field I talked with said things like "well, if they want to use blue material," or "how do they get away with that stuff." The only comedian I talked with at the time who did not object to the show was the late Jack Benny. I asked Jack what he thought of its stance on bigotry and politics and Jack said: "I'm always laughing too hard to notice."

What the program did for television is inestimable. It opened the door to the use of themes and language and situation reflecting the human condition that broadcasting had never dared explore before. Before "All in the Family" no TV husband and wife had ever slept in the same bed.

Though the obvious offspring of the show were "Maude" and other Lear products, plus its reflection in the new approach of on-going comedies, like "The Mary Tyler Moore Show," the widening scope of television involvement moved also into drama, making possible "That Certain Summer," "A Case of Rape" and other innovative dramas, including the recent "A Question of Love."

Perhaps it's true that we've gone the full cycle in the '70s from the nitwit, escapist comedy that preceded "All in the Family" to the nitwit, escapist comedy that seems to have followed it ("Mork and Mindy," "Laverne & Shirley") as the mood of the nation changed. But television will never again be the same. In the wake of the acceptance of "All in the Family," TV became a place where ideas were welcome—a theater of ideas—the only one we have now that the movies have become comic strips and the comic strips Broadway hits.

"All in the Family" might not make it today. It would probably be cancelled after a couple of showings. But the doors it opened remain ajar.

Cecil Smith
TV Critic
Los Angeles Times

I hated "All in the Family" the first time I saw it—which, as I recall, was about the second or third episode. Carroll O'Connor seemed to be doing an obnoxious imitation of Jackie Gleason in "The Honeymooners." Sally Struthers whined too much. Edith's sniveling was grating. Archie's much publicized racial slurs struck me as entirely gratuitous. And the yelling drove me up the wall.

A second viewing confirmed my first impression. So, since I didn't own a TV set at the time (I had been watching at my parents' home), I dismissed the show and the critics who were praising it.

I guess I picked the series up again in the third season, resolving to give it another chance since it had managed (somehow) to survive that long without my support. To my surprise, the things I had found so abrasive initially apparently had been smoothed out. I still didn't love "All in the Family" but I found myself coming back to it because it was interesting.

The show that turned me around all the way, or at least the one that sticks in my memory like few other TV shows I've ever seen, came on February 24, 1973 (I went back and checked). It was the episode in which a militant Jewish activist paid a call on the Bunker household and got entangled in a provocative debate with Archie and Mike over the merits of violence to affect change or to extract revenge. At the end of the show he left and went out to his car. Offscreen there came a tremendous explosion. The Bunkers and Stivics ran to the door and looked out; we stared into their horror-stricken faces as the episode closed.

Wow, I thought when I recovered from the emotional shock of that totally unexpected turn of events. There was obviously a hell of a lot more going on here than I had suspected. "All in the Family" was not just another situation comedy—not by a long shot. It was dealing with real life. It had the courage to tackle tough subjects and to probe all sorts of human foibles. Perhaps most unusually, it didn't feel obligated to be funny at all costs. This was television with relevance.

I was hooked after that. It was so refreshing to see current events and complex relationships reflected and commented upon in a TV show that also happened to be damn funny. "All in the Family" set new qualitative standards for all the shows that came after it.

The curious thing is that when I think back on the episodes that meant the most to me, it isn't the "socially relevant" ones that come to mind at all, though they clearly were what first drew me into the series. But over the years I got so wrapped up in the lives of Archie and Edith and Mike and Gloria—so fully explored were they by the actors, directors, writers and producers—that what I remember best are the personal moments. Especially after I married and began raising a family of my own, "All in the Family" frequently touched me deeply: The shows leading up to the birth of baby Joey, Edith's emergence as a whole woman able to stand up to her husband, Archie and Gloria sharing an intimate father-daughter moment. There were many more, all leading up to that beautiful, wrenching episode in which Mike and Gloria said their goodbyes en route to a new life in California. I cried as if it were my own kin bidding me farewell.

That is the real triumph of "All in the Family." None of its other achievements would have been possible if that foundation of belief in and affection for the characters wasn't there. I never did come to believe that people who thought like Archie Bunker were learning to laugh at themselves through him; I figured they probably considered him a prominent spokesman who validated rather than ridiculed their views. Ultimately, though, it didn't matter: Archie was Archie. I didn't see eye to eye with him but I understood him and had compassion for him. If his philosophical confederates felt the same way about Mike, that's good enough for me.

The show, in other words, was about people first, issues second. Life comes down to that order of priorities, too. Alas, television, when it tries at all, usually gets the two backwards, which is one reason so much of what we see is profoundly unsatisfying. "All in the Family" raised our sensibilities as to what the medium could accomplish: At its best it offered enlightenment to the mind and nourishment to the soul. I'll miss it.

Lee Margulies
Los Angeles Times

"All in the Family" is the kind of landmark show that defines all other programming as having come before or after it. The demarcation resembles that between adolescence and maturity: All that came before "Family" existed in television's age of innocence and may be excused for silliness and shallowness; everything since has had a richer pallette and must be measured against the high standard set by the program that introduced realistic characters, mature themes and frank dialogue to episodic television series.

Like any serious work of art, "All in the Family" overcomes the limitations of its form. In outline, it is straight out of the situation-comedy tradition of "I Love Lucy" and "The Honeymooners," essentially built around the interaction of two blue-collar couples whose members perform according to type in a range of situations. But while the others survived largely on bizarre antics fostered by contrived situations, the Norman Lear series built comedy on such grim and homely themes as racial tension, impotency, adultery, unemployment and pregnancy. It marked the end of pro forma mindlessness.

Most importantly, it has broken the mass medium's taboos without flouting them. The series almost unfailingly has dealt with sensitive topics responsibly, and while profiting from the sensational it has resisted sensationalizing. Stated another way, it has been more humane than opportunistic.

Les Brown
Television Correspondent
The New York Times

Alone again far up on the sand as the lesser waves of purely "commercial" television series comedy swirl and eddy close by the shoreline, "All in the Family" serves as a high-water mark for what television was in the decade of the 1970s. Most of what television offers is aimed solely at popularity, with quality an incidental consideration and bringing the mass audience close up to understanding themselves and others a troubling specter to be avoided. "All in the Family" was popular, excellent and driven by the mainspring of the laughter of human self-recognition.

At times preachy, at times noisy, the show hammered home its originally daring points with remarkable effectiveness in an era of search and turmoil in major areas of social concern—Vietnam, Watergate, abortion, sexual roles. The ratings proved, as creator Norman Lear said so often, that the network executives had for years underestimated the receptivity of the public toward material which made them think while it made them laugh.

Television, however, is a cyclical medium, and no trend in any direction remains dynamic for very long. The networks found it all too easy to pull away from what some executives considered high-decibel uplift at the first sign that new waves of more youthfully-oriented programming were rolling in. What is left is the example of a television show which attempted much in speaking to its time of birth and which found in its maturity that the audience was still listening, but indulgently and distractedly. At the end of the decade we thus see Archie Bunkerism enjoying surprising respectability in a middle class overtaken by affirmative action, inflation and growing competition with minority groups for a shrinking economic pie. It has become steadily more acceptable for bewildered parlor conversationalists who once vaguely considered themselves social liberals to voice opinions only subtly different from those of the key figure in "All in the Family." The difference is that at least now there are rueful smiles, all around, at what we have become.

It was a good try, "All in the Family," the closest the point-walkers of the traditional Army of liberal Hollywood writers have come to shaping social attitudes for a longer period than measured in the overnight ARBs. But, at bottom, "All in the Family" was only a television show. And no television show can hope to overcome the perceived self-interests of its viewers—and of the medium itself. What we can say about "All in the Family" is that it has imposed a veneer of civility on the worried seashore frolickers. And that is as much as television has ever ventured, or ever gained.

Martin Kasindorf
Los Angeles Bureau Chief
Newsweek Magazine

It is my belief that "All in the Family" has had the greatest single affect on the television industry than any other series since the inception of television.

"All in the Family" opened new vistas for writers and producers. It shattered many of the taboos that this new industry had grown up with.

In a very short period of time it allowed the industry to grow from childhood to manhood. I know of no other program that has had greater impact on this medium than "All in the Family."

Lee Rich
President
Lorimar Productions, Inc.

271

Appendix: Chronological Listing of Episodes 1971–1979

The following is a list of each of the episodes of All in the Family *broadcast from January 1971 through the 1978-79 season. Although they are listed (and numbered) in the order in which they were produced, many episodes were aired in a different sequence.*

In the writers' credits, it should be noted that when names are connected by an ampersand (e.g., Paul Harrison & Lennie Weinrib), the writers worked as a team; when names are connected by "and" (e.g., Burt Styler and Norman Lear), the writers worked individually.

1970-71 SEASON

0101   MEET THE BUNKERS
Written by Norman Lear   Air date: January 12, 1971

Introductory show. It is Edith and Archie Bunker's wedding anniversary. Edith manages to drag Archie to church for once in awhile . . . and daughter Gloria and her husband Mike Stivic try to whip up a party atmosphere for the parents.

0102   WRITING THE PRESIDENT
Teleplay by Paul Harrison &   Air date: January 19, 1971
    Lennie Weinrib and Norman Lear
Story by Les Erwin & Fred Freiberger

Mike writes a letter of criticism to the President of the United States—a fact which enrages Archie who immediately writes his own letter of praise to Nixon and day-dreams that the President thanks him for the letter on national TV.

0103   ARCHIE'S ACHING BACK
Written by Stanley Ralph Ross   Air date: January 26, 1971

Archie tries to sue for whiplash after a minor auto accident, and seeks out a Jewish lawyer to fight the case for him.

0104 JUDGING BOOKS BY COVERS
Written by Burt Styler and Norman Lear   Air date: February 9, 1971

Archie ridicules one of Mike and Gloria's friends for being a fairy. The boy isn't . . . but Mike discovers that one of Archie's tough, beer-drinking buddies *is*.

0105 ARCHIE GIVES BLOOD
Written by Norman Lear   Air date: February 2, 1971

Archie's shamed by Mike into being a blood donor, but retains his suspicions that "black blood" is different than "white blood."

0106 GLORIA HAS A BELLY FULL
(GLORIA IS PREGNANT)
Written by Jerry Mayer   Air date: February 16, 1971

Gloria gets pregnant but suffers a miscarriage. A traumatic experience for Archie who had just come around to loving the idea of being a grandfather.

0107 NOW THAT YOU KNOW THE WAY,
LET'S BE STRANGERS
Story by Philip Mishkin & Rob Reiner   Air date: February 23, 1971
Teleplay by Philip Mishkin & Rob Reiner
   and Don Nicholl & Bryan Joseph

Two young hippies are invited to stay overnight at the Bunkers by their friends Mike and Gloria. But Archie turns them out . . . He won't let the boy and girl sleep together under his roof after he discovers they're unmarried.

0108 LIONEL MOVES INTO THE NEIGHBORHOOD
Written by Don Nicholl and Bryan Joseph   Air date: March 2, 1971

Archie tries in vain to prevent a black family from moving into his neighborhood. The family turns out to be the Bunkers' friend Lionel Jefferson and his folks.

0109   EDITH HAS JURY DUTY
Teleplay by Susan Harris and Don Nicholl   Air date: March 9, 1971
    & Bryan Joseph
Story by Susan Harris

Edith serves on a jury and Archie's jealous of the attention she gets.
Edith hangs the jury and helps to save an innocent man.

0110   ARCHIE IS WORRIED ABOUT HIS JOB
Teleplay by Norman Lear and   Air date: March 16, 1971
    Don Nicholl & Bryan Joseph
Story by William Bickley, Jr.

Archie spends a sleepless night worrying because he thinks (wrongly)
that he's about to lose his job. And when Archie's up worrying—the
rest of the family has to be up worrying too!

0111   WOMEN'S LIB
Written by Norman Lear and Sandy Stern   Air date: March 23, 1971

Gloria and Mike quarrel over feminine equality in marriage and
Gloria leaves home. The Bunkers have temporarily lost a daughter
and gained a meathead son-in-law.

0112   SUCCESS STORY
Written by Burt Styler   Air date: March 30, 1971

A reunion of old army buddies at Archie's house. Staged by an ex-
buddy who's now a rich auto salesman. Archie and his pals admire
the auto man's material success and fail to see that the guy's a
lonely failure in his personal life.

0113   THE FIRST AND LAST SUPPER
Written by Jerry Mayer   Air date: April 6, 1971

Guess who's coming to dinner? It's the neighboring black family
the Jeffersons. But Mrs. Jefferson's "husband" turns out to be her

brother playing the role. The real Mr. Jefferson did an Archie on Archie and refused to eat with Whitey!

1971-72 SEASON

0201   GLORIA POSES IN THE NUDE
Written by Michael Ross &   Air date: September 25, 1971
  Bernie West & Norman Lear

Despite Archie's objections, Mike consents to let Gloria pose in the nude for a young artist friend of his. Mike, the liberal, becomes Mike, the jealous husband, when Gloria seems to be posing overtime.

0202   THE SAGA OF COUSIN OSCAR
Teleplay by Burt Styler &   Air date: September 18, 1971
  Norman Lear
Story by Burt Styler

Cousin Oscar a mooching distant relative who used to "sit on Archie's face", dies while staying at the Bunkers'. Archie is faced with the problem of paying for the funeral.

0203   FLASHBACK—MIKE MEETS ARHICE
Written by Philip Mishkin &   Air date: October 16, 1971
  Rob Reiner

On the eve of the first marriage anniversary of Mike and Gloria, we flashback to the day that Mike and Archie meet for the first time. And they've been arguing ever since.

0204   EDITH WRITES A SONG
Written by Lee Kalcheim   Air date: October 9, 1971

Edith and the kids wish to spend the "family pot" to set a lyric she has written to music. Archie would rather buy a gun to protect the house. When the house is actually invaded by two black burglars, Edith's song proves to be more powerful than the gun.

0205   ARCHIE IN THE LOCK-UP
Teleplay by Paul Wayne and   Air date: October 2, 1971
    Michael Ross and Bernie West
Story by Paul Wayne

Archie, urged by Gloria and Edith, goes to a protest demonstration to warn Mike of an impending free-for-all. Archie, the innocent bystander, is arrested and winds up in jail with a bunch of hippies, weirdos and freaks.

0206   ELECTION STORY
Written by Michael Ross &   Air date: October 30, 1971
    Bernie West

It is election eve. Mike and Gloria are stumping for a liberal candidate whom Archie despises. His opposition drives him to the extreme of voting against her—only to find, when he reaches the polls—that he is not registered and cannot vote.

0207   EDITH'S ACCIDENT
Teleplay by Michael Ross &   Air date: November 6, 1971
    Bernie West
Story by Tom & Helen August

Edith accidentally dents the fender of a parked car with her shopping cart. She leaves a note on the car which angers Archie, who is sure the owner will cheat them with an inflated bill. The owner calls and turns out to be a Catholic Priest.

0208   MIKE'S PROBLEM
Teleplay by Alan J. Levitt and   Air date: November 20, 1971
    Philip Mishkin
Story by Alan J. Levitt

Due to pressures and anxieties brought on by final exams, Mike is impotent. Worrying about this heightens the problem and causes friction between Mike and Gloria. After exams with the pressure off, and with the aid of Archie and Edith, Mike happily finds it was only a temporary problem.

0209 THE BLOCKBUSTER

Teleplay by Michael Ross & Air date: November 13, 1971
    Bernie West and Austin & Irma Kalish
Story by Austin & Irma Kalish

When a black real estate operator tries blockbusting techniques, Archie is willing to sell his house for the big profit, and renege on the neighborhood Lily-White Pact.

0210 THE INSURANCE IS CANCELLED

Teleplay by Lee Kalcheim and Air date: November 27, 1971
    Michael Ross & Bernie West
Story by Lee Kalcheim

Archie has to fire one of his men. At the same time, his home insurance is cancelled. Arbitrary prejudice causes Archie to fire a good worker, because he's Puerto Rican. The same arbitrary reasoning which places Archie in an "undesirable" area, results in the termination of Archie's insurance.

0211 CHRISTMAS DAY AT THE BUNKER'S

Written by Don Nicholl Air date: December 18, 1971

Christmas Day at the Bunker's is less joyous than usual. Archie is very subdued, claiming that the firm didn't pass out the annual bonus as usual. When this proves to be a lie on his part, he's in deep trouble with the family.

0212 THE MAN IN THE STREET

Teleplay by Don Nicholl and Air date: December 4, 1971
    Paul Harrison & Lennie Weinrib
Story by Paul Harrison & Lennie Weinrib

Archie is interviewed for the Walter Cronkite News and gives his views on President Nixon. Unfortunately, his TV set picks that day to break down.

0213 COUSIN MAUDE'S VISIT
Teleplay by Philip Mishkin Air date: December 11, 1971
  and Michael Ross & Bernie West
Story by Philip Mishkin

The entire Bunker family is hit by the flu bug at the same time, and Archie's *bete noire*, Edith's Cousin Maude, is called in to look after them.

0214 EDITH'S PROBLEM
Written by Burt Styler Air date: January 8, 1972

Edith's problem—and Archie's too—is the fact that she's entering menopause.

0215 THE ELEVATOR STORY
Written by Alan J. Levitt Air date: January 1, 1972

Archie is trapped in a stalled elevator with a black intellectual, a hysterical white woman and a Puerto Rican couple. The Puerto Rican woman chooses this moment to give birth.

0216 ARCHIE AND THE F.B.I.
Written by Michael Ross & Air date: January 15, 1971
  Bernie West and Susan Harris

How suspicion can destroy friendship. Archie and his colleague at the plant are interrogated by a government inspector.

0217 ARCHIE SEES A MUGGING
Teleplay by Philip Mishkin and Air date: January 29, 1972
  Don Nicholl
Story by Henry Garson

A local shoemaker is mugged and Mike is sure that Archie was a witness. Archie denies this and in trying to talk himself out of being a witness manages to "finger the Mafia".

0218　　　　　MIKE'S MYSTERIOUS SON
Written by Warren Murray　　　　　Air date: January 22, 1972

An old flame of Mike's deposits a 4-year-old child on the Bunkers' stoop with the information that it is his son.

0219　　　　　ARCHIE AND EDITH ALONE
Teleplay by Lee Kalcheim and　　　　　Air date: February 5, 1972
　　Michael Ross & Bernie West
Story by Tina & Les Pine

When Mike and Gloria leave to spend some days in a commune, Edith and Archie find themselves facing up to the problems of living together, without the kids for company.

0220　　　　　EDITH GETS A MINK
Teleplay by David Pollack &　　　　　Air date: February 12, 1972
　　Elias Davis and Don Nicholl
Story by David Pollack & Elias Davis

A relative gives Edith an old mink cape as a thank-you gift. Archie resents the present and orders Edith to give it back because he doesn't "want to take charity".

0221　　　　　SAMMY'S VISIT
Written by Bill Dana　　　　　Air date: February 19, 1972

Sammy Davis, Jr. in the Bunker household—after leaving his briefcase in Archie's cab.

0222　　　　　EDITH, THE JUDGE
Written by Lee Kalcheim　　　　　Air date: February 26, 1972

Archie and a local laundromat owner in a violent argument when Archie claims that the man's machine ruined his clothes and the laundromat owner counter-claims that Archie broke one of his machines. Edith is asked to settle the dispute.

0223   ARCHIE IS JEALOUS
Written by Rod Parker   Air date: March 4, 1972

Archie learns, for the first time, that Gloria and Mike spent a weekend together before they were married and isn't pleased when Edith tries to prove its innocence by remarking that she once spent a weekend with another man before she married Archie.

0224   MAUDE
Written by Rod Parker   Air date: March 11, 1972

Cousin Maude's daughter is about to be married and Archie and Edith are invited to the wedding.

1972-73 SEASON

0301   ARCHIE AND THE EDITORIAL
Teleplay by George Bloom and   Air date: September 16, 1972
    Don Nicholl
Story by George Bloom

Archie goes on TV to rebut an editorial on gun control and is mugged by two of his "fans".

0302   ARCHIE'S FRAUD
Written by Michael Ross and   Air date: September 23, 1972
    Bernie West

Archie has to explain to the Internal Revenue Service why he failed to include some money earned moonlighting in Mr. Munson's cab.

0303   GLORIA AND THE RIDDLE
Written by Don Nicholl   Air date: October 7, 1972

Even Mike is surprised to find himself a chauvinist when the men in the family cannot answer a riddle posed by Gloria and her friend.

0304   THE THREAT
Teleplay by Lila Garrett &   Air date: September 30, 1972
    Michael Elias
Story by Bill Manhoff & Lila Garrett &
    Michael Elias

The second wife, attractive and young, of an old army buddy of Archie's comes to stay for the night. Archie finds her attraction hard to handle.

0305   LIONEL STEPS OUT
Teleplay by Michael Ross and   Air date: October 14, 1972
    Bernie West
Story by Terry Ryan, Michael Ross and
    Bernie West

Archie's niece and Lionel Jefferson is a coupling devoutly not to be wished in Archie's eyes.

0306   THE BUNKERS AND THE SWINGERS
Teleplay by Michael Ross and   Air date: October 28, 1972
    Bernie West and Lee Kalcheim
Story by Norman Lear

Edith answers an ad for pen pals and her guests turn out to be a pair of wife-swapping swingers.

0307   MIKE'S APPENDIX
Written by Michael Ross and   Air date: December 2, 1972
    Bernie West

Mike has to have his appendix removed and despite his liberalism wants the operation to be performed by a man. Gloria wants it to be performed by a woman surgeon. Gloria wins.

0308   EDITH FLIPS HER WIG
Written by Sam Locke &   Air date: October 21, 1972
   Olga Vallance & Don Nicholl

Edith is arrested for shoplifting by mistake. Archie makes things worse by trying to put them right.

0309   THE LOCKET
Written by Robert Fisher and   Air date: December 23, 1972
   Arthur Marx

When Edith loses her locket Archie wants the insurance money for his own purposes and tries to get it by cheating the insurance company.

0310   MIKE COMES INTO MONEY
Written by Michael Ross and   Air date: November 4, 1972
   Bernie West

Mike receives a small inheritance from an uncle. Instead of giving the money to Archie for his room and board and expenses, he donates it to the McGovern Campaign Fund. This leads to a family split.

0311   FLASHBACK—MIKE AND GLORIA'S WEDDING
                        Part I
Written by Rob Reiner and   Air date: November 11, 1972
   Philip Mishkin

The wedding almost does not take place when an argument ensues between Archie and Mike's Uncle Casimir as to who will officiate.

0312   FLASHBACK—MIKE AND GLORIA'S WEDDING
Part II

Written by Rob Reiner and   Air date: November 18, 1972
Philip Mishkin

We finally see Mike and Gloria married in a civil ceremony.

0313   EDITH'S WINNING TICKET
Written by Don Nicholl   Air date: December 9, 1972

Edith wins a lottery prize and Archie's planning great things with
the money until he learns that the ticket really belongs to his black
neighbors. Then he's planning how to do them out of ownership.

0314   ARCHIE IS BRANDED
Written by Vincent Bogert   Air date: February 24, 1973

The Bunkers wake up to discover a swastika painted on their front
door. This is the start of a fantastic Sunday for the family. A day
that leads to them being "protected" by the Hebrew Defense Association and eventually to death.

0315   ARCHIE AND THE BOWLING TEAM
Teleplay by Allan Katz &   Air date: December 16, 1972
Don Reo
Story by Don Nicholl

Archie gets a chance to audition for a spot on the district's crack
bowling team—but finds himself "black-balled".

0316   ARCHIE IN THE HOSPITAL
Teleplay by Don Nicholl   Air date: January 6, 1973
Story by Stanley Ralph Ross &
Martin Cohan

Archie's incapacitated and Mike believes that the trouble is psycho-
somatic. Archie denies this and is sent to the hospital by a doctor

283

who is equally baffled. In the hospital Archie unwittingly shares a room with a black patient.

0317   OH SAY CAN YOU SEE
Teleplay by Michael Ross &   Air date: January 20, 1973
    Bernie West
Story by Joe Kerr

Archie has reached the stage of life where he needs to have his arms lengthened to read the newspaper. A chance meeting with an old school friend who looks years younger than Archie also troubles him.

0318   ARCHIE GOES TOO FAR
Written by Austin & Irma Kalish   Air date: January 27, 1973

Mike is incensed when Archie invades his privacy and begins to read from a book of love poetry that he discovers in Mike and Gloria's bedroom closet. After a blazing family row Mike leaves home . . . so does Gloria . . . and so does Edith!

0319   CLASS REUNION
Teleplay by Don Nicholl   Air date: February 10, 1973
Story by Stanley Ralph Ross and
    Don Nicholl

Edith goes to her high school class reunion and is looking forward to meeting an old beau. Archie's also looking forward to meeting the man who turns out to be a far cry from the handsome youth who used to be the school hero.

0320   THE HOT WATCH
Written by Sam Locke and   Air date: February 17, 1973
    Olga Vallance

Archie buys a watch from an ex-convict and Mike is convinced that it is stolen property.

0321   EVERYBODY TELLS THE TRUTH
Written by Don Nicholl   Air date: March 3, 1973

The family arguing about what *really* happened when a white man and his black assistant came to repair the refrigerator.

0322   ARCHIE LEARNS HIS LESSON
Teleplay by Michael Ross and   Air date: March 10, 1973
    Bernie West
Story by John Christopher Strong III and
    Michael R. Stein

Archie never finished high school as a boy and now needs to go to night classes in order to try for a promotion at work. He gets the diploma but not the job.

0323   GLORIA, THE VICTIM
Written by Austin & Irma Kalish &   Air date: March 17, 1973
    Don Nicholl

Gloria is the victim of an attempted rape but Archie and Mike refuse to let her press charges after a detective shows them how she would be treated in court.

0324   THE BATTLE OF THE MONTH
Written by Michael Ross &   Air date: March 24, 1973
    Bernie West

Menstrual tensions lead to a knock-down drag-out fight between Gloria and Edith and Gloria and Mike.

1973-74 SEASON

0401   ARCHIE THE GAMBLER
Teleplay by Michael Ross &   Air date: October 13, 1973
    Bernie West
Story by Steve Zacharias and
    Michael Leeson

Edith is horrified to find that Archie's old sickness of gambling has returned. When confronted, Archie promises to stop betting on the horses. An inadvertent phone call reveals that Archie has broken his promise!

0402   HENRY'S FAREWELL
Written by Don Nicholl   Air date: October 20, 1973

Henry Jefferson is leaving to set up business upstate. The Bunker's house is the scene of his farewell party. His brother, George, won't show up because it's a "honky's" house, but he is tricked and provoked into coming.

0403   WE'RE HAVING A HEAT WAVE
Written by Don Nicholl   Air date: September 15, 1973

The Bunkers learn that their new neighbors (and regulars on the series) are Irene and Frank Lorenzo. Frank is Italian, semi-retired and loves to cook. Irene is Irish and a whiz with tools and repairs.

0404   WE'RE STILL HAVING A HEAT WAVE
Written by Michael Ross &   Air date: September 22, 1973
    Bernie West

The heat wave is still with us, and Archie's nerves are frazzeled what with his air-conditioner breaking down, Frank Lorenzo's singing keeping him awake nights, and the fact that the Lorenzos have invited the Bunker family to dinner, only it's at Archie's house!

0405   EDITH FINDS AN OLD MAN
Teleplay by Michael Ross &   Air date: September 29, 1973
    Bernie West
Story by Susan Harris

Edith finds an old man wandering the streets and brings him home. Archie doesn't want Justin Quigley around because his presence reminds him he's getting old.

0406   ARCHIE AND THE KISS
Written by John Rappaport   Air date: October 6, 1973

Irene Lorenzo gives Gloria her statue of Rodin's "The Kiss". Frank is upset because it's his favorite piece of art and Archie is furious because to him it's pure pornography.

0407   ARCHIE AND THE COMPUTER
Written by Lloyd Turner and   Air date: October 27, 1973
    Gordon Mitchell and Don Nicholl

Computers that run amok complicate the Bunker's household. One keeps sending Edith quarters, another declares Archie dead, with Edith the beneficiary.

0408   THE GAMES BUNKERS PLAY
Teleplay by Michael Ross &   Air date: November 3, 1973
    Bernie West
Story by Susan Perkis Haven & Dan Klein and
    Michael Ross & Bernie West

The Bunker house is the setting for an "Encounter" Group Therapy game. The participants are: Gloria, Mike, Edith, Lionel Jefferson, and the Lorenzos. Archie refuses to play and leaves for Kelsey's Bar. It's an evening of surprises as everyone's true feelings come out.

0409   EDITH'S CONVERSION
Written by Ray Taylor   Air date: November 10, 1973

Archie is fearful that Edith is converting to Catholicism and is convinced that Irene Lorenzo and Father Majeski are the culprits.

0410   ARCHIE IN THE CELLAR
Written by Don Nicholl   Air date: November 17, 1973

Archie is alone for a weekend and is happily planning what a wonderful time he's going to have, when he accidently locks himself in the cellar and spends the whole weekend there.

0411   BLACK IS THE COLOR
           OF MY TRUE LOVE'S WIG
Written by Michael Morris   Air date: November 24, 1979

Gloria buys a black wig which turns Mike on so much he insists she wear it to bed! This upsets Gloria and Mike winds up sleeping on the couch. He finally convinces her it's not the wig that appeals to him, but Gloria herself.

0412   SECOND HONEYMOON
Teleplay by Warren S. Murray and   Air date: December 1, 1973
    Michael Ross & Bernie West
Story by Warren S. Murray

Edith has saved up to surprise Archie on their 25th Wedding Anniversary with a second honeymoon trip to the same hotel in Atlantic City where they spent their first honeymoon. Archie refuses to go as he has tickets for a big basketball game, but Edith puts her foot down and they go.

0413   THE TAXI CAPER
Written by Dennis Klein   Air date: December 8, 1973

Archie has been robbed in his cab and is all set to press charges against the boy until the boy's father sends his attorney around with a 100 dollar payoff to drop the charges. Which he does!

0414   ARCHIE IS CURSED
Written by John Rappaport and   Air date: December 15, 1973
    Michael Ross and Bernie West

Irene Lorenzo challenges Archie to a pool game. He is putting her down much to Frank's dismay, who in turn puts a Sicilian "hex" on Archie. Archie uses this curse as an excuse for getting out of the game when he realizes Irene can play. Suddenly, his back goes out!

0415 EDITH'S CHRISTMAS STORY
Teleplay by Austin & Irma Kalish   December 22, 1973
    and Don Nicholl
Story by Austin & Irma Kalish

Edith has a lump in her breast and goes to the hospital. The family
has kept the news from Archie, but when he finds out he rushes
to the hospital only to find out the lump was just a cyst but that
Edith has a broken ankle sustained by jumping off the examining
table upon hearing the good news.

0416 MIKE AND GLORIA MIX IT UP
Written by Michael Ross and   Air date: January 5, 1974
    Bernie West

When Mike and Gloria are left alone for an evening, we learn that
Mike is resentful of Gloria's recent sexual advances. This leads to a
discussion as to who has the right in a marriage to make the "first
move".

0417 ARCHIE FEELS LEFT OUT
Written by Paul Lichtman and   Air date: January 12, 1974
    Howard Storm and Don Nicholl

Archie is 50 years old and refuses not only to admit to it but also
to come to his birthday party.

0418 ET TU, ARCHIE
Written by Mickey Rose &   Air date: January 26, 1974
    Lila Garrett

Archie's old friend whom he hasn't seen in 18 years comes to town,
looking for a job. Archie is convinced he is after his job and reacts
by putting Joe Tucker down to the personnel manager down at the
plant.

0419   GLORIA'S BOYFRIEND
Written by Bud Wiser and   Air date: February 2, 1974
    Don Nicholl

A retarded boy who works as a box boy at Ferguson's Market has a crush on Gloria. Archie is made to realize although the boy is mentally handicapped, he can lead a normal life and should not be treated like a child.

0420   LIONEL'S ENGAGEMENT
Written by Michael Ross and   Air date: February 9, 1974
    Bernie West

The Jeffersons give a party to celebrate Lionel's engagement. The Bunkers and the Jeffersons have something in common when they meet the prospective bride's parents and discover she's black and he's white.

0421   ARCHIE EATS AND RUNS
Written by Paul Wayne and   Air date: February 16, 1974
    George Burditt

Archie thinks the mushrooms he's eaten are poisoned and runs to the hospital. The treatment is very painful, more so when he doscovers the mushrooms were okay and he doesn't have botulism.

0422   GLORIA SINGS THE BLUES
Written by Michael Ross &   Air date: March 2, 1974
    Bernie West

Gloria comes home depressed and confides to Edith she thinks she's fallen out of love with Michael. Edith tells her this once happened to her but that it passed as it will with Gloria. When Michael returns a little later, Gloria realizes Edith was right.

0423   MIKE'S GRADUATION
Written by Don Nicholl   Air date: March 16, 1974

After four years, Mike is graduating! Edith has mixed emotions as it means he and Gloria will be moving out of the Bunker home. Archie is ecstatic until he learns that Mike has been offered a Fellowship and will be staying on at school for another year!

0424 PAY THE TWENTY DOLLARS
Written by Robert L. Goodwin and   Air date: March 9, 1974
   Woody Kling

Archie receives a counterfeit twenty dollar bill from a fare and unknowingly passes it on to George Jefferson to pay for Edith's cleaning. When George discovers it's a phony, he confronts Archie with it.

1974-75 SEASON

0501 WHERE'S ARCHIE?
Written by Barry Harman &   Air date: November 2, 1974
   Harve Brosten

Edith's first Tupperware party is a night she will nver forget. She finds out that Archie, who was due in Buffalo at a union convention, never arrived and no one's heard from him.

0502 ARCHIE IS MISSING!
Written by Lloyd Turner &   Air date: November 9, 1974
   Gordon Mitchell

There is still no word from Archie and certain evidence leads the family to believe he may have run off with another woman.

0503 THE LONGEST KISS
Teleplay by Lou Derman &   Air date: November 16, 1974
   Bill Davenport
Story by Dawn M. Stephens and
   Lou Derman & Bill Davenport

Archie has mistakenly ended up in Rochester at a foot doctors' convention. He arrives home to find Gloria and Mike trying to set a record for kissing; Irene standing on her head; Louise and George dancing and Edith twirling a hula hoop.

0504   THE BUNKERS AND INFLATION
Written by Don Nicholl and   Air date: September 14, 1974
    Michael Ross & Bernie West

Archie's union down at the plant decides to go out on strike.

0505   ARCHIE UNDERFOOT
Written by Don Nicholl and   Air date: September 21, 1974
    Michael Ross & Bernie West

Archie is still on strike and when he's not out picketing, he's getting in Edith's way at home.

0506   EDITH THE JOB HUNTER
Written by Don Nicholl and   Air date: September 28, 1974
    Michael Ross & Bernie West

With no money coming in, Edith is forced to take a job—in the Jefferson's cleaning store!

0507   ARCHIE'S RAISE
Written by Don Nicholl and   Air date: October 5, 1974
    Michael Ross & Bernie West

The strike has been settled and Archie goes back to work with a 15% raise. He is pleased until Mike points out he's already behind the cost of living rise!

0508   MIKE'S FRIEND
Written by Roger Shulman &   Air date: December 14, 1974
    John Baskin

Mike makes Gloria feel intellectually inferior when his college friend spends an evening at the Bunkers.

0509   LIONEL THE LIVE IN
Teleplay by Woody Kling   Air date: October 12, 1974
Story by Jeffery Mackowsky

After an argument with his father over his girlfriend, Lionel spends the night at the Bunkers, much to Archie's chagrin!

0510   ARCHIE'S HELPING HAND
Written by Norman & Harriet Belkin   Air date: October 19, 1974

Archie gets Irene a job at his plant never dreaming she'll be working with him on the loading dock!

0511   GLORIA'S SHOCK
Written by Dixie Brown Grossman   Air date: October 26, 1974

Mike's announcement that he and Gloria are not going to have children comes as a complete shock to Edith and Archie—and Gloria!

0512   THE JEFFERSONS MOVE UP
Written by Don Nicholl and   Air date: January 11, 1975
    Michael Ross & Bernie West

The Jeffersons leave Bunkerville for a high-rise apartment in Manhattan.

0513   ARCHIE AND THE MIRACLE
Written by Lloyd Turner &   Air date: November 23, 1974
    Gordon Mitchell

After a narrow escape at work, Archie becomes a believer and a church-goer.

0514   GEORGE AND ARCHIE MAKE A DEAL
Written by David P. Harmon   Air date: November 30, 1974

George Jefferson is running for a political office and needs Archie's signature on his petition. Archie signs in return for a discount on the Bunker's cleaning.

0515   ARCHIE'S CONTRACT
Written by Ron Friedman   Air date: December 7, 1974

Archie is taken in by a con man selling aluminum siding. If it weren't for friends like Irene, George and Louise, the Bunker house would be covered with aluminum and $2000.00 poorer.

0516   THE BEST OF ALL IN THE FAMILY
                                Air date: December 21, 1974

This is the 100th Anniversary Special comprised of clips from 71 shows. Narrated by Henry Fonda.

0517   PRISONER IN THE HOUSE
Teleplay by Bud Wiser and   Air date: January 4, 1975
    Lou Derman & Bill Davenport
Story by Bud Wiser

Archie fears for his life and his family's safety when he learns the plumber's assistant working in the Bunker house is on a work furlough program from prison.

0518   ALL'S FAIR
Written by Lloyd Turner &   Air date: January 18, 1975
    Gordon Mitchell

Edith takes Gloria's advice and uses "Fair Fighting" in her marriage. Archie says her cousin Estelle cannot come to visit—and Edith stands up to him and tells him what she feels.

0519   AMELIA'S DIVORCE

Written by Lou Derman &   Air date: January 25, 1975
     Bill Davenport

Edith is shocked when she finds out her Cousin Amelia's "perfect" marriage is headed for a divorce.

0520   EVERYBODY DOES IT

Written by Lou Derman &   Air date: February 8, 1975
     Bill Davenport and Susan Ware

Mike accuses Archie of being a thief when he brings home a box of nails from the plant. Archie contends that 'everybody does it' and almost proves his point when both Mike and Gloria are found wanting.

0521   ARCHIE AND THE QUIZ

Written by Michael Morris   Air date: February 15, 1975

Archie takes a magazine life expectancy test and is ready to move to Arizona and lead a "clean" life when he finds he may pass on at 57!

0522   EDITH'S FRIEND

Written by Barry Harman &   Air date: February 22, 1975
     Harve Brosten

Edith goes to a family wedding in Scranton and has a "brief encounter" with her cousin Roy, whom she finds out is not really a blood relative.

0523   NO SMOKING

Written by Lou Derman &   Air date: March 1, 1975
     Bill Davenport

Archie and Mike have a bet going. Archie says Mike cannot give up eating for two days and Mike says Archie cannot give up cigars for two days.

0524   MIKE MAKES HIS MOVE
Teleplay by Lou Derman &   Air date: March 8, 1975
    Bill Davenport
Story by Robert Arnott

Mike and Gloria are moving out of the Bunker household. Archie is delighted until he learns they are moving next door into the old Jefferson house!

1975-76 SEASON

0601   ARCHIE THE HERO
Written by Lou Derman &   Air date: September 29, 1975
    Bill Davenport

Archie gives mouth-to-mouth resuscitation to a woman in his cab who turns out to be a transvestite.

0602   ARCHIE THE DONOR
Written by Bill Davenport and   Air date: September 22, 1975
    Larry Rhine

In an attempt to influence his boss for a promotion, Archie unknowingly signs up to donate his body to medical science.

0603   CHAIN LETTER
Teleplay by Lou Derman and   Air date: October 20, 1975
    Milt Josefsberg
Story by Lou Derman

Irene sends the Bunkers and Stivics a chain letter, which Archie believes causes a series of mishaps, including a case of hepatitis.

0604   EDITH BREAKS OUT
Written by Lou Derman &   Air date: November 3, 1975
    Bill Davenport

Archie objects to Edith's activities as a Sunshine Lady at a Home for the Aged because he feels she is neglecting him.

0605   THE VERY MOVING DAY
Written by Hal Kanter   Air date: September 8, 1975

When Gloria announces she is going to have a baby, Mike's initial joy and surprise at the big news soon disappears when he begins to feel that Gloria tricked him.

0606   ALONE AT LAST?
Written by Hal Kanter   Air date: September 15, 1975

As Gloria and Mike move next door to the old Jefferson house, their first night is complicated when Mike admits he forgot to have the utilities turned on.

0607   THE LITTLE ATHEIST
Written by Lou Derman   Air date: November 24, 1975

At Gloria's first Thanksgiving dinner, Archie insists that his coming grandchild be raised as a Christian. Mike, the atheist, and Gloria believe the decision will be up to the child in due time.

0608   MIKE'S PAINS
Written by Lou Derman and   Air date: October 6, 1975
   Milt Josefsberg

Though Mike and Gloria have decided to have the baby by natural childbirth, Mike suddenly gets cold feet at the thought of joining Gloria in the delivery room.

0609   MIKE FACES LIFE
Written by Mel Tolkin and   Air date: October 27, 1975
   Larry Rhine

As Mike faces the financial responsibilities involved in becoming a father, Gloria announces she's been fired from her job because of pregnancy.

0610   GRANDPA BLUES
Teleplay by Mel Tolkin   November 10, 1975
   and Larry Rhine
Story by John Rappaport

In order to pass a company physical, Archie's doctor orders a weekend of complete calm just as an argument over the coming baby's name is brewing.

0611   GLORIA SUSPECTS MIKE
Written by Lou Derman and   Air date: November 17, 1975
   Milt Josefsberg

Gloria, feeling fat and unattractive in her final months of pregnancy, suspects Mike of being unfaithful with an attractive student he is tutoring.

0612   ARCHIE'S CIVIL RIGHTS
Written by Larry Rhine and   Air date: December 1, 1975
   Mel Tolkin

Archie squirts tear gas at a would-be mugger in his cab and winds up in court facing a possible stiff jail sentence.

0613   ARCHIE THE BABYSITTER
Written by Lou Derman &   Air date: January 12, 1976
   Bill Davenport

Archie, unwilling to leave his grandson with a young babysitter, winds up babysitting during a poker game.

0614   GLORIA IS NERVOUS
Written by Milt Josefsberg and   Air date: December 8, 1975
   Ben Starr

Mike gets a lesson in the LaMaze method of prepared childbirth when he hyperventilates at Gloria's baby shower.

0615   NEW YEAR'S WEDDING
Written by Lou Derman &   Air date: January 5, 1976
    Bill Davenport and Milt Josefsberg
    & Ben Starr

Without consulting Gloria, Mike moves the setting of their best friends' wedding to the Stivic home, proving Gloria's claim that Mike makes all the decisions without consulting her.

0616   BIRTH OF THE BABY
                     Part I
Written by Lou Derman &   Air date: December 15, 1975
    Bill Davenport and Larry Rhine
    & Mel Tolkin

As Archie reluctantly rehearses for his lodge's minstrel show, Mike and Gloria have their final pre-baby fling at an Italian restaurant. Gloria feels contractions while imprisoned in a phone booth.

0617   BIRTH OF THE BABY
                     Part II
Written by Milt Josefsberg &   Air date: December 22, 1975
    Ben Starr

Archie goes to the hospital in blackface as Mike assists Gloria in the delivery of the baby.

0618   ARCHIE FINDS A FRIEND
Written by Mel Tolkin &   Air date: January 26, 1976
    Larry Rhine

Archie sees dreams of riches as partner in watchmaker Bernstein's invention. Bernstein dies, and with him the dream.

0619   MIKE'S MOVE
Written by Milt Josefsberg &   Air date: February 2, 1976
   Ben Starr

Mike is up for a teaching job in Minnesota. He tussles with his principles when a black man gets the job because of his color.

0620   ARCHIE'S WEIGHTY PROBLEM
Written by Larry Rhine &   Air date: February 9, 1976
   Mel Tolkin

Edith puts Archie on a strict diet. Archie fights it until he sees the effect of diet on a spry eighty year old man.

0621   LOVE BY APPOINTMENT
Written by Lou Derman &   Air date: February 16, 1976
   Bill Davenport

Gloria, full-time mother to infant Joey, has little time for the physical needs of Mike.

0622   JOEY'S BAPTISM
Written by Milt Josefsberg,   Air date: February 23, 1976
   Mel Tolkin & Larry Rhine

Archie wants his grandchild to be a Christian, against the wishes of Mike and Gloria. Archie sneaks the child to church and baptizes Joey himself.

0623   GLORIA AND MIKE'S HOUSE GUESTS
Written by Larry Rhine,   Air date: March 1, 1976
   Mel Tolkin & Milt Josefsberg

Due to a non-functioning furnace during a cold spell. Archie and Edith must spend the weekend with the Stivics. Their battling is ended by a power blackout, bringing the two families together—for a moment.

0624 EDITH'S NIGHT OUT

Teleplay by Lou Derman, Air date: March 8, 1976
  Douglas Arango & Phil Doran

Archie continues to refuse to take Edith out. Edith decides to go on the town by herself and winds up the life of the party at Kelcy's Bar.

1976-77 SEASON

0701 ARCHIE'S SECRET PASSION

Written by Michael Loman Air date: December 4, 1976

When Edith invites a schoolmate of Archie's to dinner she discovers schoolboy Archie enjoyed a quickie affair with their guest. In retaliation, Edith hints at an affair of her own.

0702 ARCHIE'S BRIEF ENCOUNTER
Part I

Written by Larry Rhine & Air date: September 22, 1976
  Mel Tolkin

With Edith busy at the Sunshine Home, Archie spends evenings alone. Goaded by his buddies, he dates a waitress at her apartment. He panics when confronted by Carlos from Kelsey's.

0703 THE UNEMPLOYMENT STORY
Part I

Written by Ben Starr & Air date: October 6, 1976
  Chuck Stewart

The family's joy over Mike winning a writing prize is shattered by the news that Archie has lost his job. Archie's ego and sex life suffers.

0704   THE UNEMPLOYMENT STORY
                    Part II

Written by Chuck Stewart &   Air date: October 13, 1976
   Ben Starr

Archie edges a college man out of a job as janitor. When the rejected applicant threatens to jump off the building ledge, Archie talks him out of it.

0705   ARCHIE'S BRIEF ENCOUNTER
                    Part II

Written by Larry Rhine &   Air date: September 22, 1976
   Mel Tolkin

After his date, Archie is coached by his pals on his alibi to Edith. Archie's alibi falls apart and Edith, deeply hurt, leaves for the Sunshine Home. (Aired as a one-hour show.)

0706   ARCHIE'S BRIEF ENCOUNTER
                    Part III

Written by Mel Tolkin &   Air date: September 29, 1976
   Larry Rhine

The Stivics invite the estranged Archie and Edith to dinner, using Joey as bait. Left alone, Archie and Edith realize how much they need each other.

0707   ARCHIE'S OPERATION
                    Part I

Teleplay by Milt Josefsberg and   Air date: October 20, 1976
   Mort Lachman
Story by Calvin Kelly & Jim Tisdale

Archie, in the hospital for a gallstone operation, learns that the only available blood for his transfusion will come from a black doctor.

0708   ARCHIE'S OPERATION
                Part II
Written by Mel Tolkin &   Air date: October 27, 1976
   Larry Rhine

In the hospital, Archie must face the reality of unemployment, soaring medical bills, and a lifetime of black blood in his veins.

0709   MIKE AND GLORIA'S WILL
Written by Bill Richmond &   Air date: November 20, 1976
   Gene Perret

The Bunkers are crushed when they discover the Stivics consider appointing a young married couple as guardians for Joey should something happen to Mike and Gloria.

0710   TERESA MOVES IN
Written by Michael Loman   Air date: November 13, 1976

To help pay off Archie's medical bills, Edith takes in a boarder. Archie remembers her as the Puerto Rican admissions clerk who gave him trouble at the hospital.

0711   BEVERLY RIDES AGAIN
Written by Phil Doran &   Air date: November 6, 1976
   Douglas Arango

When Archie's buddies play practical jokes on him, he tries to get even by arranging a date for one of his tormentors with a transvestite.

0712   MR' EDITH BUNKER
Written by Mel Tolkin &   Air date: November 27, 1976
   Larry Rhine

When Edith saves a life at the Sunshine Home and is featured on a local television program, Archie feels his position as head of the family is threatened.

0713   GLORIA'S FALSE ALARM
Written by Phil Doran &   Air date: December 18, 1976
    Douglas Arango

When Gloria discovers she might be pregnant again, she and Mike decide it's time he has a vasectomy.

0714   THE BABY CONTEST
Teleplay by Larry Rhine &   Air date: December 11, 1976
    Mel Tolkin
Story by Marion Zola & Ed Haas

Mike and Gloria are furious when they discover Archie has entered Joey in a baby contest. They're even more furious when Joey loses thanks to Archie's ballot-box stuffing.

0715   THE DRAFT DODGER
Written by Jay Moriarty &   Air date: December 25, 1976
    Mike Milligan

Two guests are invited to the Bunkers' Christmas dinner. Mike's draft-dodger friend, in from Canada, incognito and Archie's pal whose son died in Vietnam.

0716   ARCHIE'S CHAIR
Written by Phil Doran &   Air date: January 15, 1977
    Douglas Arango

Mike panics when he accidentally breaks Archie's chair. In an effort to have it repaired before Archie finds out, the chair ends up as an exhibit in a far-out art shop.

0717 THE BOARDER PATROL
Written by Mel Tolkin & Air date: January 8, 1977
   Larry Rhine

Archie and Edith return unexpectedly from a weekend trip to discover their boarder Teresa is sharing her bed with her boyfriend.

0718 MIKE GOES SKIING
Written by Ben Starr & Air date: January 22, 1977
   Chuck Stewart

Mike goes off for a skiing weekend with the boys leaving an unhappy Gloria to attend a party alone. His sympathy for her fades when he finds out Gloria didn't come home alone.

0719 STRETCH CUNNINGHAM, GOODBYE
Written by Phil Doran & Air date: January 29, 1977
   Douglas Arango and Milt Josefsberg

Archie agrees to deliver the eulogy at the funeral of a co-worker. To his surprise, he winds up wearing a yamulkah at a synagogue.

0720 THE JOYS OF SEX
Written by Erik Tarloff Air date: February 5, 1977

Edith reads a sex manual and concludes her sex life could stand improving. Gloria assigns Mike the chore of a man-to-man talk with Archie.

0721 MIKE THE PACIFIST
Written by Phil Doran & Air date: February 12, 1977
   Douglas Arango

Pacifist Mike gets involved in a subway dispute and winds up slugging a passenger, then suffering the pangs of guilt.

0722   FIRE
Wirtten by Michael Loman and   Air date: February 19, 1977
   Larry Rhine & Mel Tolkin

A fire breaks out in the Bunker home. Attempting to collect more than is coming to him from the insurance company, Archie winds up with much less.

0723   MIKE AND GLORIA SPLIT
Teleplay by Mel Tolkin &   Air date: February 26, 1977
   Larry Rhine
Story by Mort Lachman and
   Milt Josefsberg

Gloria accuses the college-educated Mike of lording it over her when he wins a word game. Their quarrel builds to Mike leaving the house and spending the night in bed with Archie.

0724   ARCHIE THE LIBERAL
Written by Ben Starr &   Air date: March 5, 1977
   Chuck Stewart

When Archie comes under pressure for discrimination in his Lodge, he satisfies two minority quotas by bringing in a black who is Jewish.

0725   ARCHIE'S DOG DAY AFTERNOON
Teleplay by Chuck Stewart &   Air date: March 12, 1977
   Ben Starr
Story by Mort Lachman and
   Milt Josefsberg

Archie's latest enemy is Barney Hefner's dog. He risks adding Barney to the enemy list when he accidentally hits the dog with his cab.

1977-78 SEASON

0801   COUSIN LIZ
Written by Bob Weiskopf and   Air date: October 9, 1977
  Bob Schiller

Archie and Edith attend the funeral of Edith's cousin Liz. Archie's shocked to learn Liz was a lesbian and has left her estate to the woman she lived with.

0802   UNEQUAL PARTNERS
Written by Chuck Stewart and   Air date: October 23, 1977
  Ben Starr

Archie's fishing trip is delayed by a wedding of two oldsters from the Sunshine home, arranged by Edith.

0803   ARCHIE GETS THE BUSINESS
                    Part I
Written by Larry Rhine and   Air date: October 2, 1977
  Mel Tolkin

When Kelsey has a heart attack, Archie, eager to buy the bar, forges Edith's signature to obtain the mortgage on their home to finance the deal. (One hour special)

0804   ARCHIE GETS THE BUSINESS
                    Part II
Written by Mel Tolkin and   Air date: October 2, 1977
  Larry Rhine

Edith discovers Archie has forged her name on the mortgage application but follows Mike's advice to let Archie have his dream. (One hour special)

0805   EDITH'S 50TH BIRTHDAY
                         Part I

Written by Bob Weiskopf and   Air date: October 16, 1977
    Bob Schiller

While a surprise birthday party awaits Edith in the Stivics' home, she fights off a rapist in the Bunker house. (One hour special)

0806   ARCHIE AND THE KU KLUX KLAN
                         Part 1

Written by Bob Weiskopf and   Air date: November 27, 1977
    Bob Schiller, Mort Lachman and
    Milt Josefsberg

Two klansmen decide Archie is good material for their organization. Archie discovers he's committed himself to become a member of the KKK.

0807   EDITH'S 50TH BIRTHDAY
                         Part II

Written by Bob Weiskopf and   Air date: October 16, 1977
    Bob Schiller

Edith wants to forget her shattering experience with the rapist, but realizes she must go to the police and identify the man. (One hour special)

0808   ARCHIE'S GRAND OPENING
Written by Larry Rhine and   Air date: October 30, 1977
    Mel Tolkin

Archie's mishandling of his staff inspires Harry and Carlos to quit. On opening night the family pitches in to help out. Archie burns his bridges by throwing out Mr. Sanders, his plant boss.

0809   ARCHIE AND THE KKK
                         Part II

Written by Bob Weiskopf and   Air date: December 4, 1977
    Bob Schiller

When Archie learns his first assignment by the KKK is to burn a cross on Mike's lawn, he informs them of his blood transfusion from a black, and scares them with a threat to round up his black brothers.

0810   ARCHIE'S BITTER PILL
                    Part I
Written by Mel Tolkin, Larry Rhine,   Air date: November 16, 1977
   and William C. Rader

Unable to cope with bad business, and worried he can lose his saloon, Archie is talked into taking drugs. The family discovers his addiction when he O.D.'s at the bar.

0811   ARCHIE'S ROAD BACK
                    Part II
Written by Larry Rhine and   Air date: November 23, 1977
   Mel Tolkin

Archie, recuperating from his pill taking, takes to bed. Unwilling to face life, he decides to stay in bed forever, until his family laughs him out of it.

0812   MIKE AND GLORIA MEET
Written by Bob Weiskopf and   Air date: December 11, 1977
   Bob Schiller

Gloria recalls her first date with Mike, and in a flashback Gloria admits that she's a virgin and Mike tries to change her category.

0813   EDITH'S CRISIS OF FAITH
                    Part I
Written by Bob Weiskopf and   Air date: December 25, 1977
   Bob Schiller
Story by Eric Tarloff

Edith's dear friend, Beverly LaSalle, a female impersonator, is murdered on Christmas Eve, which shakes Edith's faith in God. (One hour special)

0814 EDITH'S CRISIS OF FAITH
Part II
Teleplay by Eric Tarloff, Mel Tolkin,   Air date: December 25, 1977
    and Larry Rhine
Story by Eric Tarloff

Shaken by the death of her friend Beverly LaSalle, Edith sees no
reason to participate in the observance of Christmas. Mike convinces her that faith goes beyond reason.

0815 THE COMMERCIAL
Teleplay by Ben Starr and   Air date: January 8, 1978
    Ron Bloomberg
Story by Ron Bloomberg

Edith is chosen to star in a TV commercial. Against Archie's advice,
she refuses to lie about her preference for the product, and loses
the job.

0816 AUNT IOLA'S VISIT
Teleplay by Albert E. Lewin   Air date: January 22, 1978
Story by Michael Loman

Edith's Aunt Iola is about to end a visit with the Bunkers but no
other relatives will have her. Archie tries to palm her off on the
Stivics, but to his surprise, Aunt Iola goes to a man with whom she
has a swinging relationship.

0817 SUPERBOWL SUNDAY
Written by Bob Weiskopf and   Air date: January 5, 1978
    Bob Schiller

Archie's plan to drum up business with a Superbowl betting pool
boomerangs when two of the participants in the pool collect the
entire take at the point of a gun.

0818 LOVE COMES TO THE BUTCHER
Written by Phil Sharp   Air date: February 5, 1978

When a widowed butcher confesses his loneliness to Edith, she invites him for an evening of singing old songs. The butcher mistakes her compassion for love and makes advances which she fields easily. Archie realizes that Edith could use more attention and brings her flowers.

0819   TWO'S A CROWD
Written by Phil Sharp   Air date: February 5, 1978

Archie and Mike find themselves locked in the bar storeroom. In an in-depth conversation, Archie reveals a relationship with his father which explains what makes Archie what he is.

0820   STALEMATES
Written by Bob Weiskopf and   Air date: February 19, 1978
    Bob Schiller

Mike and Gloria think they've fallen out of love. To rekindle their passion, they go to a hotel in the country. There they realize the importance of friendship to a marriage, and they consummate the friendship.

0821   THE BROTHER
Written by Larry Rhine and   Air date: February 26, 1978
    Mel Tolkin

The brother Archie never talks about appears and old enmities surface. Archie softens when he learns his brother is about to have a serious operation.

0822   MIKE'S NEW JOB
Written by Mel Tolkin and   Air date: March 5, 1978
    Larry Rhine

Archie learns Mike's accepted a job in California and plans to take away Archie's daughter and grandson. He tries to sabotage the move. Then George Jefferson sells his house, causing the Stivics to move back in with the Bunkers for the next two weeks.

0823   THE DINNER GUEST
Written by Larry Rhine and   Air date: March 12, 1978
    Mel Tolkin

Edith has planned a going-away dinner for the Stivics. But when
Mike accepts a date for Gloria and himself with an important professor, Archie shames Mike into staying home. This leads to an old-
time no-holds-barred family argument.

0824   THE STIVICS GO WEST
Written by Bob Weiskopf and   Air date: March 19, 1978
    Bob Schiller

As the Bunkers and Stivics exchange final goodbyes, Mike confesses he has always loved Archie. There is a general declaration of
love, but Archie is unable to express his feelings.

1978-79 SEASON

0901   END IN SIGHT
Written by Nate Monaster   Air date: October 1, 1978

Archie and Harry apply for partnership insurance and have to have
physicals. Archie's x-ray comes back with a spot on the liver. He
has to go the next day for more x-rays but spends the night thinking
he is going to die.

0902   REUNION ON HAUSER STREET
Written by Milt Josefsberg and   Air date: October 8, 1978
    Phil Sharp

Blanche and Barney are still separated. Harry and Archie try to fix
Barney up with Boom Boom. Meanwhile, Blanche visits Edith and
tells her the exterminator dumped her and wonders if Barney will
take her back. She and Edith pay a surprise visit to the bar to see
Barney.

0903   WEEKEND IN THE COUNTRY
Written by Phil Sharp and   Air date: October 29, 1978
   Milt Josefsberg

Edith, Archie, Blanche and Barney spend a weekend in Barney's cabin. Barney and Blanche get into a fight over a monopoly game and Archie and Barney have to sleep in Barney and Blanche's room and Edith and Blanche are together in Archie and Edith's room. During the night Archie ends up in bed with Edith and Blanche.

0904   LITTLE MISS BUNKER
Written by Mel Tolkin and   Air date: September 24, 1978
   Larry Rhine

Edith's cousin Floyd pays a visit to the Bunkers and leaves his young daughter with the Bunkers. Stephanie overhears Archie and Edith talking and finds out Archie doesn't want her. She runs away. Archie goes looking for her and finds her at the bus station. She tells him why she is leaving.

0905   EDITH'S FINAL RESPECTS
Story by Sam Greenbaum   Air date: October 22, 1978
Teleplay by Bob Schiller and
   Bob Weiskopf

Edith's Aunt Rose has died so she goes to pay her last respects. Nobody in the family liked Aunt Rose except Edith, who finds good in everyone. Edith gets to know Aunt Rose at the funeral home.

0906   WHAT'LL WE DO WITH STEPHANIE
Teleplay by Larry Rhine and   Air date: October 15, 1978
   Mel Tolkin

Sephanie's father is coming to pick her up today, except in the mail there is a letter from him to Stephanie. Edith opens it and finds he isn't coming. Archie gets angry and calls the authorities to report Floyd for abandonment. A social worker pays them a visit.

0907   ARCHIE'S OTHER WIFE
Written by Bob Schiller and   Air date: November 5, 1978
    Bob Weiskopf

Archie and his buddies go away for a big caucus. Pinky, as a practical joke, has a black stewardess sneak into Archie's bed in the middle of the night. Archie awakens thinking he took her to bed with him.

0908   EDITH VERSUS THE BANK
Written by Mel Tolkin and   Air date: November 19, 1978
    Larry Rhine

It's the Bunkers' anniversary and the television blows up. Edith decides to surprise Archie with a new one for an anniversary present. She goes to their bank to get a loan. The bank turns her down because she is just a housewife and doesn't own anything that can be used as collateral.

0909   RETURN OF THE WAITRESS
Written by Milt Josefsberg and   Air date: November 26, 1978
    Phil Sharp

Boom Boom quits her job as waitress at the bar and Harry hires another girl without asking Archie. It turns out to be Denise, the girl Archie almost had an affair with. Edith comes to the bar later and thinks she recognizes the new waitress.

0910   A NIGHT AT THE P.T.A.
Written by Larry Rhine and   Air date: January 7, 1979
    Mel Tolkin

Edith and Stephanie are going to sing a duet at the P.T.A., Archie doesn't want Edith to sing in public. During practice sessions Edith loses her voice, tells Archie he is going to have to do the song with Stephanie.

0911 BOGUS BILLS

Written by Bob Schiller and   Air date: December 3, 1978
   Bob Weiskopf

Edith is arrested for passing a counterfeit bill. Archie goest to jail and picks her up. During an interview it comes to light that Archie gave her the bill. Archie goes back to the bar and has his own investigation as to who passed him the bill.

0912 BUNKERS GO WEST

Written by Mel Tolkin and   Air date: December 10, 1978
   Larry Rhine

Archie and Edith are preparing for Mike and Gloria's Christmas visit. Gloria calls telling them Mike's back is out and they won't be able to come. After the tremendous disappointment, Edith decides they should go to California.

0913 THE APPENDECTOMY

Written by Phil Sharp and   Air date: January 21, 1979
   Milt Josefsberg

Tomorrow is Stephanie's birthday, but she is sick. Dr. Shapiro comes and tells Archie she needs an appendectomy, Archie refuses, he wants a second opinion. Later in the night they have to take her to the hospital. Archie and Edith face the reality that her father may never come back for her.

0914 CALIFORNIA HERE WE ARE
Part I

Written by Milt Josefsberg and   Air date: December 17, 1978
   Phil Sharp

Archie and Edith arrive in California with Stephanie and Turkey in tow. Gloria and Mike are separated and Gloria spends an uncomfortable night on the chair in their room. They have a fight and Edith and Gloria end up in the bathroom talking. Edith learns of the separation.

0915 CALIFORNIA HERE WE ARE
Part II

Written by Bob Schiller and   Air date: December 17, 1978
    Bob Weiskopf

Edith finds out Gloria has been seeing another man. When Archie finds out they are separated he immediately assumes the Meathead has been cheating on Gloria. Gloria tells him the truth. Archie turns his back on her and sides with the Meathead.

0916 A GIRL LIKE EDITH

Written by Bob Schiller and   Air date: January 14, 1979
    Bob Weiskopf

Klemmer the butcher runs into Edith at the laundromat and tells Edith he has found a girl just like her and is in love. Edith invites them over to dinner so she and Archie can meet his new love.

0917 STEPHANIE AND THE CRIME WAVE

Written by Larry Rhine and   Air date: January 28, 1979
    Mel Tolkin

Archie and Edith are called by the school principal to come in for a meeting. He tells them Stephanie has been suspected of stealing things in her classroom. Archie and Edith deal with this possibility, each in their own way.

0918 STEPHANIE'S CONVERSION

Written by Patt Shea and   Air date: February 18, 1979
    Harriett Weiss

Reverend Chong pays the Bunkers a visit to advise them that Stephanie is Jewish. Archie and Edith have different ideas about how to deal with the situation.

0919 BARNEY THE GOLD DIGGER

Story by Winston Moss   Air date: February 5, 1979
Teleplay by Bob Schiller and Bob Weiskopf and
    Phil Sharp and Milt Josefsberg

Blanche has run away from Barney again and Barney is threatening suicide. Archie decides to fix him up with a friend of Edith's who is a widow with a lot of money.

0920   EDITH GETS FIRED
Written by Harriett Weiss and   Air date: February 25, 1979
    Patt Shea

A lady at the Sunshine Home dies while Edith is watching her. Edith is accused of negligence and is fired. Archie questions Edith as to whether or not she knew the lady was dying.

0921   THE FAMILY NEXT DOOR
Written by Mel Tolkin and   Air date: March 18, 1979
    Larry Rhine

Louise Jefferson pays Edith a visit and asks her to please show people their house next door. Archie sees the perfect chance to rent the house to whom he wants. Edith sees things differently.

0922   THE RETURN OF ARCHIE'S BROTHER
Story by Tom Sawyer and   Air date: March 11, 1979
    Bob Schiller and Bob Weiskopf

Archie's brother pays Archie a visit. With him he brings his new wife. Archie is pleased that Fred is settling down again until he meets Fred's new wife.

0923   THE RETURN OF STEPHANIE'S FATHER
Written by Larry Rhine and   Air date: March 25, 1979
    Mel Tolkin

Stephanie's father comes back and wants to see Archie and Edith but not Stephanie. Edith is afraid he wants to take Stephanie away. Her father has something very different in mind.

0924   TOO GOOD EDITH
Written by Harriett Weiss and   Air date: April 8, 1979
    Patt Shea

Archie is having a big Saint Patrick's Day party at the bar which he
wants Edith to cook corned beef and cabbage for but Edith is sick.
The doctor tells her she has phlebitis and must stay off her feet.
Archie won't listen when Edith tries to tell him.

Further Reading

1. Scripts

Five episodes of *All in the Family* have been published as theatrical scripts (New York: Samuel French and Co., 1975). They are:
"Archie and the Computer"
"Archie and the Editorial"
"Archie in the Hospital"
"Gloria Poses in the Nude"
"Mike's Appendix"

2. Empirical Research

Bock, Gabrielle, "Alf Garnett, Archie Bunker, and Alfred Tetzlaff: Different Societies—Different Bigots," Paper presented to the International Communication Association, Chicago, April 1978.

A cross-cultural content analysis of the British, American and German versions of *All in the Family*.

Christie, Lee, "Review of 'Archie Bunker's Bigotry' by Neil Vidmar and Milton Rokeach," Unpublished paper, Wells/Christie Associates, Beverly Hills, CA., n.d. (Commissioned by Tandem Productions).

Cooper, Eunice and Marie Jahoda, "The Evasion of Propaganda: How Prejudiced People Respond to Anti-Prejudice Propaganda," *Journal of Psychology*, 23, 1947, pp. 15-25.

Classic study which provided the model for most of the research conducted on *All in the Family*.

Felsenthal, Norman, "The Audience and the Reviewers: An Analysis of Viewer Letters and Critics' Columns Relating to the Television Program 'All in the Family,' " Paper presented to the

Speech Communication Association, Houston, Texas, December 1975.

Gross, Leonard, "Do Bigots Miss the Message?" *TV Guide*, November 8, 1975, pp. 14-18.

Popular, non-technical summary of research findings to date on *All in the Family*.

Leckenby, John D. and Stuart H. Surlin, "Incidental Social Learning and Viewer Race: 'All in the Family' and 'Sanford and Son,' " *Journal of Broadcasting*, Fall 1976, pp. 481-494.

Surlin, Stuart H., "Bigotry on Air and in Life: The Archie Bunker Case," *Public Telecommunications Review*, April 1974.

Surlin, Stuart H., "Five Years of 'All in the Family'—A Summary of Empirical Research Generated by the Program," *Mass Comm Review*, Summer 1976

Surlin, Stuart H. and Beth Bowden, "The Psychological Effect of Television Characters: The Case of Archie Bunker and Authoritarian Viewers," Paper presented to the Association for Education in Journalism, College Park, Maryland, August 1976.

Surlin, Stuart H. and Eugene D. Tate, " 'All in the Family': Is Archie Funny?" *Journal of Communication,* Autumn 1976, pp. 61-68.

Tate, Eugene D. and Stuart H. Surlin, "Agreement with Opinionated TV Characters Across Cultures," *Journalism Quarterly*, Summer 1976, pages 199-203; 210.

3.   Behind the Scenes

Adler, Dick, "Lear Kingdom: One Big Happy Family," *Television International*, January-February 1975.

Cowan, Geoffrey, *See No Evil*. New York: Simon and Schuster, 1979.

An account of the origins and ultimately successful challenge to the networks' Family Viewing Time policy. FVT's impact on *All in the Family*, and Lear's response, is an important part of the story.

Kasindorf, Martin, "Archie and Maude and Fred and Norman," *The New York Times Magazine*, June 24, 1973.

Lear, Norman, Interview, *Playboy*, March 1976.

Lear, Norman, "Dialogue on Film" (interview), *American Film*, June 1977.

O'Connor, Carroll, Interview, *Playboy*, January 1973.

Time, "The Team Behind Archie Bunker & Co.," September 25, 1972.

Whitney, Dwight, "An American Institution Rolls On," *TV Guide*, January 6, 1979.

4.   Critical Analyses

Adler, Richard, "Why Archie Bunker's Ratings Ain't So Hot," *Wall Street Journal*, February 18, 1977.

Alley, Robert S., *Television: Ethics for Hire?* Nashville, Tenn.: Abingdon, 1977.

An examination of TV as a shaper of values and attitudes. Includes a discussion of Lear as a "modern American moralist."

DeMott, Benjamin, "The Viewers Experience: Notes on TV Criticism and Public Health," in *Television as a Social Force*, Douglass Cater and Richard Adler, eds. New York: Praeger Publishers, 1975.

Reviews the Hobson-Lear debate and appraises *All in the Family*.

Hano, Arthur, "Can Archie Bunker Give Bigotry a Bad Name?" *New York Times Magazine*, March 12, 1972.

Marsh, Spencer, *Edith the Good*. New York: Harper and Row, 1977.

—————, *God, Man, and Archie Bunker*. New York, Harper and Row, 1975.

> Two books of moral and ethical commentary based on the characters and events in *All in the Family*, written by Presbyterian clergyman. Both books were written for Lear's Tandem Productions.

Newcomb, Horace, *TV: The Most Popular Art*. Garden City, N.Y.: Anchor Press/Doubleday, 1974. (paperback)

> Contains a useful history of the TV situation comedy genre as well as a critique of *All in the Family* and other Lear series.

Pierce, Kenneth M., "The Bunkers, the Critics, and the News," in *Television as a Cultural Force,* Richard Adler and Douglass Cater, eds. New York: Praeger Publishers, 1976.

Sanders, Charles S., "Is Archie Bunker the Real White America?" *Ebony*, June 1972.

Stark, Stanley, "Toward an Anthropology of Dogmatism: Traditionalism, Modernism, Existentialism, and the Counterculture: 'All in the Family,' " *Psychological Reports*, 29, 1971, pp. 819-830.

Stein, Howard F. " 'All in the Family' as a Mirror of Contemporary American Culture," *Family Process*, 13:3, 1974, pp. 279-315.

ABOUT THE EDITOR

RICHARD ADLER is a writer and researcher with a special interest in television. He has edited several books about television, including (with Walter Baer) *The Electronic Box Office,* and (with Douglass Cater) *Television as a Social Force* and *Television as a Cultural Force.* Recently, he has contributed a column of television criticism to the *Wall Street Journal* and articles to *American Film, Skeptic,* and *Learning* magazine, and has taught Television Aesthetics at the Stanford University Mass Media Institute.

Educated at Harvard and Berkeley, Mr. Adler is the former director of the Aspen Institute Workshop on Television and assistant director of the Aspen Institute Program on Communications and Society. He also served as principle investigator of a National Science Foundation supported project that produced the widely cited *Research on the Effects of Television Advertising on Children.* He is currently writing a book on children and television to be published by Prentice-Hall.

DATE DUE

OCT 26 '82			
OCT 6 1982			
NOV 22 1983			
NOV 7 1983			
OCT 31 91			
NO 30 '91			
DE 18 91			
GAYLORD			PRINTED IN U.S.A.